MK LEARNING

CH

Robots
for Kids
Exploring
New
Technologies
for Learning

The Morgan Kaufmann Series in Interactive Technologies

Series Editors

Stuart Card, Xerox PARC
Jonathan Grudin, Microsoft
Jakob Nielsen, Nielsen Norman Group
Tim Skelly, Design Happy

Robots for Kids: Exploring New Technologies for Learning, edited by Allison Druin and James Hendler

GUI Bloopers: Don'ts and Do's for Software Developers and Web Designers, by Jeff Johnson

Information Appliances and Beyond: Interaction Design for Consumer Products, edited by Eric Bergman

Information Visualization: Perception for Design, by Colin Ware

Readings in Information Visualization: Using Vision to Think, written and edited by Stuart Card, Jock D. Mackinlay, and Ben Shneiderman

The Design of Children's Technology, edited by Allison Druin

The Usability Engineering Lifecycle: A Practitioner's Handbook for User Interface Design, by Deborah J. Mayhew

Contextual Design: Defining Customer-Centered Systems, by Hugh Beyer and Karen Holztblatt

Human Computer Interface Design: Success Stories, Emerging Methods, and Real World Context, edited by Marianne Rudisill, Clayton Lewis, Peter Polson, and Tim McKay

Robots for Kids

Exploring New Technologies for Learning

Edited by
Allison Druin
University of Maryland
and
James Hendler
University of Maryland

MORGAN KAUFMANN PUBLISHERS

AN IMPRINT OF ACADEMIC PRESS

A Harcourt Science and Technology Company

SAN FRANCISCO   SAN DIEGO   NEW YORK   BOSTON
LONDON   SYDNEY   TOKYO

Senior Editor	Diane D. Cerra
Director of Production	
and Manufacturing	Yonie Overton
Senior Production Editor	Elisabeth Beller
Cover Design	Ross Carron
Cover Image	© 1998 Sony Corporation
Text Design	Rebecca Evans
Copyeditor	Ken Della Penta
Proofreader	Carol Leyba
Composition	Susan Riley, Mark Ong
	—Side by Side Studios
Indexer	Steve Rath
Printer	Courier Corporation

Most art has been supplied by contributing authors.

Designations used by companies to distinguish their products are often claimed as trademarks or registered trademarks. In all instances where Morgan Kaufmann Publishers is aware of a claim, the product names appear in initial or all capital letters. Readers, however, should contact the appropriate companies for more complete information regarding trademarks and registration.

ACADEMIC PRESS
A Harcourt Science and Technology Company
525 B Street, Suite 1900, San Diego, CA 92101-4495, USA
http://www.academicpress.com

Academic Press
Harcourt Place, 32 Jamestown Road, London NW1 7BY, United Kingdom
http://www.hbuk.co.uk/ap/

Morgan Kaufmann Publishers
340 Pine Street, Sixth Floor, San Francisco, CA 94104-3205, USA
http://www.mkp.com

Library of Congress Cataloging-in-Publication Data

Robots for kids: exploring new technologies for learning / edited by Allison Druin and James Hendler.
  p. cm.
 Includes bibliographical references and index.
 ISBN 1-55860-597-5
 1. Robotics. I. Druin, Allison, date II. Hendler, James A.

TJ211 .R5749 2000
629.8'92–dc21   00-022074

This book is printed on acid-free paper.

To our daughters, Dana Druin Bederson and
Sharone Horowit-Hendler, who are growing up
in a future we are helping to create.
—A. D. & J. H.

Table of Conten.

Contents

Contents

Contents

Contents

Acknowledgments

When we began thinking about this book, it was right around the time Furby was making its mark in toy shows, the Sony dog was still in the labs, and we were just beginning our robot collaboration at the University of Maryland. Since that time, much has changed in the world of robots for kids. This book represents those changes. But throughout our work on this book, one thing has not changed and that is the team effort that has been needed to make this book a reality.

Each of our many authors has spent countless hours in writing their chapters. Our book reviewers have contributed their advice in making critical suggestions. Our editor, Diane Cerra, and the staff at Morgan Kaufmann painstakingly sifted through our manuscripts and made them a book. To all of you, we are grateful for your efforts and support throughout the development of this book. In addition, this book could not have happened without our supportive colleagues at the University of Maryland's Institute for Advanced Computer Studies (UMIACS). It is there that we met and established a shared research group in making robots for kids. It is there that we continue to have just too much fun to be called work!

Finally, no acknowledgments would be complete without giving thanks to our families for the patience they had with us when we needed to stay late at the office, answer one more email, or send last-minute FedEx packages. This book took our time and our attention when we least expected it to. But through it all, we learned that the time was right for this book and our efforts.

Allison Druin and Jim Hendler
University of Maryland
Institute for Advanced Computer Studies

Part I

New Robot Technologies for Children

Robots for the Rest of Us
Designing Systems "Out of the Box"

 **James Hendler**

*University of Maryland, Institute for Advanced Computer Studies,
Computer Science Department*

A funny thing is happening in the field of robotics. A revolution is occurring without being noticed by many in the robotic research community. The robotics journals and conferences have largely missed the fact that robots are starting to leave the laboratory and make it out into the world. With embedded processors making their presence felt in everything from Furby, 1998's toy of the year, to AIBO, Sony's robotic dog, we're seeing entirely new types of toys that challenge the very nature of the relationship between children and technologies. We see the beginning of a time when children are no longer anchored to a PC on the desktop, but able to bring the technology into their everyday world.

Roots of a Revolution

The primary cause of this revolution is the convergence of two trends. First, we see a relatively flat trend that represents advances in mechanical systems. Although we see improvement over time, the upward trend is slow and change moves at a near-glacial pace. To get a significant improvement in performance, you must either spend more—doubling the performance of the system will cost nearly double—or wait a very long time. Robots, being mechanical systems, have this curve as a dominant factor in their performance—or did, at least until recently.

Robots, after all, also include electronic components, and particularly processors, which have been improving at a very different rate. According to Moore's law, processor performance doubles every 12 to 18 months. Doubling the performance of the mechanical system takes many years; doubling processor performance is a short wait. This linear growth of mechanics, coupled with the exponential growth of processing power, has led to the inevitable—the ability to overcome poor mechanical performance with complex but cheap (!) processing. Instead of spending significantly more money for better control, you invest in a better processor and more complex processing.

As an example of this, consider a project we had at the University of Maryland, where we programmed the "Robot with a Dustbuster"—a small mobile robot that carried a cordless portable vacuum cleaner to sweep up the dust bunnies in our laboratory (Seeliger and Hendler 1997). This robot was designed originally as a research prototype developed by IS Robotics, Inc. To keep costs down, the control system was not very precise—in fact, controlled turns that were supposed to result in a 90-degree change could be anywhere from about 80–120 degrees. Since the robot was supposed to vacuum in nice neat lanes, these turns made its behavior very erratic, and the robot quickly got "lost"—with no way to know where in the room it was. To fix the mechanical system to get better turns would have been very expensive. Instead, a software solution was used.

Two small bump sensors were wired to the robot. A program was added that simply monitored where the robot was supposed to be and "took control" whenever the robot was expected to be perpendicular to the wall. The robot would back up until the two sensors would both report bumps. This meant, of course, that the robot was backed to the wall, and then it would proceed as normal. This "self-correction" induced by software made the robot perform significantly better and kept the cost of improved control low.[1]

While this is a simple example, it shows the key innovation in the new robotics—using simple sensors and "rule-based" programming to circumvent problems in mechanics and control. This lowers the cost of robotics and, perhaps more importantly, makes robotics far more accessible to the many programmers of the world—from professionals to grade-school hackers, any of whom can now get their hands on a low-cost robotics kit. In fact, LEGO is marketing one such kit, Mindstorms, aimed directly at the children's market (see Chapter 1). Although the sensors and effectors are far below the quality of what it takes to do factory robotics, they are controllable by end-user programmable software, and thus the robots can achieve complex behaviors from these imperfect components.

Behavior-based robotics, usually attributed to the work of MIT's Rodney Brooks (1985), deals with developing robots and software that focus on autonomous robotic behaviors, rather than on tethered control (as used for robotic factory arms) or telerobotic work. Autonomous robots, particularly mobile ones that interact with humans in everyday environments, must interact with relatively unpredictable worlds. The focus in this body of work

---

1. Interestingly, people watching the robot found this behavior to be "endearing"—making the robot seem more lifelike, as if it decided to back up sometimes "just to be sure." This tendency to anthropomorphize robots is another reason they are getting so much attention in the entertainment arena.

is therefore on robustness as opposed to precision. Making the robot work all the time and in a wide range of environments required new ways of approaching robotic problem-solving and the design of the architectures on which robots could run.

Putting this all together is leading to an inevitable result. The crossover to software is causing a precipitous drop in the cost of robots and making them available outside traditional factory (or laboratory) environments. The robustness and autonomy of behavior-based robots is making them less brittle and able to function in a wider range of environments. The natural result? Robots that are available at consumer prices and that are able to perform a wide variety of tasks while running untethered from a human controller. And this, of course, means an ever-increasing number of robotic devices aimed at interacting with us and our children, in the home, in schools, and on the playground.

Robot Roll Call

The world of robotics is changing rapidly. A decade ago most of the robots in the world were to be found in automotive and other assembly plants as well as in a few high-end university laboratories. Today, most colleges and universities offer some sort of robotics course, and a wide range of robots are being found in all sorts of interesting places. Here are some types of robots that you and your children will soon be seeing more of:[2]

- *Toys:* Robotic toys have become a rage in the toy industry, with most of the major manufacturers producing, or working on, robots for the children's market. A few of these, such as the Mindstorms product mentioned earlier, are aimed at letting the child design and build robots, but most have the robotic components embedded in a stuffed animal. Although Furby is probably the best seller of these, its robotics is somewhat minimal and most of its interaction with children is very simple. A more complex line of toys uses wireless communication to control robotic toys from a PC. Microsoft was the first company to release such a beast, with its "animate" line of interactive toys. The Microsoft Barney, for example, interacts with the child both directly (for example, if the child covers Barney's eyes, he says something like "Oh it got dark in here") and via the PC (for example, when the child picks a correct choice on a game, Barney says, "You got that right"). Other characters include Microsoft's Arthur, Disney's robotic Pooh, and

---

2. This list is meant to be illustrative, not exhaustive. In addition, inclusion on the list is not meant in any way to be an endorsement for any commercial products.

even a Yoda being produced by the makers of Furby. (A discussion with one of the designers of this toy is presented in Chapter 4.)

- *Pets:* In 1999, Sony released AIBO, the robotic pet dog. AIBO goes beyond being a "toy" in two ways. First, its range of behaviors is much more sophisticated than those of the toys above. It runs completely autonomously and interacts with people. Sony has even gone so far as to program AIBO with moods—how it responds to the user depends on its emotive state. Second, AIBO costs far more than the toys above. Where a toy typically sells for no more than a couple of hundred dollars, Sony's dogs sold for about $2500. However, despite this high cost, the initial production run, sold via the World Wide Web, reportedly sold out completely within the first couple of days. With successes like this, more such robotic companions can be expected. (AIBO is described in Chapter 2.)

- *Interactive displays:* Another exciting use of robots is in interactive displays in museums and zoos. Several museums are now fielding robot tour guides, which lead visitors to displays and recite information about the exhibits. An exciting example of this is the robotic insect developed by researchers at Carnegie Mellon University (All and Nourbakhsh 1999). This bug is a small robot that works inside a cage of large African cockroaches and that can be controlled from outside by a simple joystick. As the visitor drives the bug, the child can see it interacting with the roaches and also gets a view from a "bug cam"—a small camera mounted in the head of the robot, which literally shows a bug's-eye view of the world. The child controlling the bug gets a new feel for what it would be like to be that size and shape, and to interact with a different world. Another exciting dimension of this work, currently just starting to be explored, is to use sensors other than cameras in the interaction with the robot's world. For example, infrared sensors could allow a child to see the world as a map of heat while navigating a burrow or nocturnal world.

- *Educational robotics:* Recent robotics research is also examining robots aimed at teaching children about the world. This research includes classes and activities focused on teaching children about robots (Part II of this book), but also includes some new projects aimed at using robots to engage children in activities while teaching concepts not easily taught with traditional computers. Chapter 3 describes work performed at the University of Maryland that looks at using robots to help children understand emotions. Teachers at the pre- and grade-school levels often have trouble with students who do not correctly respond to, nor appropriately display, emotions. Additionally, most young children have problems with some of the subtle difference between emotions (for example, differentiating between "excited" and "happy"). The Personal Electronic Teller of Stories (PETS) is a robot that acts out the emotion words in a story written by a child (while the computer reads the story out loud). This lets the child explore the use of these words in context while watching the robot. In addition, the child can interact with the robot in one of its emotive states and can "program" the robot's emotions (varying the way it acts out emotive words).

- *Service robotics:* Service robotics (also called assistive robotics) deals with helping the disabled to interact with the world via the use of robotic technologies. One area of special interest to researchers in service robotics is developing robots that help children with disabilities to enjoy greater freedom of movement and interaction with the world. Robotic wheelchairs, for example, can help provide more mobility and a greater measure of safety to a physically challenged child. Other projects being explored include using robots to obey voice commands for mobility-impaired children ("get the red ball," "pick up the marker," etc.) and allowing autistic children to interact with and control robotic toys. For example, the PETS robot we are developing at the University of Maryland displays a range of emotions via action and sounds. We are exploring whether enabling autistic children to use such a system might support them in learning more about emotions in others.

As can be seen, this wide range of new robots is a far cry from either the factory arms of traditional robotics or the clanking humanoids so popular in 1950s science fiction.

In fact, it is this plethora of possibilities that provides such a challenge to the developer of software, robots, games, toys, educational products, and so on. The ability of the technology to emerge from the box on the desktop into an interactive component of everyday life is profoundly different from the traditional human-computer interface design or software development.

The Developer's Challenge—Out of the Box!

This new robotics has a tremendous impact on those of us who care about designing software and systems for children—at home and at school. After all, those of us who design software have worked hard to get kids to "come to the box," that is, to focus on the desktop and interact with their computer. Key issues have been attracting and maintaining children's interest, and an attempt to understand what can make an active child sit still and pay attention.

But now the equation is changing! The new robotics allows more of the interaction to take place "out of the box." With low-cost robotics, and with the embedding of powerful processors in toys, exhibits, and so on, children can now interact with technology that comes into their worlds. No longer must we draw the child to technology. The new goal is to bring the technology to the child!

Part I of this book focuses on techniques that provide examples of this new approach to technology. We present four chapters, previously discussed in this introduction, that are representative of a number of the techniques being explored, and which will help the reader to understand both the challenges and the promise of bringing robotics out of an industrial setting and into the home.

In addition, you will notice the stories of children throughout the book. We felt it was important to include the perspective of children in their own words. Children discuss their experiences with robots or their ideas for the future of robots. In either case, their words offer the reader another way to see robots for kids.

References

All, S., and I. Nourbakhsh. 1999. Insect telepresence: Using robotic tele-embodiment to bring insects face to face with humans. *www.cs.cmu.edu/~illah/PAPERS/insect.pdf.*

Brooks, R. A. 1986. A robust layered control system for a mobile robot. *IEEE Journal of Robotics and Automation* 2(1):14–23. Also MIT AI memo 864, September 1985.

Seeliger, O., and J. Hendler. 1997. Supervenient hierarchies of behaviors in robotics. *Journal of Experimental and Theoretical AI* 9(2/3).

Chapter One

To Mindstorms and Beyond
Evolution of a Construction Kit for Magical Machines

Fred Martin
MIT Media Laboratory

Bakhtiar Mikhak
MIT Media Laboratory

Mitchel Resnick
MIT Media Laboratory

Brian Silverman
MIT Media Laboratory

Robbie Berg
MIT Media Laboratory

Abstract

This chapter traces the 30-year history of robotic construction kits for children, beginning with Seymour Papert's Logo language developed at the MIT Artificial Intelligence Laboratory, through to the LEGO Mindstorms Robotics Invention System launched in 1998, and beyond. In the future, physical and computational construction kits will be commonplace, and children will use them for their own purposes, inventing their own toys and using technology to reveal the world around them.

1.1   Introduction

When does something stop being a machine and become a creature?

From a very early age, children find movement captivating. For centuries, we have been fascinated by the inanimate brought to life. The Jewish legend of the Golem, a hunk of clay brought to life by God, has been succeeded by the story of Frankenstein, mechanical automatons, *2001*'s Hal, and a myriad of other myths. For the last 50 years, computers have allowed us to create worlds that live inside of the electronic box, creating artificial creatures in the sense of these stories. And over the last 15 years, children have been able to play in these worlds (e.g., video games) and build in them, using tools like the Logo programming language.

But only now can children embed computation into physical artifacts. In doing so, they create objects that, in a real sense, are brought to life, animated by a computer program also created by the child. These playthings, enabled by computational construction kits and living at a boundary between the animate and inanimate, allow children a special relationship to the world of technology we are living in. The magic of technology, so much a part of all of our lives, is both revealed and revered. Children realize that sophisticated behaviors can emerge from interactions of rules with a complex world but, at the same time, are still captivated by the wonder of a machine acting like a pet.

Designing tools that allow children to add computation to traditional construction—and recognizing the learning opportunities afforded by this activity—has been the focus of our work over the last number of years. This chapter explores this work as part history, part design narrative, and part vision.

In the first section, we explore a 30-year trajectory of computational design environments for children, beginning with Seymour Papert's original Logo work at the MIT Artificial Intelligence Laboratory, and ending with our recent Cricket computers. We refer both to Seymour Papert's vision of children's learning in his book *Mindstorms* (Papert 1980) and also to the Mindstorms Robotics Invention System, launched by the LEGO Group in 1998.

This section of the chapter may seem overly technical. Indeed, the focus is on the evolution of a particular set of technologies (the robotics construction kit). But our intent is to illuminate a set of design issues around which many people have explored different avenues based on their own passions. For instance, Umaschi and Urrea's work on "Con-science" (Chapter 6 of this book) proposes robotic design activities for learning about values and identity. Turkle (1984) has explored psychological implications of computational artifacts and the process of creating them. So while we focus on technology, the intent is to reveal the process by which we were led along in creating these systems, not just the particular waypoints themselves.

In the second section, we describe a set of activities oriented around science experiments, where children investigate various phenomena from a computational standpoint. We give an in-depth narration of the kinds of activities that are possible with the latest versions of our materials. This discussion is oriented around our present "Beyond Black Boxes" project, in which children perform scientific investigations with the computational construction kit. Here, we share the quality of children's experience with our tools and their relationship to them. Our hope is that the fluid, serendipitous, and yet rigorous investigations that we describe would become a commonplace replacement for the school science we are all too familiar with.

In the conclusion, we discuss new technological directions and our work in building a library of application ideas around these materials. We present a vision of the future in which children are as fluent in combining a diverse collection of computational tools—handheld, tangible, and interconnected—as they are with video games and CD players today.

1.2   From Floor Turtles to Crickets

Since the late 1960s, our research group has been developing robotic construction kits for children. Early work, led by Seymour Papert, included the development of the Logo programming language. A popular use of Logo was in conjunction with "floor turtles"—wastebasket-sized robots tethered to mainframes. With pens mounted in their bodies, floor turtles made drawings on butcher paper, commanded by children's Logo programs.

In 1972, Papert and Cynthia Solomon published a memo entitled "20 Things to Do with a Computer" (Papert and Solomon 1972). Many of these activities involved hooking some kind of contraption up to a computer and programming it to perform—for instance, a puppet show, a yo-yo, or a yard-stick-balancer. In essence, these projects proposed robotic design activities before a general-purpose robotic construction kit for children was available.

The Road to LEGO/Logo

Over the 1970s and into the 1980s, Papert's vision of computing, in which children explore ideas by constructing their own computer programs, came into reality as the first microcomputers entered schools. Logo as a computer programming language, a philosophy of learning, and a culture of users grew with the publication of *Mindstorms: Children, Computers, and Powerful Ideas* (Papert 1980). *Mindstorms* presented us with *constructionism*—the philosophy of learning by building ideas in one's mind as part of building artifacts in the world.

In the mid-1980s our research group began a collaboration with the LEGO Group. Combining the LEGO Technic product (which includes beams, gears, and motors) with the Logo language, we created the LEGO/Logo system. With LEGO/Logo, children could build various mechanical contraptions—a Ferris wheel, elevator, robot creature—connect them to an interface box, and then write Logo programs to control their movement (Resnick and Ocko 1991).

The LEGO/Logo system became commercially available in the late 1980s, sold to schools by the LEGO Group with the name LEGO tc logo. LEGO/Logo was a fantastic innovation—in an important sense, it was the first true robotic construction kit ever made widely available—but it had limitations. Children's machines had to be connected to a desktop computer with wires, which greatly limited projects' mobility. If the machine just had one motor, it was not too inconvenient, but once a machine had a couple of motors and sensors, each with its own cable, pretty soon there was a whole wiring harness connecting the interface box to the LEGO project. This was both a practical nuisance, making it clumsy to build a machine that moved about, but also a conceptual one: logically, the "intelligence" behind a machine's operation should be bundled with the machine, not sitting on a desktop.

The First Programmable Brick

At about the same time as LEGO/Logo was reaching schools, we began thinking about its successor.

Figure 1.1

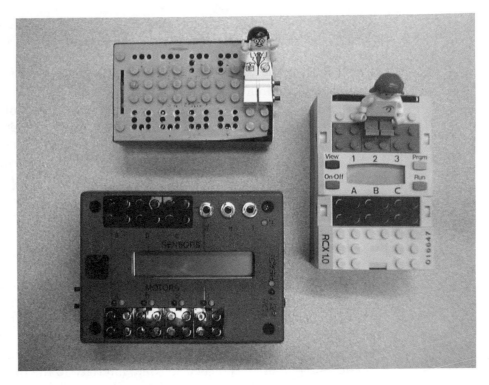

Progression of Programmable Bricks. Counterclockwise from upper left: MIT Logo Brick (1987), MIT Red Brick (1995), LEGO RCX Brick (1998).

This would clearly involve putting electronics into bricks. The question was, could we fit an entire computer into a block small enough to be carried around by a LEGO model? The answer turned out to be yes, and in 1987 we had the first prototypes of a "Programmable Brick," ready to be used with children in focused research play (see Figure 1.1, upper-left gray brick; see also Color Plate).

A set of experiments done using our first Programmable Brick with fifth- and seventh-grade students is described in *Children, Cybernetics, and Programmable Turtles* (Martin 1988). In this work, we worked closely with a small number of students who built projects using the Programmable Brick along with a LEGO turtle (a small robot). With our assistance, the children wrote programs to give different behaviors to the turtle, such as light seeking and obstacle avoidance. We paid close attention to the children's relationship to the technology. Some children liked to treat the turtle-robot like a pet and enjoyed when it displayed unpredictable behavior. Others were more interested in having the turtle perform a specific set of actions and were challenged by the difficulty in getting it to do so.

The first-generation Programmable Brick was a success in that it allowed us to conduct closely monitored work with children. But it would wait for later designs before we had Bricks that were sufficiently reliable that they could truly become part of a classroom environment, honestly owned by the teachers and children who were using them.

Over the period from 1992 to 1996, we created second-generation Programmable Bricks, including the "Gray Brick" (Sargent et al. 1995) and the "Red Brick," both named for the color of their plastic housings. The Red Brick (see again Figure 1.1) was specifically designed for robustness and ease of manufacture; over its lifetime more than 100 copies of it were built for extended use in schools and community centers.

The Red Brick

The Red Brick was not fundamentally different from the original Logo Brick. In the basic concept of its use, children built a LEGO machine (often which carried the Brick), and then plugged the Brick into a desktop computer for programming. While the Brick was attached to the desktop, children could type Logo commands directly to the Brick, or compose Logo procedures and download them. (The Logo software interface to the Brick is shown in Figure 1.2.)

But the Red Brick was stable and robust enough to be used extensively in classroom situations; we worked in three classrooms in the United States (Martin 1996) and in Project Lighthouse in Thailand (Cavallo 1999). In the United States, two classrooms were in a rural elementary school, and one was at an urban vocational high school. In this work, we developed a semester-long set of activities around the Brick in elementary school (called "Robotic Park") and engaged vocational school students in developing robots for an international contest. This field work helped serve as the foundation for the development of the LEGO RCX Brick, a version of the programmable brick concept that is now commercially available.

During this period of work, when the Red Brick was being used heavily, we engaged in design discussions as to what characteristics the next Brick should have. One concern was size. Our Brick was approximately the size of a child's juice box or a small personal cassette stereo. Also, it was reasonably heavy, about 13 oz. This made it a challenge for kids to construct a model that could carry the Brick around.

We critically evaluated the Logo programming environment that children used to develop control programs for their robots. Many children found Logo programming appealing, but others did not. We explored the idea of putting the Logo statements into on-screen blocks that could be dragged around

Figure 1.2

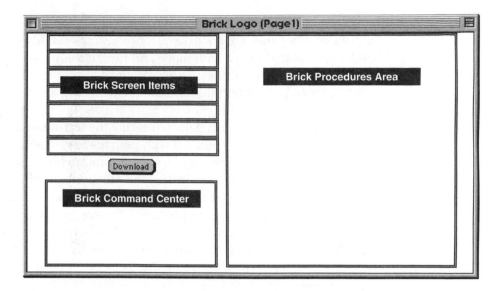

Brick Logo software interface. In the lower right, the Brick Command Center is used to type Logo statements directly to the Brick. Procedures are composed in the Brick Procedures Area, and the Brick Screen Items are used to indicate which procedures can be started up from the Brick itself. Programs are downloaded into the Brick by clicking the Download button.

and clicked into place, allowing children to assemble their control program much in the same fashion as they might assemble a LEGO project (Begel 1996). This software, which we called "Logo Blocks," served as the basis for the LEGO Group's later commercial implementation of the Programmable Brick idea.

Also, we revisited the discussion about how many inputs and outputs the Brick should have, and whether it should have an LCD screen. The Red Brick had four motor outputs and six sensor inputs. We considered the six inputs generous—four would have probably been enough—even though project work with children had shown that all six sensor inputs were often put into use.

We considered the LCD screen a critical feature. Time and time again, children would use the screen's sensor display to gain an understanding of how sensors performed. Especially in the case of light sensors, a robot needed to be in its "natural habitat"—that is, the playpen specifically designed for the robot—in order for the sensor readings to be valid. So it would be no help to have to bring the robot back to the desktop computer in order to view its sensor values; the sensors had to be seen in the context of where the robot had to perform. So the display was essential.

We also discussed the number of motor outputs. Some of us felt that two outputs were not enough. For example, two outputs would be just enough to build a vehicle that could both move and turn; if there were only two, none would be for other purposes (like actuating an arm or shovel, or spinning a turret). Others did not find this argument convincing and believed that two outputs would be enough.

So essentially we convinced ourselves that the feature set of the Red Brick was basically correct. We could go with perhaps fewer motors and sensors, but the LCD screen was necessary. So only one option presented itself: reengineering the Brick to have more or less the same circuitry but packed into a smaller box. Unless the box were substantially smaller, however, making a slight tweak to the size would not be worth the engineering effort involved.

The Red Brick and the work we did in schools served as a foundation as the LEGO Group determined what sort of product should follow up on their tethered-interface control products. The LEGO RCX Brick (see again Figure 1.1, right side) shares many features with the MIT Red Brick, including motor outputs, sensor inputs, and an LCD screen.

The LEGO Group believed in the robot design concept so strongly that they launched the LEGO Mindstorms brand, a new product line to bring these ideas directly to children in their homes (the previous control products had been marketed exclusively to schools). Our work on iconic programming, which we called Logo Blocks, was adapted by LEGO to serve as the programming environment for the retail version of LEGO Mindstorms (known as "RCX Code").

These design issues are all part of providing tools that are both flexible and powerful. We thought that we had reached the end of the line with the Red Brick, that it was optimal in some sense of these trade-offs. We then took what we thought might be a detour in creating "Thinking Tags," but which we later realized set us off in a direction that would circle back to computational design environments for children.

Thinking Tags

Postponing the task of designing a new small Programmable Brick, our team created the Thinking Tag, an electronic name tag that had infrared communications capabilities (Borovoy et al. 1996). The Thinking Tag was created to experiment with people's behavior at social gatherings, allowing people first meeting each other to learn quickly a bit about their shared interests.

We performed the initial trial of the Thinking Tag application at a Media Laboratory research consortium meeting. At the meeting, visitors each received a Thinking Tag in place of the traditional name tag. In addition to having one's name printed on it, the Thinking Tag had five LED lamps that could light either red or green.

Set up in the reception hall were five kiosks, each displaying a multiple-choice question and three buckets representing the answers. The questions were designed to be provocative, humorous, and relevant to the technology-savvy audience of research sponsors: for example, "How would you like to spend your 15 minutes of fame? a. Profile in the *New York Times*; b. Interview with Oprah Winfrey; c. Hyperlink off main page of Yahoo."

When visiting a kiosk, participants could program their Tag with an answer simply by dunking it into the bucket color-coded to correspond to their answer. An infrared transponder in the bottom of each bucket would program the Tag with the selected response. If they changed their mind about an answer, participants could simply dunk their tags into a different bucket.

Later, when two participants met, their Tags would invisibly exchange their answer data and light up LEDs to indicate how closely they matched. For each answer the pair had in common, a green LED would light. For each answer the pair disagreed upon, a red LED would light. The LEDs were unsorted, so the participants would have to have a conversation to determine which questions they had answered similarly and which they differed on—the point of the Tags was to stimulate conversation, not replace it.

In the several meetings in which we performed "Tag events," we found the Thinking Tag to be a great conversation starter. When two people met, the Thinking Tag effectively displayed something about their *relationship*— what they had in common—not just the typical static display of name and affiliation. Since a main benefit of the research consortia is to bring together people from different companies into informal relationships leading into professional collaborations, it was quite valuable for sponsors to find it easier to meet each other.

After the Thinking Tag consortia, we collected the Tags from our sponsors. The design of the Tag had been driven by the particular concept of the question/answer kiosk and red/green affinity displays just described, but afterward we stepped back from this specific application and thought about the technology we had created. What we had on our hands was a collection of several hundred tiny computers that could be worn on one's shirt and that could communicate with each other. Surely these could be instrumental in a wide variety of learning and play scenarios, not just the affinity party game! In brainstorming that followed, we realized that the Tags could keep track of who had met whom (in a rudimentary way, subject to limitations of their computational power). In the affinity application, other than the programming of the answers to the kiosk questions, the Tags were stateless. How your

Tag reacted to another person was not affected by whom you or your conversation partner had met in the past.

But the Tags' operating program could readily be redesigned to perform such tasks as passing a "magic token" from person to person. This idea was taken up by Vanessa Colella, a graduate student in our research group, who created a classroom activity for high-school students around a Tag redesigned to model the propagation of a virus throughout a population. In Colella's project, called "Participatory Simulations," a classroom of students each received a specialized "Virus Tag" that could propagate a simulated virus to other such Tags (Colella 1998).

From Tags to Crickets

In parallel to the continuing work on wearable computers, we realized that the core hardware of the Thinking Tag could be put in place in a new and radically smaller Programmable Brick. Whereas the Red Brick was about the size of a juice box, a Brick based on the Tag design could be truly tiny—about the same size as the 9-volt battery that would serve as its power source.[1]

Core Cricket Design

This new Brick, which we called the "Cricket," was substantially smaller, lighter, and less expensive to manufacture than any of our earlier designs (see Figure 1.3). Also, Crickets had the ability to communicate with one another—each of them had bidirectional infrared communications capability built in. We coined the name "Cricket" based on the idea of a chorus of little computers talking to one another.

The first Cricket was demonstrated at a Media Lab event in March 1996. This Cricket had the following feature set:

- an infrared communications system for inter-Cricket messaging and program download

- two motor output ports

---

1. This was possible because of two important technology shifts: (1) the Microchip PIC processor, and (2) our byte-coded interpreter software strategy. The PIC processor (coupled with a serial memory connected by just two wires to the PIC processor) allowed us to put the processor/memory into a much smaller space than with traditional processor/memory architectures. In our software design, begun with the Red Brick, much of the complexity was off-loaded to the desktop, allowing us to build a device that is programmable by children and yet requires only the computational horsepower that is typically put into a standard computer mouse.

Figure 1.3

The MIT Cricket (right), with LEGO Mini-Fig for size reference.

- two sensor input ports

- a pushbutton switch for starting and stopping the Cricket's program

- an audio beeper and three status LEDs

- powered by a 9-volt battery

One significant shift in our thinking that led to the Cricket was the success of the Red Brick in the classroom. We realized that a single design did not have to satisfy all needs; we could use Red Bricks where they were best suited and Crickets where they were best suited. For instance, the Crickets do not have a built-in display; if one were important, the project could use a Red Brick. (This limitation was removed with the addition of bus devices, described shortly.)

Because Crickets were simple and easy to revise, we created a plurality of Cricket designs. We realized the limitations of the first Cricket (two motors and two sensors), so we designed other Crickets:

- A "Display Cricket" that had a bank of eight bicolor (red/green) LEDs that could be lit under user program control. It also had three sensor inputs but no motor outputs.

- A "MIDI Cricket" that contained a versatile waveform synthesizer chip, along with sensor inputs.

- A "Science Cricket" that provided true analog-to-digital converters on the sensor inputs (allowing the use of a greater variety of sensor devices), along with support for 16-bit numbers in the Cricket software. (The Science Cricket employed a more powerful version of the Microchip PIC controller.)

The Cricket Bus System

In parallel with this development of multiple Crickets, we were working on a different way of supporting multiple devices—the Cricket Bus system.

As we were designing devices to interface with the Crickets, we realized that often a custom circuit would be required to connect a particular device to the Cricket. Up to this point, we had been designing entirely new Crickets each with different capabilities. For example, to get an LED display, we created the Display Cricket; to get music, we created the MIDI Cricket.

We came to realize that instead we could bundle the specific circuitry required to make a new device work with that device itself, in a sort of object-oriented hardware strategy. Then, a simple communications protocol could let the new devices talk to an existing Cricket. Thus was born the idea for the Cricket Bus.

Our first Cricket Bus device was an optical distance sensor that employed a special part manufactured by the Sharp Microelectronics Group. This component used a specific, unusual communication method to interface with an external circuit. By conceiving the Sharp distance sensor as a bus device, we were able to bundle the special hardware and software required to talk to the device with the device itself, yielding a common protocol to talk between the Cricket and the bus device.

Over time, we have come to develop a large collection of bus devices, all of which can communicate with a standard Cricket design (see Figure 1.4; see also Color Plate).

The Bus system also allowed us to converge on a single Cricket. Our so-called "Classic Cricket" (with two built-in motor drivers and two resistive sensor ports) merged with the "Science Cricket" (true analog sensor inputs and 16-bit number support) to become, with the addition of the Bus Port, our standard design. The need for different Cricket versions became drastically reduced, since nearly any device can be interfaced to this standard "Blue Dot" Cricket using the Bus system.[2]

---

2. We labeled our software revisions of the Cricket operating program by the colored dots we physically placed on the Crickets to identify them.

Figure 1.4

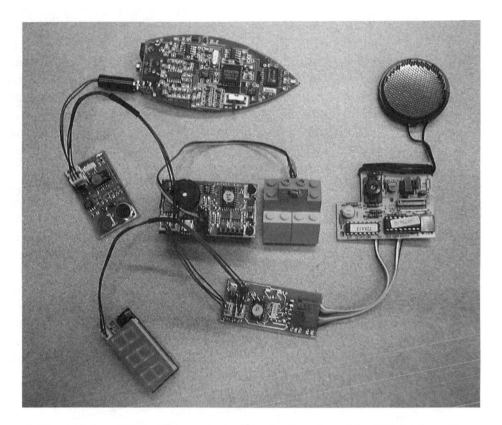

Cricket with bus devices. At center is the "Blue Dot" version of the MIT Cricket with a simple light sensor to its immediate right. Arranged around, from top clockwise, bus devices: MIDI Boat music synthesizer, Polaroid ultrasonic distance sensor, three-digit numeric LED display, and sound sensor.

1.3   Applications and Research Focus

> The things that scientists do are the same things that you have to do to help you design technology.
>
> *—A fifth-grade student*

The design of Crickets was heavily influenced by its anticipated applications in our work with children in the context of the Beyond Black Boxes (BBB) project. The BBB project provides a theoretical framework, computational construction kits (both hardware and software), and a collection of project ideas for a constructionist approach to science education.

An example of a project in the spirit of our Beyond Black Boxes work is an augmented bird feeder designed by one of the children in our project. This bird feeder included a switch for detecting when a bird alighted on the platform; the switch sent a signal to a Cricket, which then operated a motor-driven apparatus that took a picture of the bird. Hence the bird feeder could record the activity of birds even when the child who built it was away at school. We hope that with our construction kits and examples of projects like this, children (and educators) will be inspired to design their own scientific instruments for investigations that they personally find meaningful. Through designing their own instruments, children gain a deeper appreciation and understanding of many scientific concepts. And this happens in two important ways: Children not only reflect on and apply already familiar concepts, but may also come in direct contact with other scientific ideas in a natural way.

In addition to gaining a deeper and more concrete understanding of scientific ideas, children also develop a much richer sense of the interplay between science and technology. In the process of building their own instruments, they come to appreciate the importance of good design and sound engineering practice. In this regard, existing technological and scientific artifacts are excellent resources for ideas. BBB projects allow children to gain a new perspective into the tools and instruments around them. By examining and critiquing the systems around them, children get to peer into these modern "black boxes," see their inner workings, and reflect on the many powerful ideas hidden behind the design of many of these devices. Since they are engaged in design activities themselves, discussions about good and bad designs give them and us a window into what they have internalized in the process of interacting with the many opaque tools and appliances around them. In this process, beyond uncovering and discovering the mechanisms and programs that they may want to use to activate and control their creations, children also express their own expectations and sensibilities towards the design of devices and systems.

We believe that it is important to encourage attention to and reflection on design not only in an engineering sense but also an artistic sense. In this regard, the BBB project differentiates itself from many other "hands-on" approaches to science education in that it recognizes the power of, and provides tools for, integrating children's interests in the arts and music with scientific explorations. The importance of enabling children to take part in projects that are multidisciplinary in nature cannot be overstated. Construction material and project ideas that appeal to a broad range of interests allow multiple entry points into science, mathematics, engineering, design, art, and music for all types of learners. These materials not only make new knowledge domains accessible, but also provide new ways for children to relate to domains of knowledge to which they have already been exposed.

As a part of the BBB project, we work with students, teachers, and mentors in a number of different settings. In this section, we will focus on a number of investigations that they have proposed and carried out. In the following discussion of some BBB projects, we will focus on the educational goals that inspired and remain at the core of our research. In presenting the following case studies and our future research plans, we invite you to think about the following core questions with us: What educational opportunities do these new tools afford? What scientific and social values do these types of projects nurture? What implications do these activities have for classroom structure and practices?

Crickets as a Scientific Tool

Martha Greenawalt is one of the many excellent teachers who have been working with us on the BBB project. She is a science coordinator and teacher in the Bronx public school system. Following our BBB workshop last summer, she designed a series of heat/temperature activities for her fourth and fifth graders, using only Crickets and temperature sensors. Having already worked with small groups of children on some Cricket projects, she wanted to try the technology in the regular school setting. She worked with groups of 25 students during the regularly scheduled science classes.

She spent a couple of weeks introducing the Crickets, hoping that as their novelty wore off they would assume the status of a tool for scientific investigations and discussions. She showed them how to write simple programs for the Crickets to collect data, upload the data to the desktop computer, and graph it using our graphing software. She also designed short activities that highlighted the communication capabilities of the Crickets.

After introducing the Crickets and some of their capabilities, she allowed her students to have some free exploration periods with the Crickets and temperature sensors. The temperature sensors for the Crickets give raw sensor readings without conversion to Celsius or Fahrenheit scale equivalents. When she shared the Crickets and the activities she had designed with her fellow science teachers, they wanted to know the conversion factors to be able to use the established temperature scales with their students. Martha could have easily modified the software to show the temperature readings in Fahrenheit, but she had a very different idea about using this feature of the Crickets. She wanted to bring her students into the discussions that would ground the process of defining a temperature scale into their everyday experiences.

On the BBB mailing list, in response to another teacher's posting in which she asked about the conversion factors, Martha posted her lesson plans and her approach to exploring the educational opportunities afforded by the

Cricket's raw sensor readings. As the discussions on the mailing list continued, she posted many of her observations and reflections. Her discussions
with her students and her fellow teachers capture the spirit of the BBB projects very well. We will reproduce one of her postings to the list to give the
reader a sense of the level and nature of the discussions in her classrooms:

> I am working with 4/5th graders who have widely varying experience with
> and understanding of traditional temperature scales and what those values
> represent. We decided that we wanted the kids to attach the Cricket tempera-
> ture number to a real value rather than another abstract number. In other
> words, we want them to equate 215 with something hot, like hot water in a
> cup, rather than to push them to connect it to (often partially grasped) num-
> bers from a temperature scale.
>
> We plowed ahead. Kids did investigations using the receive box [on-screen
> display of sensor values] and recorded the Cricket's temperature value of a
> variety of items. (In retrospect this was a good move, because it grounded the
> numbers in real life. We can look at our notebooks and say x value is cold, y
> value is hot etc.) One class went on to collect temp data over time on a vari-
> ety of walks. When they started looking at the graphs there were absolutely no
> questions about the values we were seeing! The kids appear to have bought
> into the Cricket system as a system. They work with it on its own terms: kid,
> Cricket, and world. They don't seem to care about the Celsius and Fahrenheit
> systems at all.
>
> I sent out those early graphs to a number of tech people in the Center for
> Collaborative Education circle for comment. The man with the most solid sci-
> entific background immediately requested translation of the Cricket values to
> familiar temp values. He also wondered if we had talked about the x and y axis
> of the graphs to clarify what they meant. His questions made me realize that
> the kids, because they had created the thing, had a deep understanding of
> how the numbers and the graph worked. The definitions he was requesting
> would have been very "teacherly" (in the old chalk and talk sense) if we had
> introduced them to the class. The kids simply don't need or want the C and F
> conversions now. Within our little intellectual circle of the classroom, there is
> no need to make conversions. My sense is that we will only develop that need
> if/when we attempt to communicate with people who don't have experience
> with the Cricket system.
>
> Of course, I had to explore this some more, so we tried something else with
> the second class. Before we did any temp walks (to explore Crickets' capacity
> to collect data and store it) we looked at the data that everyone collected in
> their initial/immediate receive investigations. As a compromise, we thought
> we would create a scale of the Cricket temp values. (One of the girls in class

suggested calling it "Cricket temp number ratings.") The idea was to create a set of benchmarks: each benchmark establishing a range of possible temp values for a given event or thing that the kids had investigated. In other words: the kids would know that x range of numbers was hot like hot water or cold like ice water, or warm like the monitor screen. I thought benchmarks would be a good compromise between absolute experiential knowledge (like the class that I already described) and conversion to another scale.

I thought. Inquiry teaching and learning is fun because you never know exactly where you're going to go! Suffice it to say that we didn't create the benchmarks. Kids left for the day with the question "Do you trust this data? Why, why not?" for homework.

The readings were not reliable at all; wacky, in fact. Which leads me to ask a number of ideas/questions about how we use Crickets and the temp data we are collecting with Crickets. (Later for that.) Calibration would seem to be the order of the day in the second classroom.

Perhaps many of the BBB students working with Crickets are older or more fluently literate/numerate than my kiddies and conversion to familiar temp scales makes sense. However, the Crickets are allowing us to discover amazing variation in thinking and understandings among our 4th and 5th graders. We're really trying not to play fast and loose with words, numbers, pictures or concepts and because it's all so new to all of us it has been easier for us (adults) to slow down, look and listen to what the kids are making of this.

I could go on and on. And have. I would be delighted to receive feedback. I am curious to hear others' experience around this topic.

Martha's reflections represent the core values of what BBB would like to cultivate in the culture of our classrooms. Our image of students and teachers is that of investigators in an active dialogue. In this image Martha and her students are colleagues in a genuine scientific exploration. They are not reproducing a known experiment with known outcomes; instead they are getting a chance to appreciate scientific inquiry as rich and engaging human activity.

The Nail Salon: An Artistic Approach to Science and Engineering

Many children, primarily boys, when they find out that Crickets can control two motors, decide to build cars as their first projects. We have designed other introductory activities that suggest other alternatives to cars. In one

Figure 1.5

The Nail Salon.

particular activity, we provide everyone with traditional construction material (such as LEGO and balsa wood) and other arts material and ask them to make kinetic sculptures that sense something about the world and generate a musical or kinetic reaction. At Sensory Design, a workshop held in the summer of 1998 at the Media Lab, Elise (10 years old) was inspired by this initial activity and decided to make something very different from a car. She made a Nail Salon (Figure 1.5).

Her Nail Salon consisted of

- a place for her to insert her hands

- a sensor to detect her hands in the proper place

- a gear system to move a number of cotton balls back and forth to polish her nails

- a rotating feather to dry off her nails when she was done

- background music for her to listen to while her nails were being done

As we have often found to be the case, the art materials were a critical addition to the construction kit. Elise spent a long time—intertwined with tweaking and fine-tuning the mechanical parts of her project—decorating her nail salon. Her attention to detail and the aesthetic quality of her project mattered to her a lot. It was her affective relationship with what she had made that kept her engaged. She worked on both the engineering and the artistic aspects of her design to make her device behave and feel as she envisioned it.

And what did Elise learn in the project? She experimented with various sensors, compared their outputs for conditions under which she thought her device would be used, and decided on the reflectance sensor or the light sensors as the best candidates for detecting the user's hands. She also went through a number of iterations for the gear mechanism responsible for polishing her nails. She tried many motor settings to determine the most suitable power levels. All through her creative process, she was mindful of the most natural and comfortable design for the actual use of the device. As an added bonus, she programmed the Cricket to play music while her nails were being worked on. Her project, even though it may not have appeared technical or scientific at first, had much science, engineering, industrial, and artistic design. These types of projects present an excellent path into and preparation for scientific thinking.

The Gerbil Maze

Another activity that interests children very much and leads to rich discussions is that of building sensors and instruments for monitoring pets. The Sensory Design workshop was held in a space where we also kept a couple of gerbils in a cage. We told the group that some of us were interested in building things for the gerbils and anyone who wanted could join us in brainstorming about what things to make. At the beginning only one student, Veronica, connected to this idea strongly, but by the end, it became a community project and everyone contributed something to it.

Veronica began by building the gerbils their first LEGO house. After observing the gerbils go in and out of their new home repeatedly, she made them a second house, which was much smaller than the first. She wanted to see which house they preferred. Her theory was that they preferred smaller and darker houses. After building the second house and observing the gerbils for a couple of days, she was beginning to see evidence in support of her theory. She wanted to have a better way of determining which house they preferred and by how much.

Her first idea was to use the sensors we had to see how often they visited each house and how long they stayed in there. She built doors for each house and used a LEGO light and a light sensor to count the number of visits made to each house. She plugged the light sensor into a Cricket, experimented to find out how much the sensor readings were affected when a gerbil passed by, and wrote a program to detect an entry/exit and counted them. She added a numeric display to see the current count easily. At this point, she wanted to know if she could determine the time they spent in the house. This led to very fruitful discussion.

One of the two high-school students who had some previous programming experience with the Crickets offered to help her write the program for tracking the gerbils' activities. The program involves using the timer primitive in Cricket Logo to calculate the length of the time interval between two consecutive events registered by the sensor at the door. At this point, they realized that they needed to detect an entry and that their current scheme was not distinguishing between entry and departure. So they designed a different doorway with two light/reflectance sensor arrangements. Now by looking at the order in which the events occurred, they could determine whether the gerbils were leaving or entering the room.

Another one of the participants, Jose, suggested using a temperature sensor for detecting whether there was a gerbil in a house or not. He added a temperature sensor to the smaller house and wrote a program that successfully detected if there was a gerbil in the house. This technique was not as effective in the larger house unless he used more than one temperature sensor. The most challenging aspect of this project for Jose was the calibration to account for the variations in the ambient temperature. What was important in this project was that he could build a system that did the right thing at least in the special case. Then as he used his setup in different conditions, he was able to build on what he had to account for the other subtleties that he was discovering.

As the workshop went on, the gerbil house got more and more attention from the other kids. They would all take a break from their own project and talk to Veronica about their ideas for the gerbils. In one case, John spent a day building a counter for the gerbil wheel. He mounted a magnet on the wheel and used a Hall effect sensor and a Cricket to write a program that counted the revolutions. Every time the magnet passed the sensor, the counter increased by one. The counter value was displayed on a numeric bus device. At our prompting, he began to change the program to display the average speed of the gerbils on the exercise wheel. John and one of the other high-school students in the group worked through the timing issues involved in writing this program.

When the other kids saw this display, there were suddenly a lot of ideas about the other things to monitor about the gerbils. For example, Monica wanted to know how frequently the gerbils drank water and exercised during the night. One idea was to videotape the cage the whole night and look through the tape the next day. John thought that reviewing hours of video would be too tedious and boring. Inspired by one of the sample projects we had shown them at the beginning of the workshop, he proposed to build a contraption that would be triggered by a Cricket to film the cage for one minute. This presented a very nice challenge.

He and one of the high-school student mentors, David, went off to design the needed mechanism. Monica was interested in working on the sensor arrangement for detecting the gerbils at the drinking bottle. She successfully used a reflectance sensor for this purpose. Everything was ready to go, and everyone went home in anticipation of the video clips on the following day. On the following day, we only had two minutes' worth of video, after which the gerbils had chewed through the cables from the sensors to the Cricket outside the cage. In addition to rebuilding and reinforcing the cables, the children decided to not only record the data about the gerbils' activity on their exercise wheel, but also tape the gerbils running. So they modified their program to start taping for as long as the gerbils were on the wheel or at the drinking bottle. The next day they had footage of the gerbils doing both those things.

The gerbils provided an enormous learning opportunity. In addition to the individual projects mentioned, the children collectively designed a maze for the gerbils, with sensors all over the maze, monitoring gerbils' food and color preferences (Figure 1.6). By the end of the project, the children had used each of the sensors in multiple contexts. They had become fluent with their use and their range of applicability. It is our hope that the tools we are designing would make it easier for many classrooms to engage their students in these types of generative and open-ended activities.

Musical Stress Meter

Marcos, after spending the first few days of the workshop on building and refining a Cricket-controlled car, started to make a musical instrument. His instrument mapped reflectance sensor readings from color fabric cutouts to musical notes. One of the early challenges in this project was that the readings from the reflectance sensor were inconsistent and at most only distinguished between four different colors. Marcos spent a day playing around with different sensors such as a light sensor to see if he got any better results. The improvement was marginal.

The next day we introduced a few body-monitoring sensors—heart-rate monitors, galvanic skin response sensors, and electrocardiogram (heart response) sensors—to the group. For a couple of hours, everyone used the graphing software to generate and analyze real-time graphs of the data from a Cricket monitoring an electrocardiogram sensor. Some students made visual displays for their heart rates. One student in particular made a display with a LEGO figure running in place at a speed that varied in response to variations in his heart rate.

Marcos was playing around with the galvanic skin response (GSR) sensor. The GSR sensor measures the skin conductivity of an individual, which

Figure 1.6

The gerbil maze. In section a, the plastic cups were covered with different colors of fabric; the children were testing to which colors the gerbils were more attracted. Section b was the "Food Court"; the gerbils' food was separated into different colors, again separately sensed. Section c was the entrance to the maze in which the path that the gerbils took was recorded.

increases when people are stressed, anxious, disturbed, or shocked. Marcos had the same Cricket he was using with his musical instrument without having reprogrammed it. When he ran the program on the Crickets, he was pleasantly surprised. He liked the variations in the notes caused by the variations in his GSR reading. This prompted a two-day investigation into other people's GSR readings. He carefully divided the most common ranges of sensor readings into pieces that mapped nicely into different notes. He set up the graphing software for the real-time data collection and invited people to try to change the musical notes being played by startling each other or asking each other embarrassing questions.

In this project Marcos's interest in music brought him much closer to the data from a sensor, which he would not have normally found very engaging. At the end, he wished he were able to control various qualities of his favorite pieces of music. We are currently working on improving the Midi and other music output and control capabilities of the Crickets.

1.4   Future Directions

Our work continues along two fronts, mirroring the structure of this paper: research into new technologies and research into new applications and ways of learning. These two activities are intertwined and interdependent; a new application idea can lead to new technology, and vice versa.

For example, in the musical stress meter project, Marcos did not have access to a high-quality musical output device; he made do with the simple piezo beeper that is built into the Cricket. After working with him, we were inspired to revisit our earlier work on the Midi Cricket, which resulted in the Midi Boat, a bus device that could be plugged into our current Cricket.[3]

As an example in the other direction, of new technology leading to a new application, consider one of our latest bus devices, an acceleration sensor. This device has many applications to the Beyond Black Boxes project, acting as a motion, inclination, and shock sensor. Yet these devices did not exist as inexpensive, easily packaged units until most recently. We are always staying abreast of new technologies that are valuable to our interests.

One of our challenges is to build a collection of project and activity examples around the theme of children pursuing scientific explorations. In the robotics domain, there are many examples of project ideas and curricula (for instance, robot contests modeled after MIT's 2.70 and 6.270 projects) to draw from, but we are only now building a collection of examples of scientific explorations (this chapter; Resnick et al. 1999). We are particularly focusing these efforts to leverage new technologies that are commercially available, such as the LEGO Mindstorms Robotics Invention System.

An important aspect of the Beyond Black Boxes program is our focus on the engineering aspects of scientific inquiry. Much of the work of real scientists involves the construction of new apparatuses that allow better observation of phenomena or exploration of a physical principle. Yet this design process is often absent from science in school settings. With the BBB program, we argue for a more integrated approach to science, mathematics, and engineering, a sort of "Engineering for All Americans" in the sense of the 1989 *Science for All Americans* manifesto of the American Association for the Advancement of Science.

In our Digital Manipulatives initiative (Resnick et al. 1999), we are exploring ways of bringing these ideas to younger children, ages five to eight. By embedding computational power in traditional children's toys such as blocks, beads, and balls, we hope to provide children with new ways of connecting to scientific and mathematical concepts. For example, we have created

---

3. The Midi Boat was designed by Josh Smith and Josh Strickon, two Media Laboratory graduate students. We adapted their design to our Crickets.

Programmable Beads, a string of beadlike elements that can pass messages and programs along the string. In one application, a string of beads passes a light down the string and back, but some beads are probabilistic and randomly reflect the light rather than passing it. With materials like this, young children have a new way of playing with ideas of chance.

As we have built more and more, smaller and smaller intelligent devices, it becomes evident that these objects need to talk with one another, and not become isolated islands of technology. These devices and the everyday devices in children's world—cassette stereos, Game Boys, and cameras— must be interlinkable. More importantly, children should see them as building blocks in a larger construction set, rather than as special-purpose devices (Mikhak et al. 1999).

One concern about the widespread introduction of technology into children's lives is that we are becoming enslaved to technologies we do not understand. Instead, it is important that the next generation of children gains a sense of control, ownership, and empowerment, and becomes actively involved in understanding and designing our future. The construction kits we propose enable children to become authors of rich and wondrous technological artifacts. Children will better appreciate the magic of technology when they not only use technology, but also create it.

1.5 Acknowledgments

We would like to express our appreciation to all of the teachers who have participated in this work, including most especially Martha Greenawalt, Mike Petrich, Karen Wilkinson, Rami Alwan, and Phil Firsenbaum. We would like to recognize the contributions of other members of our research group, including Claudia Urrea, Vanessa Stevens Colella, and Genee Lyn Colobong. Michael Rosenblatt contributed helpful comments to drafts of this chapter. Finally we would like to thank all of the children who have participated in this work. We hope that they got as much out of the experience as did we.

1.6 References

American Association for the Advancement of Science (AAAS). 1989. *Science for All Americans.* Washington, DC: AAAS.

Begel, A. 1996. *LogoBlocks: A Graphical Programming Language for Interacting with the World.* Unpublished undergraduate thesis, Department of Electrical Engineering and Computer Science, Massachusetts Institute of Technology.

Borovoy, R., M. McDonald, F. Martin, and M. Resnick. 1996. Things that blink: Computationally augmented name tags. *IBM Systems Journal* 35(3):488–495.

Braitenberg, V. 1984. *Vehicles: Experiments in Synthetic Psychology.* Cambridge, MA: MIT Press.

Cavallo, D. 1999. Project Lighthouse in Thailand: Guiding pathways to powerful learning. In *Logo Philosophy and Implementation.* Montreal, Quebec: Logo Computer Systems Inc.

Colella, V. S. 1998. *Participatory Simulations: Building Collaborative Understanding through Immersive Dynamic Modeling.* Unpublished Master's thesis, Media Laboratory, Massachusetts Institute of Technology.

Martin, F. G. 1988. *Children, Cybernetics, and Programmable Turtles.* Unpublished Master's thesis, Department of Mechanical Engineering, Massachusetts Institute of Technology.

Martin, F. G. 1996. Kids learning engineering science using LEGO and the Programmable Brick. Presented at the 1996 meeting of the American Educational Research Association.

Mikhak, B., F. Martin, R. Berg, M. Resnick, and B. Silverman. 1999. The children's machines: Handheld and wearable computers too. *Proceedings of the 1999 International Symposium on Handheld and Ubiquitous Computing.* Karlsruhe, Germany.

Papert, S. 1980. *Mindstorms: Children, Computers, and Powerful Ideas.* New York: Basic Books.

Papert, S., and C. Solomon. 1972. Twenty things to do with a computer. *Educational Technology Magazine* 12(4):9–18.

Resnick, M., R. Berg, and M. Eisenberg. 1999. Beyond Black Boxes: Bringing transparency and aesthetics back to scientific investigation. *International Journal of the Learning Sciences.*

Resnick, M., R. Berg, M. Eisenberg, S. Turkle, and F. Martin. 1996. Beyond Black Boxes: Bringing transparency and aesthetics back to scientific instruments. Proposal to the National Science Foundation. Available from MIT Media Laboratory.

Resnick, M., M. Eisenberg, R. Berg, and F. Martin. 1999. Learning with digital manipulatives: A new generation of Fröebel gifts for exploring "advanced" mathematical and scientific concepts. Proposal to the National Science Foundation, May.

Resnick, M., and S. Ocko. 1991. LEGO/Logo: Learning through and about design. In I. Harel and S. Papert (eds.), *Constructionism,* Norwood, NJ: Ablex Publishing.

Sargent, R., M. Resnick, F. Martin, and B. Silverman. 1995. Building and learning with Programmable Bricks. *Logo Update* 3(3). New York: The Logo Foundation.

Turkle, S. 1984. *The Second Self.* New York: Simon and Schuster.

Kid's View

   My Dragon Helper

By Sharone Hendler, age 12

Hi. My name is Sharone. I am in the seventh grade. When I was in fourth grade I built a robot for the school's science fair. My dad helped too. I built all the parts with a little help from my dad: the gears, the structure, wrote the program, and all the other parts. I programmed my robot to dump a LEGO dragon when something hit its bump sensor. I also programmed it to go towards a very bright light.

I put a very bright light in a box and cut a hole so the light could shine through it. I decorated the box, and called it a castle. My robot would go to the light, hit the box, and dump the dragon in the box. For this reason I named my robot "Dragon Helper."

The six parts of a robot are

1. The computer: The computer is on the board of my robot. You also type the program into a computer and connect the computer to the robot so the robot knows what to do.

2. The sensors: The sensors help the robot sense whatever they need to. Example: light sensors help the robot find light, heat sensors help the robot find heat, and bump sensors help the robot sense if they bump into something.

3. The structure: The structure is the shape of the robot and what the robot is made of.

4. The motor: A motor is what makes a robot move things. Example: the motors in the gearboxes in my robot make the gears move, which moves the wheel.

5. The batteries: The batteries charge the robot up so that the robot can move.

6. The program: To tell the robot what to do, you need to write a program. You type the program into the computer and the computer should have a plug that plugs into a special place on the board and you should be able to load the program onto the robot.

I think making robots is fun. You should try it. Here are some basic instructions. They are in order.

1. You decide what you want your robot to look like and what you want your robot to do.
2. Make a gearbox.
3. Make another just like it but mirror image.
4. Attach the gearboxes together.
5. Build some of the body onto the robot.
6. You build places to put the battery and board.
7. You build a place for heat/light/infrared sensors.
8. You connect the heat/light/infrared sensors.
9. You type a program.
10. You build a place for bump sensors.
11. You connect bump sensors.
12. You make something special to make the robot do what you want it to (my robot has the special platform that dumps the dragon into the castle).
13. Make the program better than before.
14. Test the robot.

Here are the steps I used to make the structure for "Dragon Helper":

1. I made the gearboxes and connected them together.
2. I built stuff onto the gearboxes including what holds the battery and what holds the board.
3. I made the wall that the light sensors are on.
4. I made the thing that pushes the bump sensor.
5. I put up the wall that attaches the platform that the motor is on.
6. I made the platform that dumps the dragon in the castle.
7. I made the stick that moves the platform that dumps the dragon in the castle and the parts that hold the stick in the right place.

This is how my dad and I wrote parts of the program:

1. To decide how fast the robot should go, we experimented by making the motor go faster, making one motor go the other way than the other motor, and making one slower than the other.

2. We made the motor that makes the stick move to see which way it would go. The first time it went "shooting" up, so we made it go the other way slower, so now it goes down and doesn't "shoot" down.

3. We made the robot spin because when we first typed into the program how to make the light sensors work, when we put the robot too far from the light the robot would just go straight. So we decided we should make it turn till it got a certain low number with the light sensors. So we did a test.

In the test we took the light sensors and pointed them at the bright light. We took the number that showed up and added a little. Then we took the number we ended up with and programmed the robot to spin till its light sensors "saw" that amount of light.

I really enjoyed making Dragon Helper. Making Dragon Helper took a long time (a few months), and would have taken a lot longer if my dad had not been helping me. Try making a robot. It probably will take a while, but your robot will be worth it. Enjoy making your robot! 'Bye!

Chapter Two

Robot Entertainment

Masahiro Fujita
Sony Corporation

Hiroaki Kitano
Sony Computer Science Laboratories, Inc.

Toshi T. Doi
Sony Corporation

Abstract

Entertainment is an important application of autonomous robotics. It is one where reliablility and safety are not as serious issues as they are in other robotics applications (e.g., in industrial settings). In this chapter, we propose to establish a new industry called robot entertainment. We describe possible application categories. To evaluate the possibilities, we developed a quadruped robot with pet-like reactions. Some technologies made the prototype robot more lifelike, especially increasing the complexity of motions and behaviors. We developed another prototype, which is a reconfigurable robot platform. We believe that a variety of robot configurations is key to the successful establishment of the robot entertainment industry. In addition, a standard interface for the reconfigurable robot platform would encourage and support the research for and development of a robot entertainment system and would help establish a robot entertainment industry. The prototype robot is a reconfigurable robot platform based on OPEN-R (which is a standard architecture) and the set of interfaces we propose. In 1999, we began to sell AIBO ERS-110, which is based on these prototypes. In the future, it will be ordinary for children to use autonomous robots and to interact with them in a friendly way, ushering in a new era of autonomous robots.

2.1   Introduction

In May 1999, Sony officially announced the market launch of the entertainment robot "AIBO." AIBO is a four-legged autonomous robot, with paws, legs, head, and tail (the effectors), run by 18 motors. Not only is the robot capable of emitting sound or noise with the use of a built-in speaker, but it also has a charge coupled device (CCD) color camera, stereo microphone, and touch sensor. While the sensors enable the robot to input external stimuli to itself, the effectors enable it to respond to stimuli by using its paws, legs, head, and sound. Unlike traditional robots, it can interact with people and its surroundings. AIBO has an accessory prerecorded 8 MB "Memory Stick." This stick contains the software program for sensor processing, control, and judgment. When this stick is inserted, AIBO can behave autonomously. AIBO was sold in limited quantities, and only in Japan and the United States. All sales were handled exclusively over the Internet. Priced beyond the reach of the average child, AIBO was meant for adult purchasers. However, AIBO is the first step in the new robot entertainment industry that we are now trying to establish. In the future we hope that children will become the main users.

There are five possible ways to enjoy this entertainment robot:

- *Watch the movements of the robot:* Many people enjoy watching movements, gestures, and behavior of animals in zoos. Recently, computer-controlled dinosaur robots have been very popular in museums, and they actually move rather smoothly. The ability to move at a certain level of complexity is essential for entertainment.

- *Interact with the robot:* We can interact with dogs through gestures and voice. In addition to just watching movements, interaction brings owners more pleasure and amusement. We believe that interaction is another vital feature of the entertainment robot.

- *Raise the robot:* Simulation games, where the players virtually raise a synthetic agent, are popular in video games. In the research fields of artificial life and artificial intelligence, researchers often discuss the possibilities of adopting this concept in the entertainment field. The popularity of this type of game may have a scientific basis—the behavior of raising pets or children comes from an inborn instinct every human has. Unconsciously, people's instincts are stimulated by this kind of game. This aspect should be included in the entertainment robot.

- *Control the robot:* There is another category of video games, called action games, where people enjoy controlling a synthetic agent to fight with another agent that is controlled by another user. A similar example is controlling a car to compete for a time record. That led us to the notion that a soccer-playing robot would be a great application. While researchers in universities and research labs are interested in making robots autonomous because of artificial intelligence, the general public would simply be interested in playing soccer using the robots.

- *Develop the robot:* We believe that developing robots is entertaining in itself. Lately, many robot contests require the participants to develop their own robots under constraints such as size, weight, cost, and so on. The contestants enjoy creating their own robots, implementing their ideas or programs, and watching the behavior that they have designed. We believe that amateurs as well as experts can enjoy creating their own robots, if we provide them with a friendly and easy-to-understand development environment.

The possibilities seem endless. We proposed the standard architecture OPEN-R or its interfaces as the standard, and ensured that this standard met the requirements of the entertainment robot so that the possibilities mentioned above could be attained (Fujita and Kageyama 1997; Fujita, Kitano, and Kageyama 1998). The main advantage of the OPEN-R architecture is the hardware and software modularity, not present in most industrial-use robots today. Interchangeability of both hardware and software with various functions and shapes means that users can assemble diverse robots, even ones with different application software. Needless to say, AIBO was born out of the superior features of OPEN-R, in which the application software consists of different software components.

This chapter describes the design concept of a prototype used as the basis for AIBO's design, and how it was implemented (Fujita and Kitano 1998). Then, we describe a reconfigurable robot platform based on OPEN-R (Fujita, Kitano, and Kageyama 1998). We conclude by discussing robots for children.

2.2   Requirements for a Pet-Type Robot

We had considered the question "What kind of entertainment robot should we develop as a prototype?"

We opted for a pet type, although we had also considered a remote-operation type. We decided to work on the pet-type robot because it would give us the challenge of solving problems, such as learning, maturing, and autonomy in particular, that would stand in our way when trying to establish this industry. Developing a remote-operated type of robot would pose fewer technical problems, which might sound attractive for short-range development, but at the same time would produce fewer business possibilities. We wanted to verify and demonstrate the robot's feasibility. We had to overcome the technical obstacles and verify the entertainment robot's viability by integrating state-of-the-art technologies in both hardware and software.

Three major points emerged when considering the possibilities of watching the robot's movement and interacting with it:

- *Natural human interaction:* We hoped to create an environment in which we could interact with the robot naturally without using special tools like an infrared device.

- *Real-world complete agent:* We hoped to ensure that the robot would work in a normal environment that we now live in. We were not interested in a robot that could only live or run in special environments. Unlike the traditional factory automation (FA) robots that run accurately at very high speed in dedicated environments, we wanted the robot to be able to adjust itself to a dynamic, complicated, and ever-changing world because that is how we believe autonomous robots should be.

- *Complexity of movements and reactions:* We wanted the robot to move, act freely, and react to the external stimuli or environment on its own, so we would never be bored. This feature is crucial. It would have a tremendous impact if it could move just like a real living creature. It would lead users to be more emotionally involved with the robot, and to become more attached to it.

Here are two guidelines we considered when establishing the robot's system.

- *Stand-alone system:* The robot's system should be stand-alone, equipped with necessities like batteries, CPU, and so on. If the robot has to be plugged into the power supply, or connected to a host PC by a cable, it would prevent the robot from moving freely and make it appear less lifelike.

- *Software component:* The software architecture must support modularity and future robot upgrades. This is partly because it makes development more effective. However, this kind of architecture is also necessary for the many and varied types of processing involved in running autonomous robots because algorithms will be reconfigured and new processes added along the way. Further, as pointed out in the list of entertainment possibilities previously, this will help users design the robot by visual programming, so that end users who are not familiar with programming languages will be able to design the motion of the robot.

2.3   Designing a Pet-Type Robot

Here is how we approached the above goals:

- *Natural human-robot interaction:* To be able to interact with the robot without depending on special tools, first we considered what kind of sensor or effector should be used. We thought that, basically, interaction through sound, touch, and colors would be possible. Sound and touch would be the basis for the natural human-robot interaction. As for the sensors for sound and touch, it was not a problem to find suitable ones for the robot because a wide variety of sensors, such as microphones, speakers, and microswitches, were viable in terms of size, weight, and price. As for color, we decided on image processing with the use of a camera. Hopefully, this method will enable the robot to perceive things by shape or motion in the future, as well as by color. We mainly focused on the image processing, simply because human beings generally act, move, or behave based on visual information, so much so that it plays a powerful role in our community and environment. In other words, we concluded that if we could successfully build autonomous robots to be able to behave and perceive things based on visual information, it would be easier for them to integrate into human society for the purpose of cohabitation.

- *Real-world complete agent:* What is required for recognizing both sounds and images? The difficulty lies in real-time processing in the real world, especially for sound. We decided to develop a tonal language with a stationary pitch component, which is robust enough in the noisy real world. For example, musical tones of an instrument would be easier for the robot to recognize in an ordinary noisy environment because tones tend to keep their frequency longer and at a constant level.

- *Complexity of movements and reactions:* What factor would be the most important in making pet-type robots? The answer is how close or how successfully we could make them look as if they are alive. We studied this challenge from another perspective and concluded that making the motions or responses as complicated as possible would be the key. Thus, (1) each joint in the robot has as many degrees of freedom as possible, so the parts corresponding to paws or legs would move effectively and freely; and (2) the robot is given multiple motivations that, when integrated, give the robot a more lifelike appearance, with complex emotions. The latter feature is described later.

With regard to the stand-alone system and software reusability, we decided to leave this up to the implementation. We targeted the robot to be as small as possible, to minimize the required motor power and battery capacity. A positive feedback relation exists between the size and the power, and this should be the main factor when choosing what kind of system should be employed.

2.4   Implementation

To accomplish the above aims, we developed an autonomous four-legged robot as a prototype (Figure 2.1).

Let's briefly touch on a few different points.

Mechanical Configuration

Figure 2.2 shows the structure of the robot, especially the sensor and mechanical configuration. Although categorized as a four-legged robot, its capacities distinguish it from any other four-legged robots designed up to

Figure 2.1

Pet-type robot: MUTANT.

now. Besides being able to walk, its unique structure enables a variety of postures such as lying down, standing up, and sitting down. In fact, the variety of postures is more important than the ability to walk. There are several reasons for choosing a four-legged type. Compared to bipedal walking, we would face fewer technical problems. Moreover, when it sits down, the robot can have its two front legs completely free in the air, so they can move freely. In short, this mechanical configuration meets the requirement of complexity of motions and reactions.

Key Components

In order to make the robot as compact and light as possible, we created several key components on our own.

Micro camera unit

As mentioned earlier, we place great value on image processing. To make the camera small, light, and affordable, we developed a micro camera unit (MCU) using a technology called multichip module (Figure 2.3). Its structure is quite simple: it has bare chips, which include a CCD, a CPU for control, and a timing generator. A single lens is placed on this, to obtain good-quality

Figure 2.2

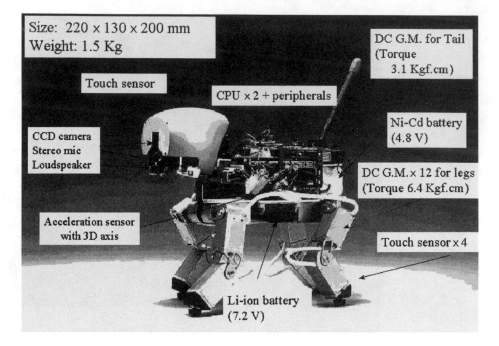

Size: 220 × 130 × 200 mm
Weight: 1.5 Kg

Touch sensor

CPU × 2 + peripherals

DC G.M. for Tail
(Torque
3.1 Kgf.cm)

CCD camera
Stereo mic
Loudspeaker

Ni-Cd battery
(4.8 V)

DC G.M. × 12 for legs
(Torque 6.4 Kgf.cm)

Acceleration sensor
with 3D axis

Touch sensor × 4

Li-ion battery
(7.2 V)

Mechanical configuration of MUTANT.

images so that the robot can recognize objects. The size of the MCU is 23 × 16 × 4 mm, with 492 × 362 pixels.

Geared motor

In addition to the MCU, we developed a DC geared motor (Figure 2.4). The gearbox functions as the outer shell for the legs. It consists of a DC motor made from four spur gears, a potentiometer, and a motor driver chip, which are all in the gearbox. A motor case made of magnesium alloy serves as the outer shell for the legs, making them light and robust.

Robust Recognition in the Real World

For the robot to be able to live in the real world, it must have robust sound recognition. However, recognition of speech, which human beings employ most often, would be too challenging because of interference from ambient noise and other voices. We decided to leave that feature for the future, and in the meantime opted for a tonal language with a stationary pitch component, which remains robust in ordinary noisy environments. In addition, a stationary pitch component such as a whistle or tone is easy to extract from

Figure 2.3

Micro camera unit.

Figure 2.4

DC geared motor with an outer shell.

Figure 2.5

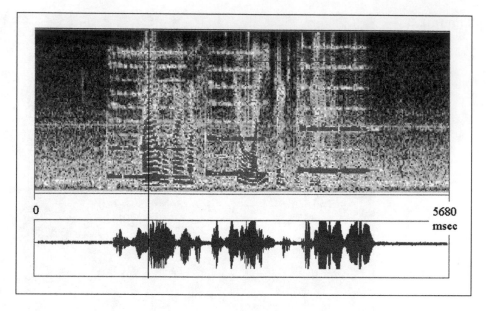

Time-frequency graph of mixture of voice and music tone.

human speech interference because of the nature of the spoken voice. In general, the pitch component of the spoken voice in natural conversation does not keep the same frequency, but fluctuates. On the other hand, a tone signal keeps a constant frequency. Figure 2.5 shows a time-frequency graph of a mixture of both natural conversation and a music tone of a synthesizer. Figure 2.6 shows a graph of the filtered version.

Figure 2.7 shows the spectrum of both the original signal and the filtered signal. The target signal is suppressed in the original signal, but is recovered in the filtered signal.

Complex Movements and Reactions

As already mentioned, the most important target feature for the pet-type robot is to make the robot move and react to any kind of stimuli as if it is alive. Complexity is the key to achieving this target.

Degrees of freedom

The simplest way to increase the complexity is to use many actuators. However, since we want to make a compact robot, we have to find a balance between the number of degrees of freedom and the size of the robot. We

Figure 2.6

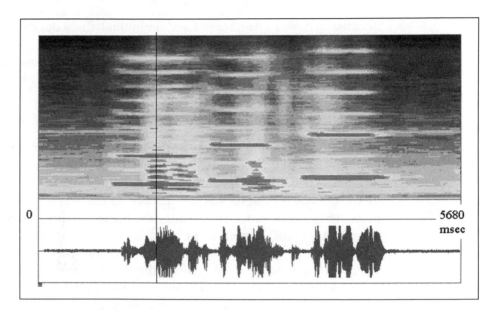

Time-frequency graph of filtered signal.

Figure 2.7

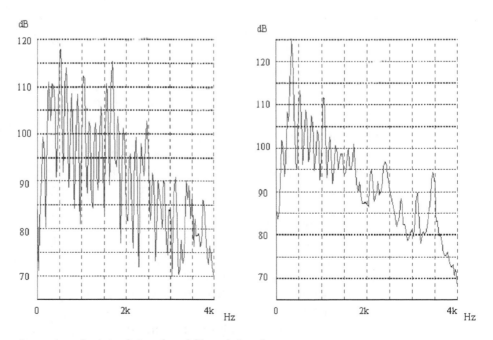

Spectrum of original signal and filtered signal.

decided to have 16 degrees of freedom in total, three degrees of freedom for each leg, three for the neck, and one for the tail. Using the 16 degrees of freedom, the robot can display abundant and impressive postures and movements, including walking, sitting down, standing up, and sleeping.

Motivations for motions/behavior

Once a robot is endowed with sufficient degrees of freedom for complex motions, we need to consider how to use these actuators so that they seem really alive. In order to give sufficient complexity to a robot with 16 degrees of freedom, we believe that complexity of motivations for motions and behavior is important. In our definition, the term "motivation" is used as a trigger that invokes motions or behavior, and the motivation itself varies constantly depending on the sensor stimuli and internal conditions. Now, the question is, how we can increase the complexity of the motivations.

Brooks pointed out that complex behavior emerges when the robot can react to a dynamic, constantly changing environment (Brooks 1986). Further, the complexity of the behavior increases if the robot continues to react to it because the reaction from the robot makes the environment change. He demonstrated this phenomenon using his robots with subsumption architecture (SSA).

The SSA succeeded in showing the importance of the reaction or reflex motion to intelligence. However, the SSA was not capable of deliberate behavior.

Recently, a layered architecture that combines reactive behavior with deliberate behavior is being proposed by another group independently (Firby 1994; Horswill 1996). It could be one solution for increasing motivations for behavior chronologically.

Reactive behavior to stimuli arising from the dynamic environment forms one group of motivations in a short time domain. Deliberate behavior, by deliberate decisions, forms another group of motivations in a longer time domain. However, the time domain is not the only factor to be analyzed in the complexity of the motivations for the motions. There are other domains. For example, if we were to give instinct, emotion, and rational ability to the robot, this could form another domain of motivation. Instinct, such as appetite or a desire to sleep, is directly linked to survival of the species. Instinctive motions or behaviors are direct actions of the creature to satisfy wants based on desire.

Emotion is similar to instinct in one sense, but it is not for survival purposes directly. It is more like an internal condition and is a motivation for expressions, such as laughter, anger, or weeping. The rational ability generates deliberate behavior and is a motivation that controls instinct and emotion.

In terms of the second domain, moving to a battery station can be considered instinctive behavior, whereas laughing and dancing can be considered emotional behavior. Moving a ball to a particular place can be considered rational behavior.

It is very natural for some parts, such as the head and tail, or the entire body, to simultaneously have independent motivations. For example, the head moves to track an object while the paw moves to touch other objects, and the entire body moves to come close to something else. An integration of these motions and behaviors generated by multiple parts makes it possible for the robot to exhibit very complex behavior.

Thus, we categorize the numerous motivations as follows:

- reactive/deliberate motivations

- instinct/emotion/rational ability motivations

- head/leg/body part motivations

To increase the complexity of motivations, we combined, integrated, and coordinated these motivation categories into one motion or behavior. If we are very successful, the robot appears lifelike. Now, let's move on to how to combine the motivation categories.

Layered agent architecture

We designed the agent architecture as a combination of reactive processes and deliberate processes. As shown in Figure 2.8, in the reactive process, sensory inputs are processed and a motor command is sent back immediately by the motor command generator. In the deliberate process, higher-level processing is programmed using action sequence generators and target behavior generators.

Tree-structured agent architecture

So that each part of the robot can move independently, we decided on a tree-structured agent architecture. As shown in Figure 2.9, this architecture decides the configuration of the robot parts. Moreover, we assign a layered agent architecture to every node in the tree structure topology. This combination of two architectures enables every part of the robot to move and behave either reactively or deliberately, thus attaining our goal of combinatory complexity. However, the motion or behavior of the body has to be coordinated with its parts. By prioritizing the architecture, the motions or behavior can be coordinated. Nodes in the upper part of the tree have higher

Figure 2.8

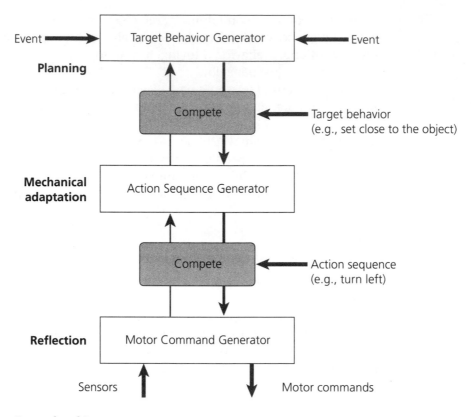

Layered architecture.

Figure 2.9

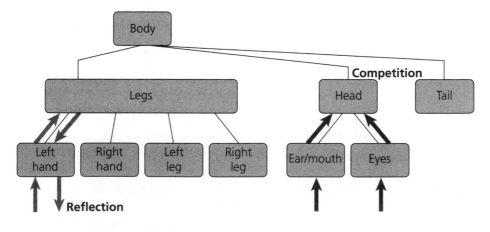

Tree-structured agent architecture.

Figure 2.10

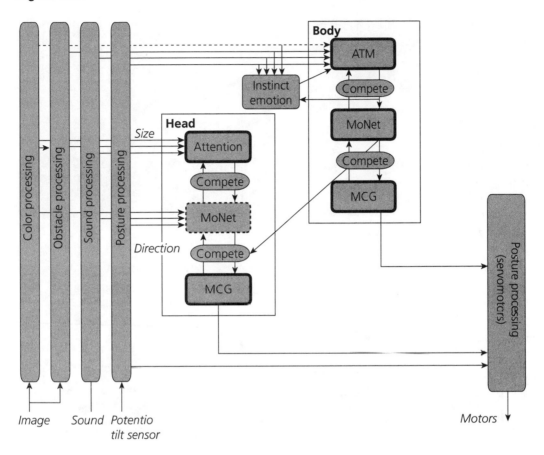

Overall agent architecture for MUTANT.

priority than those in the lower part. In other words, controls/motivations in the upper part have more power in coordinating the motion of the robot.

Figure 2.10 shows the overall agent architecture of the prototype, including the layered architecture and the tree-structured agent architecture for the body and head parts. The instinct/emotion model is also realized in this architecture for the instinct/emotion/rational behavior category.

Figure 2.11 shows the complex motions and behavior displayed by the prototype with the quadruped mechanical configuration and the agent architecture. Tracking a yellow ball is one good example of the reactive behavior of the head part. Karate motion is motivated by an anger state of the instinct/emotion model, and offering a paw is motivated by both color detection of hand color and an estimation of distance to obstacles in the higher-level recognition. Sleeping is motivated by the fatigue state of the instinct/emotion model.

Figure 2.11

Examples of complex motions and behaviors.

2.5   Reconfigurable Robot Platform

In developing the pet-type robot to study the feasibility of an entertainment robot, we proposed OPEN-R, a standard architecture and interface for robot entertainment systems.

Requirements for OPEN-R

OPEN-R is defined to satisfy four technical requirements: (1) extensibility, (2) style flexibility, (3) software portability, and (4) interoperability.

Extensibility

OPEN-R must be extensible for diverse system configurations. In a minimum configuration, a robot may have just a few components and perform a set of behaviors as a complete agent, without any external systems. This robot can be scaled up, in terms of the numbers of components, by adding physical components. It should also be possible to scale up such a system by including these robots as subsystems of a larger robot system. Each robot should be able to work as part of a larger system, functioning as a remote-operated system.

Style flexibility

Style flexibility ensures that different kinds of robots can be built with OPEN-R components. Two very different styles of robots, such as a wheel-based robot and a quadruped robot, can use the OPEN-R standard. These robots may have different types of sensors, such as cameras, infrared sensors, and touch sensors, as well as different motor controllers.

Software portability

Software must be portable among different systems and robots. OPEN-R should ensure portability among different mechanical configurations of robots. Application software should operate both for wheel-based robots and quadruped robots. Note that an open architecture for computer systems does not need to consider the problem of portability among different styles of mechanical configurations. Rather it is central to a robotics software standard.

Interoperability

Robot entertainment systems must be interoperable so that two or more robot systems can exchange information and make use of it transparently.

Development environment

In addition to the above requirements, it should be emphasized that the development environment for robot entertainment is also very important. OPEN-R must provide a development environment, both for professional developers/researchers and for end users who are not familiar with technical matters. End users may develop or compose their own programs using the development environment.

Figure 2.12

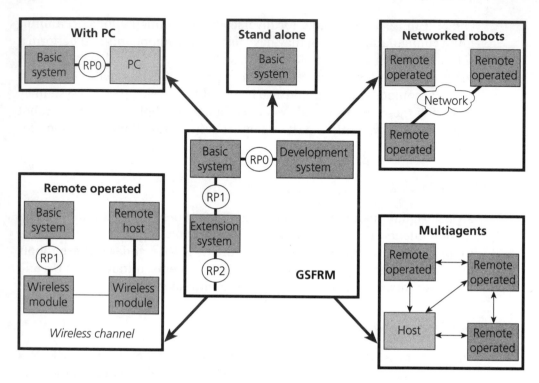

Generic system functional reference model.

Key Technologies for OPEN-R

Our key technologies to meet these requirements are summarized as follows.

Generic system functional reference model

To meet the requirements of extensibility and a development environment, we have defined a generic system functional reference model (GSFRM) composed of the basic system, the extension system, and the development system. Based on GSFRM, we are able to construct various kinds of robot systems with extensibility and with a development environment (Figure 2.12).

GSFRM also supports style flexibility, enabling stand-alone robot systems, remotely operated robot systems, and networked robot systems.

Layering

For interoperability and a friendly development environment, we utilize the layering technique that is often used for multivendor open architecture.

Figure 2.13   **CPU recognizes the robot configuration automatically**

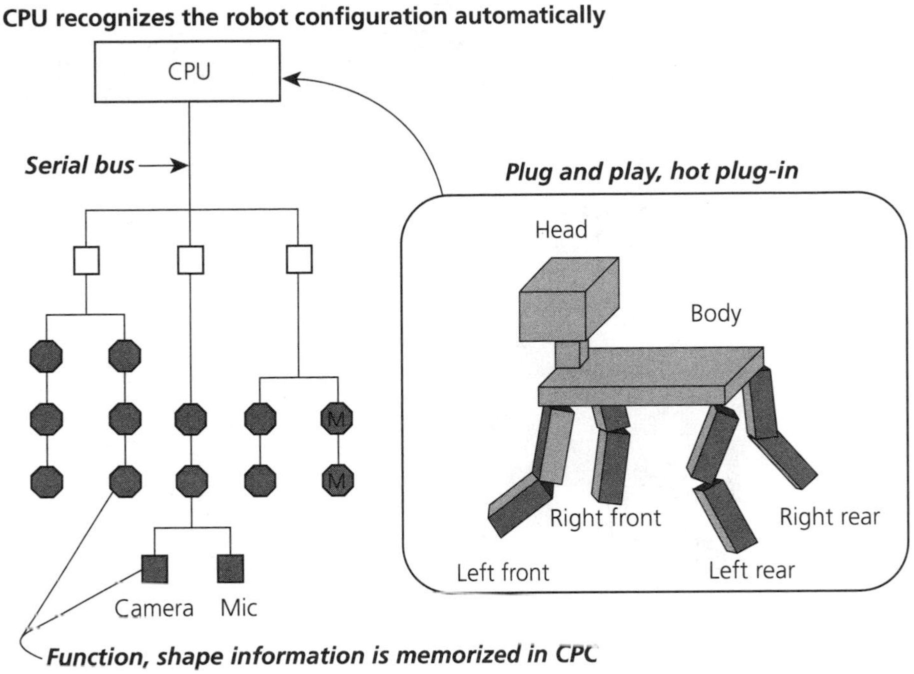

Configurable physical component (CPC).

OPEN-R divides each functional element into three layers: the hardware abstraction layer (HAL), the system service layer (SSL), and the application layer (APL).

Configurable physical component

For flexibility and extensibility, we devised the idea of configurable physical components (CPC). The physical connection between the robot components is via a serial bus (Figure 2.13). In addition, every CPC has nonvolatile memory for plug-and-play features. We will discuss this later.

Object-oriented programming

To achieve software portability, the object-oriented programming (OOP) paradigm is employed for reusable software components. The object-oriented operating system (OS) Aperios is also employed for the same reason. The details are described below.

Figure 2.14

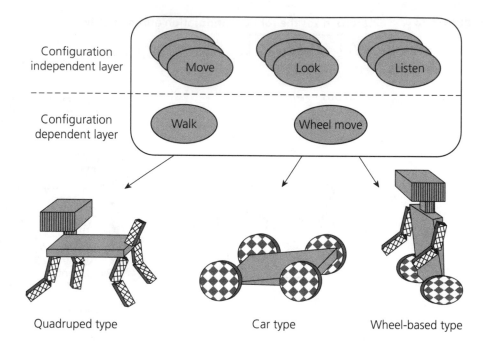

Configurable independent APIs.

Configuration-independent APIs

To achieve software portability among the different styles of robots, we separate the application software into two layers, the configuration dependent layer (CDL) and the configuration-independent layer (CIL). We define application interfaces (APIs) between the two layers so that we can achieve portability of software objects in the CIL (Figure 2.14).

Style Flexibility

Here, we mainly focus on the issue of style flexibility. (For other issues, please refer to Fujita, Kitano, and Kageyama 1998 and Fujita, Kitano, and Doi 1999).

First, let's consider the feasibility of style flexibility. The true semantic meaning of the robot parts cannot be defined until the entire mechanical configuration of the reconfigurable robot is completed. For that reason, an important topic is what kind of information should be written in the previously mentioned CPC devices. If style flexibility can be realized only after we reprogram based on the new mechanical configuration, we cannot achieve our other goals of software portability and plug-and-play. To achieve these goals

Figure 2.15

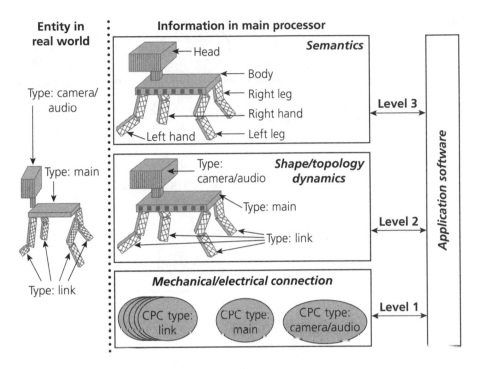

Three levels of style flexibility.

together with style flexibility, the software of the reconfigurable robot must understand its semantic meaning as well as its mechanical configuration. How should the software of the configurable robot understand not only its configuration, but also the semantic meaning of the reconfigurable robot parts?

Three levels of style flexibility

We divide the implementation of style flexibility into the following three levels (Figure 2.15):

- *Physical connection and device driver:* This is the level where we can attach and detach CPC devices to create different styles of robot. Moreover, the device driver (such as a servomotor) used for each CPC device is automatically assigned by the operating system, just as is done with current personal computers. Figure 2.16 explains the procedure for controlling CPC devices (shown in the bottom box of Figure 2.15). In order to control these CPC devices, the application software objects send messages to them through the assigned device drivers. However, this level accomplishes only mechanical or electrical connection. In other words, this completes loading of the device driver only. Other elements, such as where to connect each CPC, and the size, shape, and weight of the CPC, are not written in

Figure 2.16

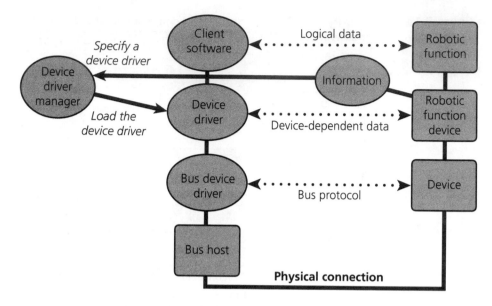

Software architecture for level 1.

the CPCs. Hence, the system software and the application software do not have all this information, unless the programmer teaches them interactively, reprograms, or reloads the program.

- *Function/shape/topology/dynamics configuration:* At this level, the CPC devices are configured automatically, and relevant information for these components is written in the CPC. The information includes the functions of the device in each component (such as a rotary actuator, an image sensor, or a stereo microphone), to where and in which direction it is being installed, its physical shape, and its dynamics parameters. On top of the details about each component, in this level, it is possible to know in which order each CPC is being connected, and to obtain the connection topology of all CPCs as a whole, so the application software objects can grasp the overall idea of the robot configuration. However, this information does not help system software or application software to recognize the semantics of the CPCs. For example, system software cannot know which part is the right paw or left leg in one robot. However, the user can apply any CPCs for any parts of the robot, as long as its physical shape and mechanical configuration and functions are suitable.

- *Semantic configuration:* At this level, an automatic semantic configuration of the CPCs is carried out. More concretely speaking, at this level, the semantic information, as well as its mechanical information mentioned earlier, is contained in the CPCs, so it becomes possible for the application software objects to know which component functions as its paw, or its leg, and have them operate properly.

However, at this level, it is no longer possible to use the right paw as the left leg even though its mechanical configuration or function is the same.

Another problem hidden in this level is that each CPC cannot know the entire robot configuration until the final connections of all CPCs are made. For example, mechanically speaking, a leg can be available for both types of robots, biped and quadruped. However, the leg does not know how it is supposed to operate until the final configuration of the robot is done because walking algorithms vary depending on the style of robot.

As you can now see, even the semantic information does not help much, unless its final configuration is complete. The goal of plug-and-play is difficult to accomplish.

Some researchers suggest that the semantics of the robot components can be learned only when the robot is put in the real world and senses the reaction from the real-world environment. The "learning and embodiment" or "internal observer" theme is one of the key issues in evolutionary artificial life or cognitive robotics (Tani, Yamamoto, and Nishi 1997). According to Matsuno (1989), an observer is embedded in an internal loop of actions, and comes to learn and understand the meaning of its actions through many experiences. Specifically, the observer understands how movement of certain parts would affect its outer world, and would actually act so it can learn the functions of each part. This is still an open issue for researchers.

We believe that our robots can be used for experiments to solve this issue. We decided to implement the CPC device at the second level, device functional/topological configuration, because the third implementation level removes the freedom of alternative uses of the CPC device as described above. We expect that many users will want to use a CPC part with different semantics, such as a leg, a hand, or a finger, depending on the situations.

In addition, we can simulate the entire robot dynamics using information at the second level. This means that we can employ simulation methods where some learning or evolutionary computationary approach can be tested as described below, instead of using the actual robots.

Portability and plug-and-play

Style flexibility means we can build many styles of robots, such as quadruped robots and wheel-based robots. However, this great advantage presents another challenge, that of guaranteeing the portability of the application program regardless of the robot's style. This is the plug-and-play challenge.

The solution to this problem is simple. OPEN-R divides the application software into two layers, the configuration-independent layer (CIL) and the configuration-dependent layer (CDL). Therefore, all the user has to do is to port only the application software objects in CIL into the differently configured robots. Through configuration-independent APIs (CI-APIs), which are APIs between CIL and CDL, the plug-and-play feature is realized as follows.

Through the CI-APIs, configuration-independent commands (CICs) are given from the higher command generator CIL to the CDL, and finally down to all robot agents, which are the software objects in a running process. Depending on the configuration, the CDL defines how each component should move and converts the commands to configuration-dependent commands (CDCs) for the robot agents. But how does the CDL convert the commands? The software in the CDL must be flexible, corresponding to the change in the mechanical configuration. However, as mentioned earlier, the semantics of each device is not written in the CPCs. Therefore, how the semantics is given to the robot would be the key factor in the implementation of portability. Moreover, the plug-and-play requires that the semantics remain flexible to dynamic configuration changes. The system software must recognize the changes made in the mechanical configuration, and consequently, if necessary, it must change the semantics and reconfigure the software in the CDL. If this process can be done automatically by the system software, plug-and-play can be accomplished. The following are three possible solutions to achieve this goal:

- *Manual setting:* Although it is not automatic, the conventional method is a manual setting. The designer of the robot manually registers the CDCs to the associative memory in the figure corresponding to the CICs. In addition, the messages must be manually set to each CPC device corresponding to the CDCs. When the configuration of the robot changes, the designer must manually change these correspondences.

- *Categorization method:* In the second level of style flexibility, the system software or the application software grasps the current mechanical configuration of the robot as a whole. Therefore, by matching a new mechanical configuration with the prerecorded finite number of configurations, the system software can choose the closest configuration, or the configuration that can operate the new mechanical configuration (Figure 2.17). The prerecorded configuration has a category number, to which the software objects in the corresponding CDL are downloaded for execution. In the prerecorded configuration, the semantic meaning of each component of the robot is already prerecorded. The objects downloaded in the CDL can convert control commands to appropriate parts according to the predefined semantics and can convert the commands to the level of the CPC devices. An automatic categorization method can be another means of accomplishing plug-and-play.

Figure 2.17

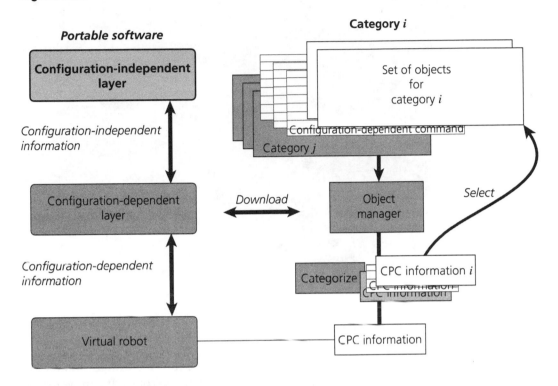

Categorization method for plug-and-play.

- *Evolutionary computing approach:* When the mechanical configuration is changed drastically, or when one wishes to minimize manual setting of the software components, evolutionary computing might be a solution, although its feasibility remains to be proved. It is not easy to work out how each component should move for arbitrarily configured robots. Also, even though the system software could recognize the style of the robot (for example, four-legged), the kind of control parameters that would be suitable remains unclear. If the robot could figure out on its own how each hand and leg should move in order to walk or to sit down through its learning ability or evolutionary methods, this would be the best solution. In this evolutionary computing approach, the CDL is expected to become a self-organization module whose inputs are CICs and whose outputs are the commands to the CPC devices.

Let's explain why it is important to write the dynamic information to each CPC. As mentioned earlier, if the style flexibility information on the second level could be written into the CPCs, it would enable simulation of the

Figure 2.18

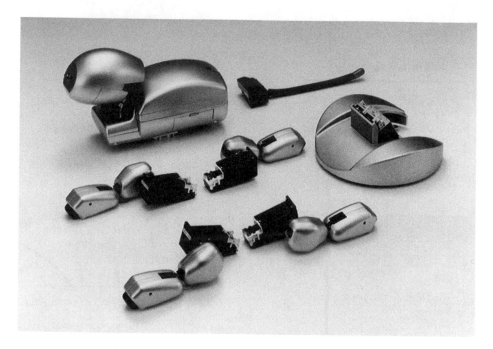

Prototype of CPC parts for reconfigurable robot.

dynamics of the robot as a whole. In order to see how a command to a CPC would work, it is not necessary to actually operate the robot. It can be tested by simulation. This yields two advantages.

One is simulation as a mental rehearsal. It becomes possible to forecast the results of a command to a CPC, helping us find how much deviation from the forecast would occur and how to fix this. The other advantage is more advanced. By using the real CPU of the robot, the simulation executes an evolutionary computation method. Consequently, software can be developed much faster than when its verification is done with an actual robot.

As you can see, the importance of writing the dynamics information in the CPC is appreciable. Not only does model-based control become feasible, but also applications such as prediction and evolution.

In the long run, we believe that the evolutionary computing approach is the key to solving the problem of automatic software adaptation. However, for the moment, we can employ the other two approaches.

Implementation

In order to realize style flexibility, we have developed the following CPC devices (Figure 2.18):

Body

The body part includes the system core of the basic system and the card slots for storage media for the program. In addition, it has four connectors for the CPC devices. For example, attaching the leg parts to these connectors makes a quadruped robot. In this implementation, the neck/head parts are unified with the body part. This part has basic sensors such as the CCD micro camera unit, a stereo microphone, and a speaker. It has three degrees of freedom to track objects and to make emotional expressions. A three-dimensional acceleration sensor is also included in the body part.

Leg

Each leg has three joints where DC-geared motors and potentiometers are used as servomotor actuators. In each foot, there is a tactile sensor that detects whether the leg touches something or not.

Wheel

Instead of the rear legs, wheel-type parts can be connected to the body part. This CPC part uses two CPC connectors so two wheels can be controlled independently.

Using these CPC parts, we can create both quadruped and wheel-based robot configurations, as shown in Figures 2.19 and 2.20.

As described in the previous section, the current implementation employs the second level of style flexibility. Since the difference between the two robot configurations, quadruped and wheel-based, is so obvious, it is easy to distinguish one from the other using the tree structure for CPC parts. However, in the future, the difference in styles of robot may not be so apparent. Therefore the categorization method described in the previous section is currently under development, so general configurations can be identified (Fujita, Kitano, and Doi 1999).

2.6   Robots for Kids

The two types of robots, the first pet-type robot and the reconfigurable robot, often appeared in conferences on artificial intelligence or robotics. However, the Legged Robot Exhibition in RoboCup-98, held in Paris in July 1998, was the first demonstration for nontechnical people. In the demonstration, we provided several opportunities for children to actually touch the

Figure 2.19

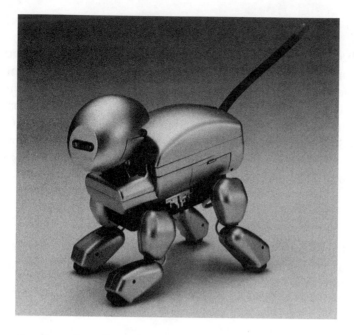

Quadruped configuration.

Figure 2.20

Wheel-based configuration.

Figure 2.21

Legged robots in RoboCup-98, Paris.

robots and play with them. (For general information on RoboCup, see Kitano, 1995.)

At the Legged Robot Exhibition, an exhibition soccer match was held (Figure 2.21). We lent out prototype robots and some sample software to three universities, who developed their own soccer robot programs. Also, between the competitions, the autonomous pet-type robot put on a performance for the crowd. At the end of the show, we let people from the audience touch the robots (Figure 2.22). The results were fascinating. When one toddler tried to feed the robot his cookie, we wondered if the robot really looked alive to him.

As we mentioned at the beginning of this chapter, AIBO, our four-legged autonomous entertainment robot, made its world debut in 1999 (Figure 2.23). The limited number of robots available, 3000 in Japan and 2000 in the United States, were sold out within 20 minutes and 4 days, respectively, via the Internet. There are now many websites devoted to AIBO, where owners can exchange information with each other or write daily accounts of AIBO's behavior.

Although this robot is not reconfigurable, it was developed and designed based on the OPEN-R. The software is based on one of the prototypes, and

Figure 2.22

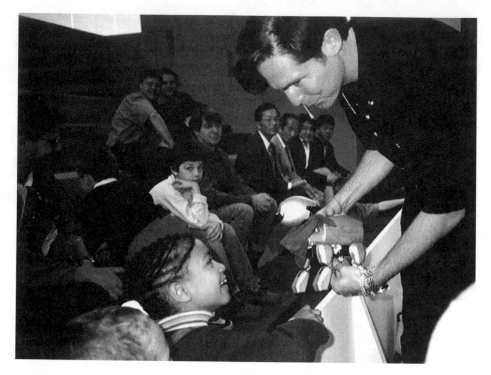

Kids with legged robot in RoboCup-98.

Figure 2.23

AIBO ERS-110.

Table 2.1   *Specifications of AIBO ERS-110.*

Dimensions	Approx. 6 1/4 × 10 1/2 × 10 7/8 inches
Mass	Approx. 1.6 kg
Movable parts	Four legs Each leg: 3 degrees of freedom Head: 3 degrees of freedom Mouth: 1 degree of freedom Tail: 2 degrees of freedom
Built-in capabilities	CCD color camera Stereo microphone Speaker Thermometric sensor
Distance sensor	Infrared
Acceleration sensor	3 axes
Battery life	Approx. 1.5 hours

the functions of learning and maturity, as well as instinct and emotion, are built in. Table 2.1 gives the specifications.

Children show their interest in the robot's motions, reactions, and emotions as expressed by the lamps (LEDs) of its eyes and sounds. Moreover, the functions of learning and growing up encourage children to interact with the robot (Figure 2.24).

We designed AIBO ERS-110 while keeping in mind the possibilities of an entertainment robot described in the previous sections. The previously mentioned tonal language enables us to interact with the robot. The robot is sold with a specially designed Sound Commander, with which the users can make the robots play soccer. A whistle can be another means of interaction. A software development kit is also commercially available. This enables users to customize the motions or the sound of the robot from their PCs. We hope the available hardware and software give users every opportunity to explore the possibilities of an entertainment robot, such as (1) watching motions, (2) interacting with the robot, (3) rearing the robot, (4) controlling the robot, and (5) developing the robot.

In addition to the activities for the commercial product, we organized the RoboCup-99 Sony Legged Robot League as an official league approved by the RoboCup Federation. Nine research groups developed their own soccer player software on a common robot platform—AIBO—but exclusively

Figure 2.24

A child plays with AIBO ERS-110.

designed for developers (Figure 2.25). The university students enthusiastically developed soccer-playing robot programs, and some even stayed overnight in the competition location to complete their development. The research and development of autonomous robots is very attractive to students whose major is pure science or engineering and may help reverse the current undesirable trend of students losing interest in studying science. We hope that by providing this opportunity and challenge for them, our activity will make a contribution.

2.7   Conclusion

The AIBO ERS-110 is only the first step toward a new application concept for the autonomous robot, which we call robot entertainment. The AIBO ERS-110 requires extensive modifications. It needs to acquire more complicated abilities of recognition, control, and learning. AIBO ERS-110 is not reconfigurable; it is a four-legged permanently configured robot. Soon we will see

Figure 2.25

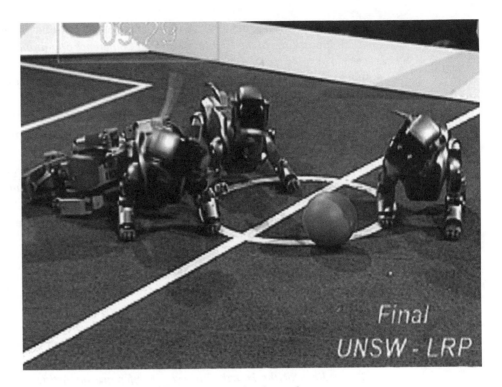

RoboCup-99 Sony Legged Robot League: final match.

reconfigurable robots. Entertainment has to cater to individual taste. Diversification of hardware and software is a must. The hardware shape, design, texture, and material and the software type will decide the success of entertainment robots. Interaction between children and robots will be far more complicated and varied in the future. We will keep our eyes on how children enjoy the robots, including programming on their PCs. When they grow older and start developing autonomous robots on their own, the robots they have dreamed about will be attainable. That will be a whole new generation of autonomous robots.

2.8   References

Brooks, R. A. 1986. A robust layered control system for a mobile robot. *IEEE Transactions on Robotics and Automations, Robotics and Automation* 2(1).

Firby, R. J. 1994. Task networks for controlling continuous process. *Proceedings of the Second International Conference on AI Planning Systems.*

Fujita, M., and K. Kageyama. 1997. An open architecture for robot entertainment system. *Proceedings of the First International Conference on Autonomous Agents,* pp. 435–440.

Fujita, M., and H. Kitano. 1998. Development of autonomous quadruped robot for robot entertainment. *Autonomous Robot* 5:7–18.

Fujita, M., H. Kitano, and Toshi T. Doi. 1999. Syntactic-semantic analysis of reconfigurable robot. Proceedings of the 1999 *IEEE/RSJ International Conference on Intelligent Robots and Systems,* pp. 1567–1572.

Fujita, M., H. Kitano, and K. Kageyama. 1998. Reconfigurable physical agents. *Proceedings of the Second International Conference on Autonomous Agents,* pp. 54–61.

Horswill, I. 1996. Variable binding and predicate representation in a behavior-based architecture. *Proceedings of the Fourth International Conference on Simulation of Adaptive Behavior,* pp. 163–172.

Kitano, H. 1995. RoboCup: The Robot World Cup initiative. *Proceedings of the International Joint Conference on Artificial Intelligence.* Workshop on Entertainment and AI/Alife. Montreal.

Matsuno, K. 1989. Physical Basis of Biology. Boca Raton, FL: CRC Press.

Tani, J., J. Yamamoto, and H. Nishi. 1997. Dynamical interactions between learning, visual attention, and behavior: An experiment with a vision-based mobile robot. *Proceedings of the Fourth European Conference on Artificial Intelligence,* pp. 309–317.

Kid's View

   ## Thomas's Robot Review

By Thomas Plaisant Schwenn, age 10

I think a robot is a machine that is programmed to perform functions such as move an arm up and down or say hello. At least one of a robot's functions is physical. In other words not all a robot's functions aren't just thinking and talking.

I started making my first robot when I joined the University of Maryland's intergenerational (many ages) design team in 1998. I think it was in February or March.

The way I, or we, made the robot was by observing current robots and brainstorming about what we liked and didn't like about the robots. Then we

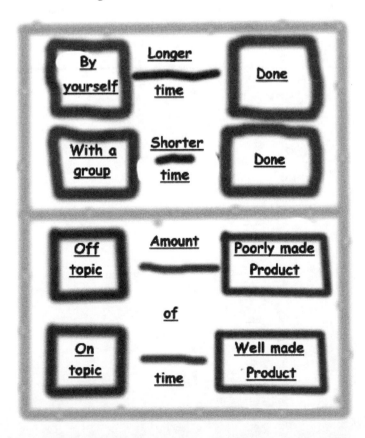

made cheap, low-tech models of robots we'd like to make. A little bit later someone gave us a robot to start with. Then we decided to split into groups that focused on certain things but the groups still interacted with each other. At the end of each session we presented to each other what we did and decided on issues. Now we're still doing these things and I don't think we'll ever be completely finished. To do these things we used our imagination, LEGOs, servos, computers, craft materials and lots of low-tech stuff.

While making this robot we noticed that some things are hard to do. One thing that is hard is interacting with others and making decisions as a group. Some other things that are hard are making things easy to use and understand, designing user interfaces, and designing the robot in general.

Not much is easy while making a robot, except having fun. It is also easy to make friends and learn about your team members while designing a robot.

Designing robots is a lot like designing a computer program. You start with something and keep on testing and then improving. Designing a robot is also a lot like an adventure. It's a huge pile of challenges that never end.

Other kids should know that designing a robot isn't easy. It isn't exactly a short process either. But it's fun and you learn about other people. If you ever make a robot *don't* design it by yourself and *don't* get off topic. The reason not to design a robot by yourself is that work in a group goes faster and more ideas are considered, making a better product quicker. And if you get off topic you don't make a well-made product.

Chapter Three

PETS: A Personal Electronic Teller of Stories

Jaime Montemayor

*University of Maryland
Institute for Advanced Computer Studies,
Computer Science Department*

Allison Druin

*University of Maryland
Institute for Advanced Computer Studies,
College of Education, Human Development Department*

James Hendler

*University of Maryland
Institute for Advanced Computer Studies,
Computer Science Department*

Abstract

In 1998, a team of 12 researchers at the University of Maryland came together to build robots for children. We were educators, computer scientists, artists, roboticists, and engineers. While our diversity in skills was not novel in ambitious interdisciplinary projects, one aspect of this team was unusual—the ages of its members: half of us were between 7 and 11 years old. A successful design team learns to find the delicate balance and respect for the disparate voices of every member. This is even more important when ages and areas of expertise are so diverse. The result of our collaboration is PETS: a Personal Electronic Teller of Stories. It is different from other robots, both in what it does and in how we conceived and built it.

In the chapter that follows, we will describe the evolution of both our robot and our team's efforts, why we needed so many different specialists, and why we included children as equal partners from the very beginning. We will also show how *cooperative inquiry* became our design philosophy. Every expert had a unique perspective and knowledge base. More important, we communicated our ideas and solved problems in very different ways. As our project progressed, we learned to leverage our individual skills and to listen with different ears to each other.

 ## 3.1   A Story

Let us start by reading a story written by a seven-year-old child, entitled "Michelle."

> There once was a robot named Michelle. She was new in the neighborhood. She was HAPPY when she first came, thinking she would make friends. But it was the opposite. Other robots threw rocks and sticks. She was SAD. Now no one liked her. One day she was walking down a street, a huge busy one, when another robot named Rob came up and ask [sic] if she wanted to have a friend. She was SCARED at first but then realized that she was HAPPY. The other robots were ANGRY but knew that they had learned their lesson. Michelle and Rob lived HAPPILY ever after. No one noticed the dents from rocks that stayed on Michelle. (Druin, research notes, August 1998)

This is just one of many stories that children have written with the help of PETS (Druin, Montemayor, et al. 1999). The author of "Michelle" did not just write this moving story; she is also an integral member of the team that built our robots. As you read on, PETS will be further described. Our motivations

Figure 3.1

PETS₂, Spaceship, and My PETS software.

behind building such an interactive robotic pet will also be discussed. In addition, the process of how we made this robotic technology with our team of adults and six children will be introduced. And with this, we will present *cooperative inquiry* (Druin 1999), the methodology that we embrace as we discover insights about technology, education, science, engineering, and art. Finally, this chapter will close with reflections on what was learned from ongoing research efforts.

3.2   Who, or What, Is PETS?

PETS is a "Personal Electronic Teller of Stories," a robotic storytelling environment for elementary school age children (Druin, Montemayor, et al. 1999). The PETS kit contains a box of fuzzy stuffed animal parts and an authoring application on a personal computer (Figures 3.1 and 3.2). Children can build a robotic animal, or pet, by connecting animal parts such as torso, head, paws, ears, and wings. After they construct their pet, they can write and tell stories using the My PETS software. Just as the robotic animal is constructed from discrete components, My PETS is also constructive. This application enables children to create emotions, draw emotive facial expressions,

Figure 3.2

The PETS₁ storytelling environment.

name their robotic companion, and compile a library of stories and story starters.

What Does PETS Do?

Each emotion that the robot performs is a sequence of physical movements that conveys a specific feeling to the audience. Our child designers defined six basic emotions: happy, sad, lonely, loving, scared, angry. They were chosen because the actions that represent these emotions are sufficiently different from each other that the audience would not confuse one with another. For example, a lonely robot droops its arms down and looks left and right for a friend. If the robot is happy, it would wave its arms quickly, turn its head left and right, and spin the spaceship it rides in. And, when the robot is sad, it droops its head and arms, and moves forward at a slow, deliberate pace (Figure 3.3).

PETS encourages creativity through interactive and iterative play. Children are constantly writing and rewriting their stories, and in the process, developing their own writing styles. They also enjoy building different kinds of animals. Whenever they want, these children can direct My PETS to tell the story and watch their animal act out emotions. As the robot

Figure 3.3

Emotions and their corresponding sets of actions.

encounters an emotional word in the story, it performs that emotion by moving its body in the sequence specified by its creators.

Collaborative learning is an important feature of PETS. Within a group of children, some enjoy writing stories; others like to construct physical things. Together, they become the authors, choreographers, and directors, creating narratives replete with emotions and actions.

A critical feature of PETS is that the child user is always in control. Unlike products such as the Actimates Barney, where the robot directs the flow of action and the child follows its instructions, we believe that children should decide their own activity patterns. Many other researchers and industry developers support this constructive approach. For example, KidSim/Cocoa (Cypher and Smith 1995), Logo (Papert 1980), and LEGO Mindstorms, and so on all place the child at the center of creative play. In short, we believe children are intelligent beings and should have the freedom to create their own imaginary worlds and invent their own playthings.

How Has PETS Changed?

Over the past two years, we designed three versions of PETS. We call them, in the order of creation, $PETS_0$, $PETS_1$, and $PETS_2$. Each successive version is a

Figure 3.4

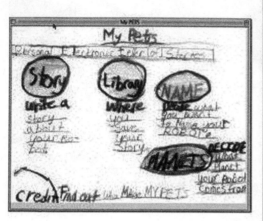 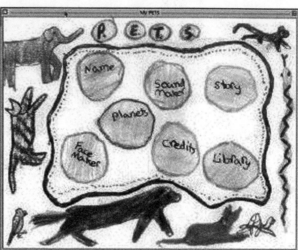

Main screens of the My PETS application. The left is from PETS₁; the right is from PETS₂.

more refined "sketch" of our group's collective vision of the storytelling environment (see Figure 3.4).

PETS$_0$ was a prototype that the adult designers created to understand the technical issues related to interactive robots. As we will show later, this version was a critical step in our design of future iterations. PETS$_0$ is in fact the result of the adult members' technology immersion process. The knowledge we gained from building this robot became a rough technology road map for future versions.

PETS$_1$ (Figure 3.5) was the first "full-featured" and demonstrable robot from our intergenerational design team. This machine had primitive reactive behaviors. For instance, its head would follow or turn away from a beam of light, depending on its mood. Also, it would move its paws toward you if it was happy, or pull away if it was scared. Most of its skeletal structure was constructed of LEGO blocks, and the limbs were simple plastic boxes. Various fabric materials covered the robot to hide the mechanical components. For instance, the head was covered with a fabric with cowhide prints; some limbs were feathers; and a furry skirt was draped over the entire body to give the robot a rounded and soft shape. A Handy Board (Martin 1998) microcontroller, within the torso, controlled various embedded motors and servos. In addition to on-board programs for the robot's primitive behaviors, the controller also received commands from My PETS through a connecting wire. Finally, sensors (e.g., light, touch) throughout the body informed the robot about its environment.

Figure 3.5

PETS₁, with a furry body, dog paw, duck foot, and cow face.

Our current prototype, PETS₂ (see Figures 3.1 and 3.6), includes many refinements over its predecessors. For example, PETS₁'s software implemented only the reactive layer of a generalized three-tiered behavior-based architecture (e.g., Bonasso et al. 1997). In contrast, PETS₂ has an additional sequencing layer. This change allowed us to transfer a large portion of the program from the microcontroller over to a more powerful and flexible desktop computer. It also greatly simplied the code underlying the user interfaces we used to control the robot.

After we completed PETS₁, we set three major goals for the next version: aesthetics, durability, and wireless communication. PETS₂ has a foam outershell covered with felt (Figure 3.7). It has far more graceful shapes and vivid colors. The foam shell not only provides the outline of the robot; it is also a buffer against abusive play from children. In addition, it has a much sturdier skeletal structure built from metal, plastic, and polycarbonate materials. Finally, the robot now communicates with the My PETS software via wireless radio frequency channels (Figure 3.8).

Figure 3.6

Children type their stories and insert emotions in the Story Screen.

Figure 3.7

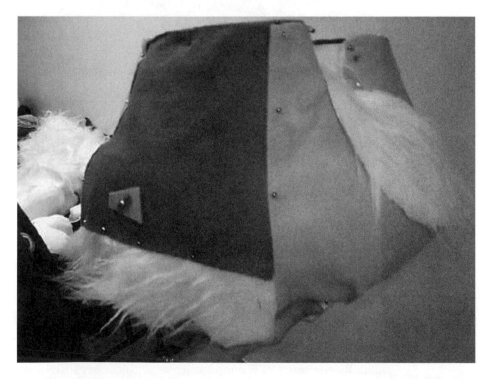

The foam shell (torso) of PETS$_2$.

Figure 3.8

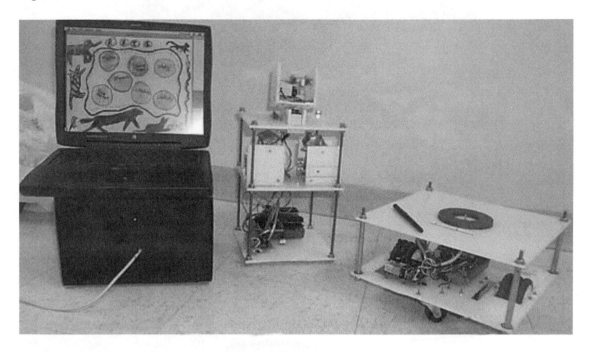

The My PETS software, the transmitter box, and the skeletal components of PETS₂.

 3.3   Why Build an Emotional Robot to Tell Stories?

We knew that we wanted a new technology that would be fun to build and to use. But what would it do, and what would it look like? Although the choice seems obvious in hindsight, it actually evolved from a vague idea to an emotional robot that can tell stories.

Why a Robot?

Children are drawn to physical playthings. They love robots! We saw this repeatedly over the past year, as we demonstrated PETS to young visitors (see Figure 3.9; see also Figure 3.10, Color Plate only). As they enter our lab, inevitably they are drawn to the robots in our room, even though it is filled with lots of other technological goodies. We believe this is because robots are inherently intriguing and highly interactive objects. Indeed, studies have shown that in settings where there are both things to observe and things to play with, young children are usually attracted to activities where they can

Figure 3.9

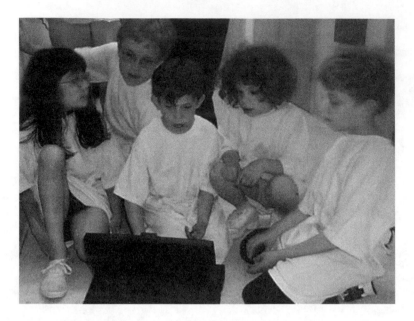

Kids (team members and visitors) play with the My PETS software.

become interactive participants. For example, in zoos, they prefer to interact with pigeons and squirrels than the more exotic animals behind bars (Greenfield 1984).

Accordingly, a robot as a design goal is useful for two reasons. The first is that it is much easier to excite children about inventing something they like than to create the next-generation toaster oven, for example. The other is that the process of building robots is inherently collaborative and physical. Since we are interested in both the process and the product, having a project that requires collaboration and lots of construction helps us study and test our design methodology in action.

But we have found that interactive, robust, and child-friendly robots are notoriously difficult to make. We believe that there are two main reasons: First, a project such as ours requires an interdisciplinary effort, thus a team with diverse talents. Putting together such a group is not easy. Second, interactions between a robot and its environment are often unpredictable. This uncertainty presents many technological and scientific challenges.

Because robots are difficult to make, and because the development process requires strong collaboration, we have found that they are ideal subjects for our research in technology and methods (see Figure 3.11, Color Plate only).

Why an Animal?

Children are naturally drawn to animals, these creatures that come in so many shapes and sizes. Animals are intriguing things: they can fly or hop or slither about. It is just plain fun to watch them and to play with them. No wonder libraries are filled with storybooks about animals. On television and in movies, Muppet and Disney characters are some of the most enduring memories for many of us. In addition, many of us can still recall the joy of visiting zoos when we were young. We have found that people make emotional connections with animals. Some visitors have observed that in our storytelling environment, children can share their feelings through a safe surrogate, which means they feel freer in discussing difficult emotional issues.

Just as important, our younger team members have been quite specific that they wanted to build things that are warm and fuzzy; they don't want the "cold," "hard," and "metallic" look-and-feel of classical robots (Druin, Montemayor, et al. 1999). Indeed, because of technical challenges related to creating "furry, fuzzy" robots, the adult members have on several occasions asked whether being "huggable and cuddly" is a requirement. And each time our kids responded unequivocally, "Yes!"

This theme has become a fertile area for commercial endeavors and academic research. Microsoft (Strommen 1998), Tiger Electronics (Furby; see Chapter 4), and Sony (Fujita and Kitano 1998; see Chapter 2) are actively promoting robotic animal products. At MIT's Media Lab, researchers are also developing plush toys to control synthetic characters in animated environments (Johnson et al. 1999). Another project, SAGE, also uses a programmable stuffed animal to tell stories (Umaschi 1997).

Why Stories?

People love stories. From their earliest moments, children love to listen to stories. Either as parents or children, many of us have fond memories of our favorite bedtime stories or books. Stories preserve our culture and history, enable us to communicate our ideas and feelings, and educate learners of all ages (Bruchac 1987; Gish 1996; Ortiz 1998).

Storytelling and story-making can be immensely creative and empowering for children. They decide what they want to say and how they want to say it. A story can be made of words, or pictures, or sounds, as long as it conveys the message of its author. From the beginning, we made this a functional requirement for our new technology, since it is such a natural way for children to explore new ideas and feelings.

Why Have Emotions?

It is difficult to imagine a robotic animal devoid of emotions. Observe how children play with stuffed animals or action figures. Their play is filled with emotive content (Goldman 1998). They attribute emotions to their toys, whether they are dolls or trucks. So it is natural that when children interact with a robot, especially one that looks like an animal, they relate to it emotionally. Indeed, how can you tell stories without including emotions within them? It just does not make sense.

3.4   Our Intergenerational Design Team

When people discuss the design process, they usually refer to the result of that process, or the technology. For us, our design goal is a new kind of educational technology, one that incorporates many different constructive and collaborative learning experiences. This is important, but we are also equally interested in the development process and the learning experience that comes from building and studying technology. Many researchers have referred to this type of learning as outcomes of the cooperative or participatory design process (Ehn 1993; Greenbaum 1993; Mumford and Henshall 1979/1983). Educators (Lave 1992) also call it a community of practice. Druin (1999) describes this as "a community of people with different skills that learn as they work toward shared goals."

We want to invent new methods for learning through technology, and we want to know about the kinds of learning that can occur in adults and children when they collaborate as equal design partners.

Our team, the *intergenerational design team* (IDT), has at least 12 members (Figure 3.12). Six of us are between 7 and 11 years of age and come from local (public and private) elementary schools. These children stay with us for a long term, at least for one year. The adults are undergraduate or graduate students, and faculty from art, education, engineering, and computer science. We share a common goal: to understand how children are interested in and wish to play with new and existing technologies. This investigation led us to develop our robot and the principles behind *cooperative inquiry*.

It is clear to many people that our team should include people with many different specialties. For example, the mechanical engineer designs and builds the physical structure of the robot. Of course, given enough time, anyone might be able to do this, and he (the non–mechanical engineer) would surely gain valuable learning experience. But although this may be an enlightening learning process, it is probably not a very efficient way to

Figure 3.12

Members of our team talk about the structure of PETS.

develop products. Similarly, we can see how the other experts are integral to the team. The educator guides us and shows us ways to collaborate with children. She also provides the framework for our design process. The artist transforms our "cold" and "ugly" machine into a huggable and lovable companion. And the computer scientist creates the programs that enable children to write the stories to make the robot come alive with emotions.

But it is not obvious to observers why we include children as equal partners on our team. This deserves a more in-depth discussion, and we will offer our reasons in the next section.

Why Children?

We are often asked why we include children on our design team as equal-voiced partners. After all, many would suggest that it's difficult enough to have a good working team of adults; there is no need to make the development process more complicated by including young people who (presumably) don't know one-tenth as much as grown-ups. Visitors of our research lab ask the following common questions: "How do you work with children?" "How do you select the 'right' child for the group?" "Won't they slow down the development process?" "Why do we need them? After all, we were all young once, so we should know what and how children think." The common underlying questions seem to be this: Can children be effective partners, and are they qualified? After spending over two years with our young members, we believe the answer is decidedly affirmative.

Here is an example that shows how adults may be less effective than children in reporting flaws in a program. Consider how grown-ups use software programs—in particular, an adult who uses a business application at her workplace. When she uses a program that does not feel intuitive, she may curse and complain about the awkwardness, but since she has a job to do, she might change her own work pattern to circumvent the flaws. So while the program may not provide her the highest productivity, it still gets some work done. Still, the user might have misgivings about her time on the computer, and she certainly would not enjoy using it. Here we see that adults compensate for flaws in technology.

Contrast this with technology that is designed for children. Any imperfections in a product become magnified many times when a child uses it. She has no patience for things that are not "just right." Furthermore, she has no incentive to change her behaviors just to complete her task; she may just as likely abandon it.

In recent years, industry has come to understand children's needs, and most commercial technological products for children are evaluated and tested by young people before they are produced commercially.

How do you work with children?

It is difficult to work with children to design technology for many reasons. For instance, young children have more difficulties verbalizing their thoughts than adults. This is particularly the case when they want to convey abstract ideas (Piaget 1971, 1973). So unless we acquire the skills to properly communicate with them, it would be difficult to involve them in development efforts. In addition, while there has been an immense amount of research into communication channels among adults of varying skills, it has only been in the past decade that we have come to understand ways to work with children. Also, traditional types of relationships between adult and child, such as speaker-listener, child-parent, or instructor-follower, are not always useful in collaborative settings. Finally, misconceptions about the proper roles of adults and children can often lead to frustration. For example, children are not just "short adults," implying they are equally capable of any task that an adult can handle. We would never expect a seven-year-old child to solder wires or operate heavy machinery. Alternatively, just because a child utters a statement does not necessarily mean that it must be followed, since she should always know what's in the best interest of young

Figure 3.13

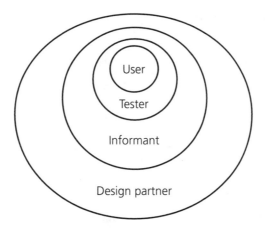

The four levels of involvement in a technology team.

people. In short, children are an entirely different user population with their own culture, norms, and complexities (Berman 1977), and they should be treated as people with special knowledge about the subject of "being a child," just as engineers are people who know a lot about building things.

As long as we understand that children are a kind of specialist, we can effectively engage them in the design process. We have found that a child can participate in the technology development process in four ways: (1) user, (2) tester, (3) informant, and (4) design partner (Druin 2000). As Figure 3.13 shows, each level of participation encompasses the lower level. For example, a tester needs to be a user in order to test a product. Below we will briefly describe each of these roles (see Table 3.1 for a summary of children's roles in technology).

Both user and tester offer feedback to designers, either directly or through observations by researchers, about the usefulness, effectiveness, and correctness of a product. The major difference is that the user tests a technology after it is completed and unchangeable, while the tester uses intermediate prereleased prototypes as well as the final product. It is clear that as a user, the child has little impact on the design of a technology except for its future iterations, if they do happen. However, the child tester can affect change in technology, since her preferences and dislikes can affect internal versions of a product. Notice that the idea for a technology originates from adults. The child is brought into the process as an evaluator of the adults' efforts and ideas. These two roles are appealing for adult researchers because adults can more easily control the design process and they are easy roles for children to assume, so little learning need happen.

Table 3.1 *A summary of the role of children in the design of technology (Druin 2000).*

Role of child	Began	Strengths	Challenges	In use by
User	Late 1960s/ early 1970s	• Easy to include children • Researcher in control • Can suggest future directions in HCI and education areas	• Less direct impact on changes in technology • Children have less say in changes • Educators need time to accomplish in classroom	Primarily academic researchers
Tester	A few examples in the 1970s; began primarily in the late 1980s/ early 1990s	• Begins to empower children • Quicker input for changing technology • Methods can be done in and out of schools	• Children don't have input until later in the design process • Can offer surprises to adults • Adults decide what can be done given limits of schedule	Academic researchers and industry professionals
Informant	A few examples in the 1980s; began primarily in the mid-1990s	• Empowers children • Brings children's input into the start of the development process • Flexible when children and researchers work together	• Adults still decide when to bring children into the design process • More time is needed to work with children	Academic researchers and industry professionals
Design partner	Mid-1990s	• Empowers children throughout development experience • Children and adults can change and learn from the experience • Instant feedback from children throughout the design process	• Team decisions must be negotiated between adults and children • More time is needed to work as partners • School environment is difficult to work within • Difficult finding researchers that can work with children	Primarily academic researchers with industry professionals beginning

The role of child as informant has become prominent very recently (Scaife and Rogers 1999). In this capacity, the child can have an impact on technology from the start of the development process. The child can participate based on what the researchers believe a child can offer at various stages during product development. Here, the researcher still holds majority control, since she decides when to involve the child. The final role, that of design partner, is where the child has the same stake throughout the entire design and research process. So, unlike the participant, the child partner is not brought in and out of the development; she is always involved. But this level of involving children can slow the development process, although this is not necessarily bad. In our experience, the slowdown is usually due to discoveries of better ways of doing things or new ideas/features that should be included in a technology because the child partners were able to see things that the adults did not.

It is up to the development team to choose the role for their young members. Depending on the team's philosophy, resources, and time constraints, a different role may make more sense. In industry, the role of child as tester can be indispensable. It would just be too expensive to release unusable technology. But educational researchers may prefer the user role because observations and evaluations can be much easier. If you want to involve children as informant or partner, then you should be prepared for longer development times. And you should be prepared to deal with the additional problems of working with young people who are far from being adults.

How do you select the "right" child for the group?

This is usually the first question we are asked after visitors sit through one of our design sessions and meet our children. Implicitly, they might believe (1) these kids are intellectually above the norm, (2) they have played with technology for years, or (3) they are natural team players. In fact, these children are no different from others in their age group. Some are bright, and some have used computers for several years. But they all have had to learn new things and forget bad habits to become productive members. Every child has her own talents and weaknesses. For example, many have never participated in groups before, so collaboration can be difficult for them. A few of our children have been shy and quiet and have not liked to express their ideas in front of the group. But, six months into our project, these children have blossomed into fully participating partners. They fought for their ideas to be heard and they openly criticized opinions that they believed were wrong. More importantly, they gained new confidence, whether in technical skills or in social skills, and they began to believe and realize that they were truly "partners."

We require only four attributes from prospective child partners. The first is that the child must be enthusiastic about playing with technology. The second is that the child must be able to express her ideas (e.g., write, speak, draw, paint, etc.). Third, she should be open to collaborate with other children and adults. Finally, she should be between 7 and 11 years old, an age we have found most appropriate for this kind of design partnership. Children are old enough to be self-reflective, but young enough to be open to new ideas.

Won't they slow down the development process?

Yes, children can slow down the design process. Products can take longer to build. This is especially true for a new team. Our experience shows that it takes about six months before an intergenerational team becomes a cohesive unit. Consequently, the ramp-up time is significant. Also, since there are many more forms of communication for adults to recognize and understand, this means that the same conversation might be repeated several times, over different channels; this extra effort translates into more time. Alternatively, the design process can slow down just because children can offer insights into better technology so that we often decide to incorporate new features and ideas that were not part of the original design goals.

But consider what might happen if adults try to build technology without incorporating children, using one of the previously defined roles, into the development process. Here is a hypothetical scenario:

1. Grown-up has a "great" idea for new technology for kids.

2. Grown-up builds it.

3. Grown-up shows the gadget to kids and asks, "What do you think?" And, "What should I do to make it better for you?"

4. Kids look at grown-up and mumble, "I dunno," or "I don't understand," or "I don't like it."

5. Grown-up tries to rephrase "What do you think?"

6. Kids mumble and walk away.

Does this sound familiar? What happened? We believe this gulf in communication is the phenomenon of two monologues. What appears to be an interaction, or dialog, is really just the two sides trying to guess at what the other is really saying. There is no transfer, or flow, of information. Let us look at steps 3 through 6 again.

Adult's Perspective	*Child's Perspective*
3. Grown-up shows the gadget to kids and asks, "What do you think?" And, "What should I do to make it better for you?"	Whah! Information overload! What's all that stuff? What's going on? Why are these things purple? Why is that thing round?
4. Kids look at grown-up and mumble, "I dunno," or "I don't understand," or "I don't like it."	Just say anything.
5. Grown-up tries to rephrase "What do you think?"	Child thinks, "Hmm. I don't like purple. Therefore, I don't like this thing." Child says, "I dunno."
6. Kids mumble and walk away.	Who was that?

The problem is that children have no context in understanding the object presented before them, and grown-ups have no context in understanding how children comprehend their environment. Consequently, when all a child sees is the technology, she cannot understand the rationale behind its features. Now the adult might try to decipher the ever-so-deep "I don't like it." But she may very easily misinterpret the child because that is just not enough information to work with. And if she does misinterpret her observations, and if she then tries to create a new iteration based on this false interpretation, then the technology may stray from its intended objective.

Why do we need them? After all, we were all young once, so we should know what and how children think.

Yes. We were all children at one time. But designing technology for children based on personal memory is probably not a good idea. First, we overestimate our ability to remember our past. Do I really remember what things I liked 20 years ago? More importantly, do I remember the reasons that I liked certain things? In addition, we grew up in a very different time from today's children. Some of us still remember the vacuum-tube television, vinyl phono albums, and so on. Compare that to what our kids have today: inexpensive home computers, VCRs, camcorders, Walkmans, and more. The context within which we grew up is not comparable to the current generation. Even if we do remember what was fun and useful, it is doubtful that knowledge easily applies to designers of technology for the future. So we need to include children's voices in our development efforts. They give us their perspectives for today, not 20 years ago.

Some Insights from Our Kids

During our many design sessions, our young members offered many refreshing insights. Some of them the adults might have come up with eventually. But there were many great ideas that may never have come to light had adults been the only ones doing the thinking. We will share four examples: the story starter, the planets, the emotions, and the emotion construction interface.

Story starter

When we were designing the PETS$_1$ story-writing screen, a child member remarked, "Let's have a story starter button." All of us looked at her and wondered what she meant. She explained that some children may have a difficult time writing stories. For this reason, we should have a way for other children, who do not have problems creating them, to write up the beginnings of stories. This way, if a child is stuck, all she has to do is to push a button and pick from a library of ideas from other kids (see Figure 3.14, Color Plate only).

Planets

An adult suggested that we should have a way to name our robotic pet. After all, real pets have names. The children really liked this idea. And then they said we should have planets too. Now, the adults were not quite sure about the purpose of the planets. Since there was no reason *not* to have this feature, we incorporated it into My PETS. We asked the kids why the planets were so important. But they could not explain why they liked the idea.

Several months later, one of the adults had an insight: Our animal does not look like anything from Earth. So it makes sense that it must have come from somewhere among the stars. And, since the robot is an actor, it must have a stage from which to tell its stories. The stage and the origin of the pet were two great reasons to include planets as a feature.

Emotions

Our team was divided into three groups (software, skins and sensors, and skeleton) to design different parts of the robot. The software group was in charge of defining the emotions (Figure 3.15). Within less than an hour of starting this task, the child members in this group asked the skeleton group what kinds of movements the robot could make. They wanted to know this before they defined the action sequences. The skeleton group's adult member was astounded by this and asked the adult member of the software group whether she had initiated this. No, she said, the children had come up with

Figure 3.15

A kid member tests an emotion.

that insight. Apparently, a couple of days before, they had gone on a field trip to the zoo to study the shapes, movements, and sounds of the animals. They must have realized that physical structures in animals impose a limit in the kinds and range of motions. So the same must be true of the robotic animal they are creating.

Emotion construction interface

During PETS$_0$, the adults had created a user interface to control the robot. While it was functionally correct, the kids had no idea how to use it. This became an important design issue for subsequent PETS. Before we asked the kids to invent a new screen, we explored a couple of issues: what did the robot need to know in order to move around, and how do we give this information to the robot? For example, we knew the robot could move its arms. To do this, it needed to know which arm to move, in what direction, and how far. After the kids understood this relationship, they went ahead and sketched a new interface. Interestingly, not only did they know how to use the controls, so did the adults. This screen, as well as the others within My PETS, reflects a child's approach to controlling technology.

Some Difficulties of Working with Child Team Members

We did not always have good days. There were times when the team worked together flawlessly. But on other days, pandemonium broke out in our lab. Children sometimes acted out. We tried to remember that the kids were, after all, still quite young. At times, a kid member became stubborn. She refused to do anything coherent. In short, she was having a bad day. This was when the power structure took a break, and the adults became caretakers. We tried to resolve the problem if we could. The key is that adult members were both adults and partners. Sometimes, we just had to be the "regular" grown-ups, whether we liked it or not.

What if the children became bored? We encountered this problem a few times. We believe the main reason is that the children were working on the longest-lasting project in their experience. It is difficult to hold an adult's attention on a difficult subject; imagine what a child must endure. As a result, we rescheduled our research calendar to include frequent rest and free-play days. These "free sessions" occurred during the regular design meetings. But the children did not have to do anything but play with their favorite toys. It was important to schedule regular decompression sessions. But these were not just free-play days; they were also great for technology immersion.

3.5 What's Different about Our Lab?

Walk into any "normal" academic research lab, and you are not likely to see a 6-foot-tall stuffed robotic animal smiling at you. You are also not likely to see boxes upon boxes of LEGO blocks, fabric swatches, playthings made out of clay, and above all, kids and adults engaged in lively debate. This pandemonium is our lab.

The Room

Our laboratory is also our design room. It is full of computers, stuffed animals, beanbag chairs, lots of sketching material, and lots of stuff made by children. It has a large open central area so that everyone can sit in a circle to chat. We have carpets on our floor because much of our initial brainstorming occurs with everyone sitting on the ground and throwing out ideas. To the child, it does not feel like a classroom; to the adult, it does not feel like a laboratory. Most importantly, our room is very comfortable and inviting for both adults and children.

Sketches

We sketch a great deal. This is the primary way we communicate to each other about our ideas. We write, we draw, we sew, and we build three-dimensional objects. Without sketches, we would not be able to get past the age difference between the child and the adult, and we would have a difficult time communicating with people from different disciplines. We use clay, paper, socks, LEGO blocks, strings, tape, pins—anything we can get our hands on. We try to have as much and as many different kinds of materials in our stockroom as possible. You never know what you are going to need to make your ideas come alive.

Mental exercise: Invent a new kind of toy house in your mind. Now sketch it. (Use any media you like.) Finally, show it to another person. How did you envision this house in your mind? Was it a written description, a drawing, or a three-dimensional object? Next, what did you use to sketch your idea? Did you use more than one medium? Did you prefer one medium to another? Did you find it impossible to convey your vision with some media but trivial with others? Different ideas require different kinds of sketches to convey the message.

A Typical Session

We meet twice a week. We always start with snack time. Our team sits around a table full of tasty foods, and we chat. We talk about everything except our design problems. That comes after the snacks. This is an important time. First, children (and grown-ups too) cannot concentrate if they are hungry. Second, they have just finished their day of regular school, and they need a transition time where they remove their student hats and put on their designer hats. In the real world, these children may still be stuck in the traditional teach-listen model. They need to shed that first before they become our partners.

After snacks, if it is a free day, the children play with anything in our lab. Sometimes they play computer games, other times they design their personal Web pages; or they may videotape each other. (They really like the camcorder.)

If we have a regular research session, then we talk about the major open issues in the project. During our discussions, no one is allowed to raise her hand, meaning that the children do not need "permission" to speak out. We discuss what worked from previous sessions and what did not work. We talk about why the ideas failed and what we can do to fix them. Next we focus on one or two specific things for the day. Here we trade ideas about technological

Figure 3.16

The skins and sensors group testing different kinds of covers.

limits, user interface ideas, the look and feel of the robot, and so on. Often we split into groups to tackle the problem of the day (Figure 3.16).

Some people mistakenly believe that designing with children means giving them some very high-level, abstract goal, and then standing back and watching the kids figure out what is needed to achieve it. We do not believe this is a good approach. Consider a farmer and his crop. The farmer prepares the land and plants the seedlings into the soil; he nurtures them by watering them, removing weeds, and fertilizing the soil; then, he stands back and watches his crop grow; finally, he harvests. In our lab, this is the same way we engage our children. We come up with a goal. We explore the motivations for the goal. We think about what is hard and what is easy. This is the first stage, where we prepare and plant the seedlings. In effect, we are providing context for the children so that they understand intuitively the "what" and the "why" behind the project. The next thing we do is to give them the material they need to solve problems. They can sketch any way they like. They can discuss scientific issues with us, and so on. Equally important, we correct them (and they us) when either goes down the wrong path. This is the weeding. Third, we stand back. Now the children have context, they know what they want to build, and they have the materials to realize their ideas. At the end, we all collect our prize.

3.6 Cooperative Inquiry

Over the past several years, our research has involved children as active research partners (Druin et al. 1997; Druin, Bederson, et al. 1999). In addition to children, these teams were composed of educators, computer scientists, and artists. Originally, these teams employed methods, such as "cooperative design," "contextual inquiry," and "participatory design," which were methods to facilitate collaboration among adults. While these were adequate starting points, we found that they needed to be modified to account for the inclusion of children as design partners (Druin 1999). Techniques such as the interview procedures and note-taking practices evolved to be more suited to child partners. For example, children can draw, rather than write, to express their ideas. These adaptations eventually led to the development of *cooperative inquiry*, a way to create new technologies for children, with children. It incorporates three complementary design methods: contextual inquiry, participatory design, and technology immersion.

The theoretical basis for cooperative inquiry comes from cooperative design, participatory design, contextual inquiry, activity theory, and situated action. The cooperative inquiry methodology includes (1) multidisciplinary partnerships with children, (2) field research that emphasizes understanding context, activities, and artifacts, and (3) iterative low-tech and high-tech prototyping (Druin 1999).

Contextual Inquiry

In *contextual inquiry*, we ask how processes work, why they are laid out in certain ways, and whether they can be improved. In order to understand a process, researchers should record data within the environment of that process (Beyer and Holtzblatt 1998). We extend this approach by having both adult and child researchers observe and take notes about the child user in her environment. As a result, we collect impressions from both the adult and the child perspectives.

Originally, we asked everyone to record their observations the same way. Table 3.2 shows an example contextual inquiry diagram. But we soon found that children do not necessarily want to take notes. They prefer to draw cartoons and write captions to describe what they saw. On the other hand, some adults shy away from graphic records because they do not have confidence in their drawing abilities. In order to accommodate individual differences, we began to ask the children to draw pictures, along with some simple text, to explain their observations (Figures 3.17 and 3.18), and adults to use the standard textual method.

Table 3.2 *Portion of a contextual inquiry diagram created by adults.*

| | Raw Data | | Data Analysis | | |
Time	Quotes	Activities	Activity Patterns	Roles	Design Ideas
10:05	E: Can you draw whatever you want? [Adult: Yes.] E: (To K) A Christmas tree? K: Yes!	K takes the mouse rapidly, draws a red tree, takes the yellow crayon,	Drawing	Artist	
		draws something in the corner, rubs out, continues	Drawing Erasing	Artist	
		E tries to take the mouse	Struggling for control of input device	Leader	Multiple input devices
	E: But I want the long one! E: Noo! [Difficult to erase.] E: There. E: But what's this? [Windows Start menu appears.]	E gets the mouse, tries to get the blue crayon, looks irritated when she cannot get the blue one, gets it	Difficulty selecting tools	Frustrated user	Easier way to select tools
		E draws a cloud, rubs it out	Drawing Erasing	Artist	
		K takes the mouse	Struggling for control of input device	Leader	Multiple input devices
		K goes on with clouds, concentrated	Drawing	Artist	
		E looks around, yawns		Bored user	

Figure 3.17

Contextual inquiry notes by a kid member observing other kids at a computer.

Figure 3.18

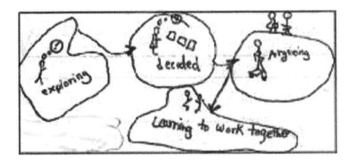

Contextual inquiry notes by a seven-year-old child.

Data we collect through contextual inquiry can provide both the adult and child a common context, or language, for discussion. This is extremely useful when the adult needs to interpret children's comments about the technology. In addition, since we have both textual and graphical data, we can study the similarities and differences between adult and child perceptions about an environment.

We have found that the most effective textual note-taking usually requires a pair of observers: one transcribes the user's quotes, and the other records the concurrent activity. Both people also log the time so that the quotes can be synchronized with their corresponding activities.

A typical observation session includes a pair of observers, an *interactor*, and a child subject in her environment. The interactor's role is to ask questions and initiate discussions about activities. This is an essential role. Without the interactor, children often feel as if they are on stage and being observed. But by actively engaging them in conversations about what they are doing, children are more likely to reveal their natural patterns. In addition, it is important that the interactor does not take notes, again because children may become self-conscious. The interactor is not an interviewer; instead she asks questions that help identify activities or patterns as they occur in the context of the target process. For example, she might ask, "Why are you doing this?" Or "What's this?" When properly captured by the note takers, the answers to these questions engender both insights about the process and new ideas to improve it.

Interestingly, both adult and child have difficulties being the interactor. Because of her role (such as parent or teacher) in a traditional power structure, the adult interactor may steer or direct the child subject. The child interactor's challenge is to remain in the role of the facilitator/observer and not be actively involved in the context being studied.

Contextual inquiry creates a common frame of reference for the adult and child as well as the people with different expertise. An adult can consult and compare the textual records with the graphical notes and understand the meaning behind a child's utterances and behavior. A child can understand the process of "doing research" and become comfortable asking questions and, through her notes, telling others about their impressions.

Participatory Design

Contextual inquiries often generate ideas that can best be understood by construction. We use participatory design to visualize concepts because it balances the power structure between adult and child and across specialties. These two techniques form an iterative prototyping cycle. Inquiry leads to new ideas, which beget prototypes, which reveal more ideas or flaws, then more prototypes, and so on.

Prototyping

Once we have an idea, we visualize it by using low-tech prototyping (for example, see Figure 3.19). This is a deceptively simple method, but it can be improperly applied. For example, since our prototyping material is the usual

Figure 3.19

Socks filled with tissue paper give the rounded shape of the head.

"kid" stuff, such as clay, paper, glue, and so on, adults may think that these are solely children's prototyping supplies. Or, if an idea is "mechanical," then the engineer should lead the design effort. Neither is correct.

We use low-tech stuff so that *everyone* can prototype with them; they are easy to manipulate for both children and adults. Also, choosing the right kinds of material to visualize a specific idea can be tricky. We have observed that a set of supplies that worked in solving one problem was frustrating and limiting to use when we applied them to another. In addition, we have found that creative ideas can come from "nonexperts," since making things with low-tech materials does not require special knowledge or tools. Notice that low-tech prototypes do not have to work. They are mainly the manifestations of our mental thoughts. In addition to our notes from contextual inquiry, these objects also become part of our shared experience and knowledge.

The insights we gain from low-tech prototyping give us the foundation to build functional high-tech prototypes. Again, we go through the iterative prototyping cycles. But this phase is more deliberate and time-consuming. For comparison, Figure 3.20 shows a shelf full of low-tech prototypes, all built within a few hours, while $PETS_0$, $PETS_1$, and $PETS_2$ required many months of labor. You might wonder whether the few hours of quick prototyping are

Figure 3.20

Some early sketches of "fluffy-fuzzy" robots using low-tech prototype materials and techniques.

truly useful. Absolutely. Without these simple objects, our team could not communicate the much more abstract requirements of the technology. Furthermore, because they can be built so swiftly, we could create many more trial sketches before deciding on a good design.

Learning from cooperation and collaboration

Participatory design teaches us how to collaborate with people from different areas and of varying ages. We have noticed that over time, our team members learn to complement each other, so that a person with expertise in one area helps the other people in the group to understand ideas related to that topic. We found this to be a powerful way for us to extend our knowledge. Much of creativity comes from making mental leaps beyond what we understand or novel connections between tidbits that we already know. When we collaborate with a diverse group, someone else inevitably helps us make that jump.

As experts in our fields, we tend to look at problems and solve them within some fixed patterns. While this may be efficient in solving problems in our domain, it can quickly become a hindrance when we are faced with situations that are not quite like anything we have seen. Now, when people with diverse perspectives gather and look at a problem, they each will see a different facet. When one person is stuck and cannot move forward, another, because she perceives the problem differently, offers the mental opening for the first person. Then they move on to the next problem. This happened with such regularity in our group that we realized it was a powerful effect of our methodology.

Here is just one example. When we were moving from PETS$_1$ to PETS$_2$, one of our goals was to design a much stronger but lighter skeleton. Our technologist considered many variations of boxlike structures. These designs were strong, to be sure. But they were heavy and required precision machining. There was an additional constraint. He wanted to give as much contact surface as possible so that the "skin," or foam shell, could attach itself to the hard structure. The extra weight and machining requirements bothered him until the next design session. Our resident artist was listening to the roboticist describe the physical structure of the robot and his need to build these boxes and how he did not like his solutions. She then said, "I don't need to glue the foam to the skeleton because the foam will hold its shape and stay in place around the box." This was so straightforward and simple, but he just could not see past the box without her help. Now all he had to build was a structure with a top and bottom plate and four columns to support them. Much easier to build and much lighter.

Technology Immersion

From *technology immersion* we understand how things work, why they are good or bad, and how we can make them better. Do we need to invent new technology, or can we reuse current technology in new and novel ways? We call this process the *creation of new metaphors in technology.*

While most adults on our team are surrounded by technology, the same is not true for our children. We believe that in order for them to appreciate fully the impact and meaning of technology in their daily lives, they need to have access to the best technology and the widest variety that we can afford—and enough so that children do not have to share. In addition to the availability of physical resources, our goal is that they also have enough time to become fully immersed in the technology. An important point: our children decide how and when they use the technology. We do not persuade them to do things "our" way. Otherwise our inquiry observations would be about the adult's interactions with the environment, not the child's experience.

Design-Centered Learning

Throughout the chapter we have mentioned the different learning experiences that our team encountered. Collaboration, familiarity with technology, and research techniques are just a few of the many enlightening topics. Druin calls the collection of learning outcomes related to cooperative inquiry *designed-centered learning* (Druin 1999). The following is a list of five areas of self-reported designed-centered learning from our team (Druin, research notes, August 1998).

1. *I learned about the design process.* All team members discussed understanding the technology design process in new ways.

2. *I learned respect for my design partners.* Both adults and children discussed their mutual appreciation for the work that the others could accomplish.

3. *I learned to communicate and collaborate in a team.* Children and adults discussed the difficulties and the rewards of learning team communication and collaboration skills.

4. *I learned new technical skills and knowledge.* All team members mentioned technical skills they had come to learn (e.g., building robots, designing software).

5. *I learned new content knowledge.* In the case of the team working on the PETS project, children and adults discussed learning more about animals.

We found that both adults and children changed from the process of building PETS. The adult began as a researcher, perhaps with some biases about the usefulness of elementary-school students as partners. Through cooperative inquiry, she began to learn that every person has a different communication method. And then, as she learned to identify her team members' individual voices and then to share her knowledge through the appropriate channels, she became a partner to the children. Our young members began the project as followers/listeners, because this is the role of the child. With time, the child realized that she had talents too and that she could contribute her knowledge to the group. She also learned how she preferred to communicate her ideas. At this point, she became a designer with an equal voice.

3.7   Reflections

We learned so many things from building PETS. Not only did we build a novel robot, but we also learned about working as a group of adult and child design partners (see Figure 3.21). And now, we close our chapter with some final thoughts.

Figure 3.21

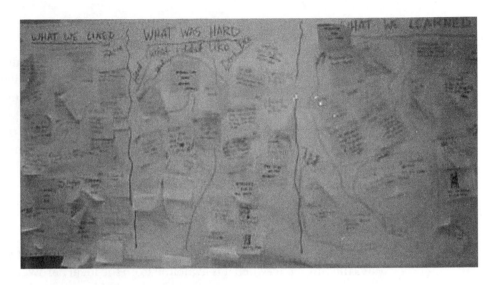

Results from a group review session.

Transformations

We learned to become more than adults and children. The computer scientist learned about educational principles, the engineer learned about art, the educator learned about robots, and the artist learned about science. Cooperative inquiry gave us the means to find a common language to share our thoughts and ideas.

Adapt Methodology to Accommodate Both Adults and Children

We did not abandon a sound methodology (for adults) just because it did not work with children; we adapted and adopted variations of the techniques so that they did apply to the different age groups. But it is important to know when an approach will not work, no matter how you vary it. This is when you abandon it and try something else.

A Good Team Takes Time to Develop

Our team became a cohesive group after about six months. This is a long time, but well worth the initial investment. In fact, our older kid members began to take on the role of task leaders after about 10 months. This level of maturity requires time and plenty of patience too.

Good Thinking Comes from Being Comfortable

Adults might be able to endure a bad design space, but children will not. Make sure your room is comfortable for everyone and that all members feel equal to each other. Our lab is filled with things we make. They remind us of what we have learned and our vision as a team.

Don't forget to feed your team. You do not want to be in the same room as six hungry and grouchy kids. Snack time also gives everyone enough transition time to mentally join the group.

Know What's out There

Get to know the available construction material. You do not want to spend days making a part when it is available from the local hardware store for pennies. Spend time visiting hardware stores, hobby stores, fabric stores, and electronics stores. Not all technology immersion is high tech!

Remember the Basics

Whenever you encounter a breakdown in communication, check to see if you are still in the cooperative inquiry mode. Did you revert to "plain" adult, or did the child stop being a designer?

When you are stuck with a technical design, don't try to solve it yourself. Remember that you are on a team. Bring up the problem during design sessions. Someone on your team just might spark the insight to help you see the answer.

Feed Your Team

Did we mention this yet?

3.8   Acknowledgments

We have had the good fortune of working with many talented people. Without their genius and talents, PETS would not have been created. To our wonderful group, our deepest gratitude.

In alphabetical order, the PETS team: Houman Alborzi, Angela Boltman, Gene Chipman, Allison Druin, Eric Fiterman, Jim Hendler, Alex Kruskal, Britt McAlister, Jaime Montemayor, Hanne Olsen, Aurelie Plaisant, Isabella Revett, Lauren Sumida, Thomas Plaisant Schwenn, Lisa Sherman, and Rebecca Wagner.

3.9 References

Berman, R. 1977. Preschool knowledge of language: What five-year olds know about language structure and language use. In C. Pontecorvo (ed.), *Writing Development: An Interdisciplinary View*, Amsterdam: John Benjamins Publishing, pp. 61–76.

Beyer, H., and K. Holtzblatt. 1998. *Contextual Design: Defining Customer-Centered Systems*. San Francisco: Morgan Kaufmann.

Bonasso, R. P., R. J. Firby, E. Gat, D. Kortenkamp, D. Miller, and M. Slack. 1997. Experiences with an architecture for intelligent, reactive agents. *Journal of Experimental and Theoretical Artificial Intelligence* 9:237-256.

Bruchac, J. 1987. *Survival This Way: Interviews with American Indian Poets*. Tucson, AZ: University of Arizona Press.

Cypher, A., and D. Smith. 1995. Kidsim: End-user programming of simulations. *Proceedings of Human Factors in Computer Systems (CHI 95)*. New York: ACM Press, pp. 27–34.

Druin, A. 1999. Cooperative inquiry: Developing new technologies for children with children. *Proceedings of Human Factors in Computing Systems (CHI 99)*. New York: ACM Press.

Druin, A. 2000. The role of children in the design of new technology. Submitted to *Transactions on Computer-Human Interaction (TOCHI)*.

Druin, A., B. Bederson, A. Boltman, A. Miura, D. Knotts-Callahan, and M. Platt. 1999. Children as our technology design partners. In A. Druin (ed.), *The Design of Children's Technology*, San Francisco: Morgan Kaufmann, pp. 51–72.

Druin, A., J. Montemayor, J. Hendler, B. McAlister, A. Boltman, E. Fiterman, A. Plaisant, A. Kruskal, H. Olsen, I. Revett, T. Plaisant Schwenn, L. Sumida, and R. Wagner. 1999. Designing PETS: A Personal Electronic Teller of Stories. *Proceedings of CHI'99*. New York: ACM Press.

Druin, A., J. Stewart, D. Proft, B. Bederson, and J. Hollan. 1997. KidPad: A design collaboration between children, technologists, and educators. *Proceedings of Human Factors in Computing Systems (CHI 97)*. New York: ACM Press, pp. 463–470.

Ehn, P. 1993. Scandinavian design: On participation and skill. In D. Schuler and A. Namioka (eds.), *Participatory Design: Principles and Practices*, Hillsdale, NJ: Lawrence Erlbaum, pp. 41–77.

Fujita, M., and H. Kitano. 1998. Development of an autonomous quadruped robot for robot entertainment. *Autonomous Robots* 5(1): 7–18.

Gish, R. F. 1996. *Beyond Bounds: Cross-Cultural Essays on Anglo, American Indian, and Chicano Literature.* Albuquerque, NM: University of New Mexico Press.

Goldman, L. R. 1998. *Child's Play: Myth, Mimesis, and Make-Believe.* New York: Berg Press.

Greenbaum, J. 1993. A design of one's own: Toward participatory design in the United States. In D. Schuler and A. Namioka (eds.), *Participatory Design: Principles and Practices,* Hillsdale, NJ: Lawrence Erlbaum, pp. 27–37.

Greenfield, P. M. 1984. *Mind and Media.* Cambridge, MA: Harvard University Press.

Johnson, M. P., A. Wilson, B. Blumberg, C. Kline, and A. Bobick. 1999. Sympathetic interfaces: Using a plush toy to direct synthetic characters. *Proceedings of CHI 99.* New York: ACM Press.

Lave, J. 1992. *Cognition in Practice.* Cambridge, U.K.: Cambridge University Press.

Martin, F. G. 1998. The Handy Board technical reference. *el.www.media.mit.edu/projects/handy-board/techdocs/hbmanual.pdf.*

Mumford, E., and D. Henshall. 1979/1983. *Designing Participatively: A Participative Approach to Computer Systems Design.* Manchester, UK: Manchester Business School.

Ortiz, S. (ed.). 1998. *Speaking for Generations: Native Writers on Writing.* Tucson, AZ: University of Arizona Press.

Papert, S. 1980. *Mindstorms: Children, Computers and Powerful Ideas.* New York: Basic Books.

Piaget, J. 1971. *Psychology and Epistemology: Towards a Theory of Knowledge.* New York: Viking Press.

Piaget, J. 1973. *To Understand Is to Invent: The Future of Education.* New York: Grossman.

Scaife, M., and Y. Rogers. 1999. Kids as informants: Telling us what we didn't know or confirming what we knew already. In A. Druin (ed.), *The Design of Children's Technology.* San Francisco: Morgan Kaufmann, pp. 27–50.

Strommen, E. 1998. When the interface is a talking dinosaur: Learning across media with Actimates Barney. *Proceedings of Human Factors in Computing Systems (CHI 98).* New York: ACM Press, pp. 288–295.

Umaschi, M. 1997. Soft toys with computer hearts: Building personal storytelling environments. *Proceedings of Extended Abstracts of Human Factors in Computing Systems (CHI 97).* New York: ACM Press, pp. 20–21.

Kid's View

  ## Making a Robot

By Rebecca Wagner, age 11

I think that a robot is a piece of machinery that you can give a personality, or make do something. We are still making our robot right now, but we started in March 1998. Our robot is now a friendly, furry storytelling robot.

Making robots is a lot harder than other things like drawing a picture. It takes a lot of hard work and time. If it takes you five minutes to draw a picture, it will probably take you about five months of very good luck, and long days of work to make a robot.

I do not really know what another kid would need to know to make a robot, but I know that they would need to know a lot. I worked in a group. There I had adults to help me and the other kids do the programming and stuff. So my advice to someone who does not know about robots would be to work in a group.

Making a robot is fun, easy, hard, exiting, and sometimes boring. I am glad to be making a robot, but when I look back over everything we have done to make the robot it just shocks me I think how did we do that? I think that you would have fun making a robot, but you should work in a group.

Chapter Four

Bolts from the Blue

How Large Dreams Can Become Real Products

Richard Maddocks

RJM Design

Abstract

This is a journey behind the scenes of toy design and development, from first concept to production, with emphasis on the steps taken to bring a "high-tech" product to market efficiently and economically. The focus is on both the drama and the routine, the overview and the detail, including preliminary design, brainstorming, "looks-like/works-like" models, value engineering, safety/reliability, design drawings, prototyping/proving, and assembly and production processes.

 ## How It All Began

It all began for me about 28 years ago in England when I accidentally stumbled into the toy business after beginning my career as a draftsman in the automotive business.

Seven years previously I began a five-year student apprenticeship sponsored by Commer, a truck manufacturer subsequently acquired by the Dodge division of Chrysler. The course consisted of six months of each year at Luton College of Technology and the other six months "hands on" in every department of the company, from machining gears to marketing. I qualified with an HNC (Higher National Certificate) in mechanical engineering. Several months were also spent in the apprentice workshop learning the basics from the ground up, sawing, filing, and hand-fabricating from different materials, and learning to operate machine tools from lathes to surface grinders. I had been drawing, painting, and building models from a very early age as soon as I could hold a pencil, so I found myself gravitating towards the drawing office during the final year of my apprenticeship. I was offered my first job as a detail draftsman in the chassis design department, relocating exhaust pipes or screen washer installations and similar scintillating challenges, but an excellent grounding nevertheless in the disciplines of mass production that would serve me well in later years.

Two years later I was lured across "the pond" by some headhunters from General Motors seeking detail draftsmen on contract rates some 10 times greater than my current earnings as an employee! Being just two years out of an apprenticeship, this 24-year-old was easily persuaded to give it a try. My plan was to respond to this challenge for a year and retire on the proceeds. Not so. The work was on a grander scale—chassis components and more of the dreaded exhaust pipe routing, for a GM bus this time—but not approaching the creative opportunities I had hoped for. Early retirement was not an option either. The contract was terminated after six months, and I spent the next six months on an extended camping trip living on Spam and exploring the United States . . . but that's another story.

Arriving back in England in the spring of 1971, I signed on with all the employment agencies as an automotive design draftsman. Yes, I promoted myself based upon my experiences at GM. (A detail draftsman traces and fully dimensions each individual component designed and drawn by a design draftsman as part of a more complex assembly.) At that time the development cycle in the industry had peaks and troughs depending on the demand for new models. No one was hiring, except one company. I returned a call.

"Draftsman, cars, trucks?" the voice said.

"Yes," I replied.

"Well . . . " the voice continued, "Matchbox Toys needs a draftsman."

"Very interesting," I replied. "But what about me? I need a proper job."

The voice went on to explain that this did indeed constitute a proper job, and even paid real money as compensation.

A couple of days later I marched into the research and development department feeling very superior, demanded what I considered to be an outrageous salary, and to my astonishment was offered the job on the spot! I later realized that inflation had raged ahead while I was away and the salary was appropriate. I was also perfectly qualified for the position. I started work the following Monday, thinking to myself this would tide me over for a few weeks until I found that proper job.

What, no more exhaust pipes? Unbelievable, I had an *entire vehicle* to draw! It would have taken another 20 years minimum had I remained in the "other" automotive business to have reached such a lofty goal. Big Banger, Matchbox No. 26, was loosely based on a Camaro, customized with drag racing slicks at the jacked-up rear end, an oversized V8 engine, massive air scoop higher than the roof line (totally obscuring the driver's view, but heck, this is a toy I had to keep telling myself). Yes, this is what it's all about. I did not fully realize it at the time, but I was hooked, no going back now. This was the headquarters and R&D for Matchbox Toys, which was rapidly expanding during the 1970s into all categories of toys, including preschool, radio-controlled vehicles, dolls, action figures, and construction kits. All under one roof were designers, draftsmen, project engineers, pattern makers, and production engineers. Located nearby, in and around the East End of London, were diecasting and injection-molding facilities and assembly lines. Later in this chapter I will be expanding on the contribution that all of these elements have to the final product on the shelf.

During my first year on the drawing board I became involved with mechanisms in the miniature diecast vehicles, such things as moving pistons in a see-through cylinder block, a rotating gun turret on an armored car, or a pig that ran around in circles in the back of a pickup, to mention a few. I became fascinated by the challenges of solving these mechanical problems, often limited to the addition of one or two additional components to produce the desired effect while staying within the same cost parameter as other non-mechanized toys in the same product line. I soon discovered it is relatively easy to design a more complicated mechanism; the greater challenge is to simplify the design without compromising performance, while staying within the parameters of cost, reliability, and "drop dead" time deadlines.

John Hawkes, the senior product designer at the time, was promoted to design manager and was inspired to offer me the opportunity as a toy designer, although I had no formal training in industrial design. Working under his guidance I found myself in the deep end but loving it, with a line of preschool toys to design.

Flashback

As a child I had always drawn, painted, and built models for as long as I could remember. My dad was an excellent model maker, mostly ships built from scratch with any materials available. I had my own bench and tools, and spent many happy hours building my own and doing joint projects with my dad including working sailing ships, a diesel engine powered warship, model canons with working firing mechanisms, and so on. The ability to draw as a means of expressing and communicating design ideas and solutions is a great asset for a designer—something that serves me well to this day, even in the CAD age.

As a designer, I realized that I was drawing from all these experiences, with additional contributions from some of those obscure and academic pursuits long forgotten, almost, from my mechanical engineering roots: fluid dynamics, strength of materials, thermodynamics. Little did I know while wading through fluid dynamics that one day I would be designing bath toys or using applied math to calculate the wing loading for a towline glider flying toy! Quite an expansion of variety from those earlier limited experiences in the automotive business.

4.2   Lessons Learned

Working in-house as a toy designer at Matchbox taught me the most, although it would have been less useful without the mechanical engineering background and my drawing, painting, and model-making hobbies. During my 14 years with Matchbox I worked on many different categories of toys:

- diecast vehicles

- dolls

- action figures

- preschool

- remote-control/electric-powered vehicles

- plastic construction kits

- games

The processes involved included

- diecasting (molding a metal alloy)

- injection-molding plastics including styrene, ABS, polypropylene, acetal, polycarbonate, rubber

- rotocasting and slush molding (vinyl paste in a mold rotated inside an oven that cures when the mold surface cools, for doll heads, etc.)

- vacuum-forming plastic ("sucking" a sheet of heated plastic over a three-dimensional form)

- extrusion (squeezing a plastic strip through a shaped aperture)

- blow-molding (inflating a "balloon" of plastic inside a mold)

Understanding the limitations and fully exploiting the features of each process are essential for good design. The properties, performance, and function of the component in the design will determine the material and the process. The designer should also think about split lines and a line of draw (see Figure 4.15 in Section 4.3) for injection-molded components at the preliminary design stage. This saves problems later when a concept model is approved by management. It is not very helpful if the design as presented is not manufacturable!

I also learned the art of improvising with bits and pieces to build the quick mock-up to rapidly prove or disprove a mechanical principle and move on, hopefully to an eventual solution, which may not even be the answer to the original problem! My mentor in those days was Bill Clark in the R&D department, who could build just about anything from his collection of motors, gears, springs, rubber bands, assorted vending cups, plastic sheets and tubes,

Figure 4.1

The Matchbox Live-n-Learn preschool range.

and a lifetime of experience. He began as a toolmaker and, like most of us, accidentally found himself inextricably involved in the toy business.

While working on the Matchbox preschool line (Figure 4.1) I realized the importance of working with the real experts in the field, those under the age of five! A visit to a local playgroup every Wednesday was an integral part of our week, observing reactions to our latest prototype, often redesigning a particular feature before returning the following week. Some of my most engaging design discussions have been with kids, always willing participants in the process when given a chance (Figure 4.2).

Following a design brief, working within strict cost and time limitations, child-testing with real live kids, trying to understand the market and the competition, staying in tune with trends, working with international safety regulations, and monitoring quality control was valuable experience gained,

Figure 4.2

Toy expert David, age four, putting a Shufflie cow through its paces during a playgroup test session.

as was the experience of working within a team (Figure 4.3); supervising the draftsmen, model makers, sculptors, pattern makers, under the leadership of John Reynolds as design manager and eventually director of R&D; and realizing the importance of following through on every detail until the design has reached its maximum potential. Each step had to be completed on schedule and presented to management and marketing on a regular basis.

Ray, one of the project engineers, wrote a poem encapsulating all the trials and tribulations of the "Tuesday meeting," a biweekly presentation to management. It was entitled "Have It by Tuesday," and it began

It ought to be original, it ought to be unique,
It must cost very little, and we'd like it by next week.

Figure 4.3

Some members of the Matchbox preschool design team discussing Shufflies, an environment featuring gravity-activated walking figures. Left to right: Colin "Chalky" White, project engineer; Peter Whibley, project engineer; John Reynolds, design manager; myself (with considerably more hair back in those days!); Bill Clark, toy development engineer. Copyright © 1978 British Toys and Hobbies. British Toy and Hobby Association.

 4.3   ## Turning a Large Dream into a Real Product: How Do Robotic Models Become Manufacturable Toy Products?

It usually begins in one of two ways—one's own impossible dream or somebody else's. In any event the designer is faced with a blank sheet of paper and has to start somewhere. Identifying the need is most important, not necessarily making what is technically possible while exploring state-of-the-art technology. Ideas can be proposed by the design team within a toy company in response to a request by marketing to compete in a particular category. Or an outside inventor's item could be brought in. I have been on both sides of the fence. Typically it is the independent inventor who will create "the bolt from the blue." In-house designers are often overloaded with line extensions, another jeep for GI Joe, or a new environment for Barbie, leaving little time for blue-sky lateral thinking. The fact is, every project is different. There are no formulas, just good "gut" sense and a thorough understanding of the market to go by. The great ideas can come from anywhere anytime; it just takes a champion on the management side of the equation to take the risk to spend some money and take it to the next stage.

The Brief (from Marketing or Management)

Let's assume that this particular large dream is a prototype robotic model demonstrating the essence of the idea or invention. It could have originated inside or outside the company, but the decision has been made by management to release the product at the following New York Toy Fair, held every year around the second week in February, when manufacturers show new products to the buyers in the retail trade. It is only six months away, and production should begin the following June or July for delivery in time for Christmas. Marketing has defined a target cost and made the design team aware of the competition as well as a forecast for sales.

Putting Together the Design and Development Team for a Robotic Project

The mechanical design team will usually consist of a project manager, a toy designer, an engineer, model makers and prototype builders, and CAD designers working with Pro/ENGINEER (Parametric Technologies, Inc.) or other solid modeling applications. This structure varies from company to company and project to project. The team will discuss the development program and report back to marketing and management with a forecast of time and resources required for each step. The ideal time from concept to shelf is around two years, but this is out of the question for robotic and interactive products. In order to respond to the latest trends and electronic developments, turnaround is needed within the year, and sometimes a few months.

Selecting the right people and processes is critical for success, particularly when time is of the essence and the pressure is on to get it right the first time. Less time to complete the project must not result in a lowering of standards or quality.

My Uncle Arthur back in England enjoyed betting with a few pounds on the horse races featured on TV on Saturday afternoons. He referred to his system as "Horses for Courses." He would select horses trained on a right-handed track if the race was to be run on a right-handed track; horses with the best track record for heavy going if it had rained the previous few days;

Figure 4.4

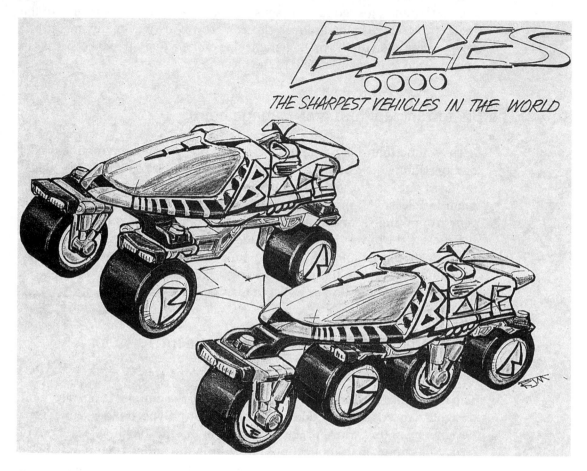

Concept drawing for Switchblade.

comparing the weight of the jockey to the weight of previous jockeys when the horse won or was placed. My uncle usually came out ahead by the end of the day! The same principle can apply when placing one's bets as to who and what is needed to get the product over the finish line on time. For example, when time and facilities are limited, designing a gearbox to reduce motor RPM using standard gears available "off the shelf" by overnight delivery is preferable to having something custom machined. Or you may have CNC (computer numerical controlled) milling facilities in-house with a programmer who can make gears to your specification in a few hours. Planning is key. If we were all clairvoyant, the R&D process would be considerably shortened!

Figure 4.5

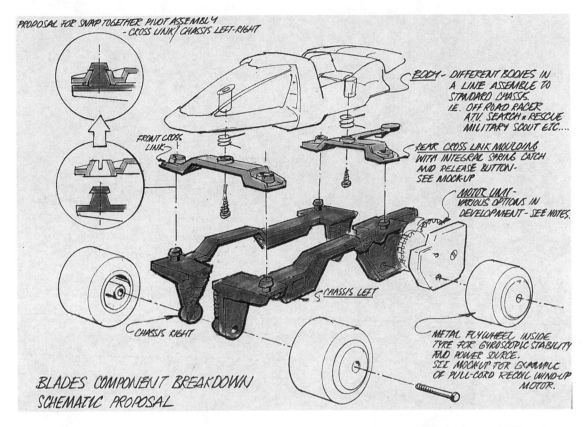

Preliminary exploded view of component breakdown. Note the one-piece molded "chassis left" and "chassis right."

A creative approach of parallel development often has to be initiated in areas where one or more options have to be investigated, and the best solution implemented when proven later in the development process.

Brainstorming

As the designer on robotic projects I have been the liaison between the mechanical and electronic development teams. When the animated features have been specified (Figures 4.4 and 4.5) and demonstrated (Figure 4.6) in the first breadboard or early prototype, the mechanical team has to decide how the whole product will be broken down for production, that is, what

Figure 4.6

Early breadboard models of Switchblade to demonstrate the parallelogram variable geometry feature (U.S. Patent No. 5,372,534).

Figure 4.7

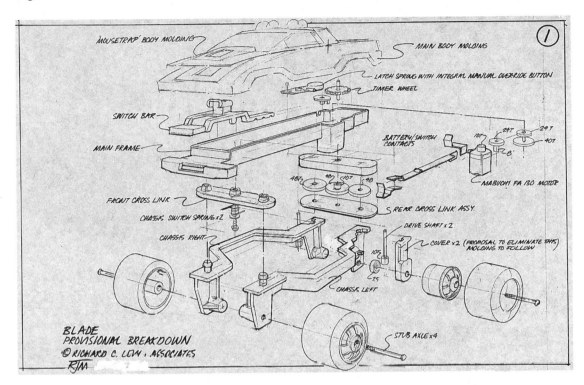

Preliminary exploded view of a more advanced design.

process will be used for each component, what materials will be selected, and what assembly sequence will be followed.

Preliminary Design Sketches

Design sketches (Figures 4.4, 4.5, 4.7–4.10) will evolve through several generations as the design develops, but they are a valuable first step to help visualize the mechanism and related parts.

Scale drawings will be made of some of the subassemblies for the layout of gearing, clutches, and lost-motion devices; for example, the motor and mechanism must be protected from abuse when a child sticks his or her finger in the toy's mouth or any other moving parts. The location of the motor, linkages, animated features, the battery compartment, and all major components will be sketched in and discussed by the team.

Figure 4.8

Styling sketch, one of a series exploring various approaches for presentation to management.

Component Breakdown and Value Engineering for Production (Including Assembly Sequence)

This is the most fundamental, "make or break" stage. Sometimes an early prototype is sent to Asia for costing and production by those who don't know any better—seems like a good idea, meanwhile everyone back here is lulled into a false sense of security, circulating emails to the effect that "it's in tooling" when challenged as to the status of the project. But someone should be asking, "*What* is in tooling?" A catastrophe could be "in tooling," not to be unveiled until much later, in the shape of a bag of first shots (the first sample injection moldings from the factory).

Early prototypes, at best, perform the essential function of proving the concept and are usually evolutionary in nature, with many changes and modifications, pieces stuck on, relocated, and generally hacked around until they work (Figure 4.11). Getting the prototype to work satisfactorily is often considered the big breakthrough, but it is just the introduction to this vital component breakdown stage (Figures 4.12 and 4.13). Foolproof assembly

Figure 4.9

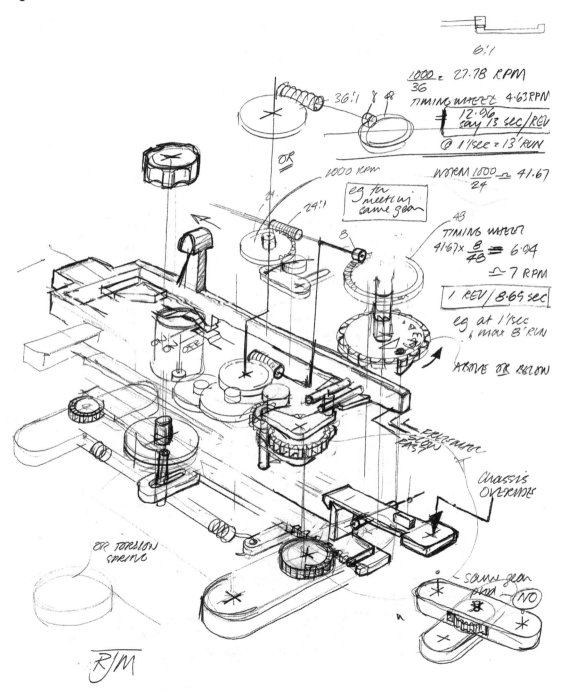

Preliminary sketch for more advanced mechanically programmed control system as a result of more brainstorming.

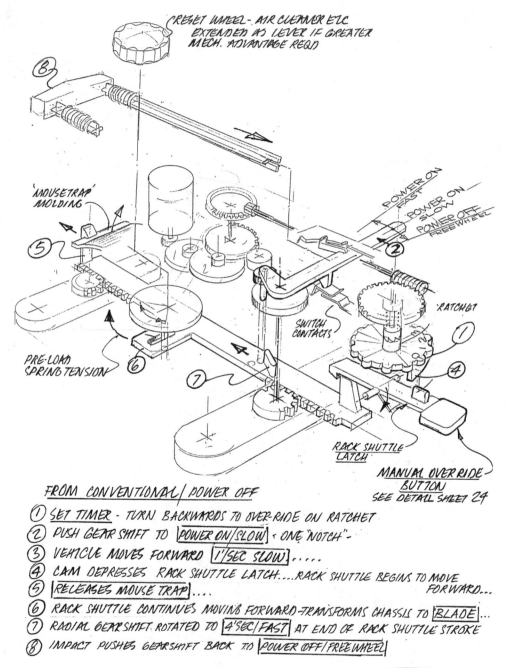

Figure 4.10

PRESET WHEEL - AIR CLEANER ETC
EXTENDED AS LEVER IF GREATER
MECH. ADVANTAGE REQD

B

'MOUSETRAP' MOLDING

5

POWER ON FAST

POWER ON SLOW

POWER OFF FREEWHEEL

2

RATCHET

SWITCH CONTACTS

1

PRE-LOAD SPRING TENSION

6

7

4

RACK SHUTTLE LATCH

MANUAL OVER RIDE BUTTON
SEE DETAIL SHEET 24

FROM CONVENTIONAL / POWER OFF

① SET TIMER - TURN BACKWARDS TO OVER-RIDE ON RATCHET
② PUSH GEAR SHIFT TO | POWER ON/SLOW | ± ONE "NOTCH" -
③ VEHICLE MOVES FORWARD | 1'/SEC SLOW | . . . . .
④ CAM DEPRESSES RACK SHUTTLE LATCH . . . . RACK SHUTTLE BEGINS TO MOVE
⑤ | RELEASES MOUSE TRAP | . . . .   FORWARD . . .
⑥ RACK SHUTTLE CONTINUES MOVING FORWARD - TRANSFORMS CHASSIS TO | BLADE | . . .
⑦ RADIAL GEARSHIFT ROTATED TO | 4'SEC/FAST | AT END OF RACK SHUTTLE STROKE
⑧ IMPACT PUSHES GEARSHIFT BACK TO | POWER OFF/FREEWHEEL |

RJM

Further development of the mechanism.

Figure 4.11

First working prototype.

Figure 4.12

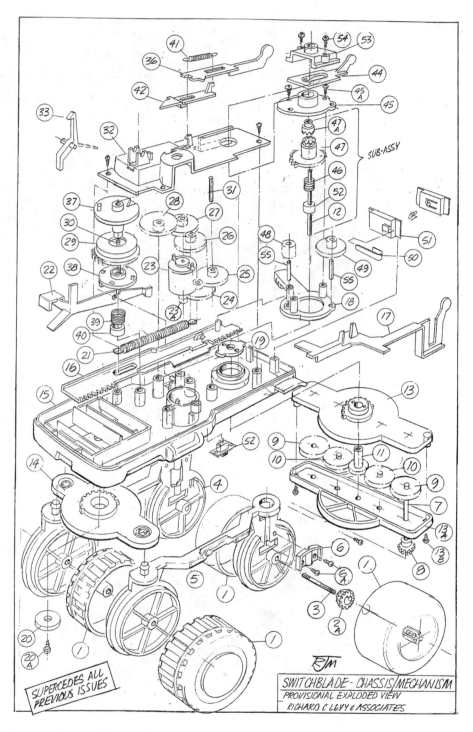

Exploded view of the production version of the Switchblade mechanism and variable geometry chassis (U.S. Patent No. 5,372,534).

Figure 4.13

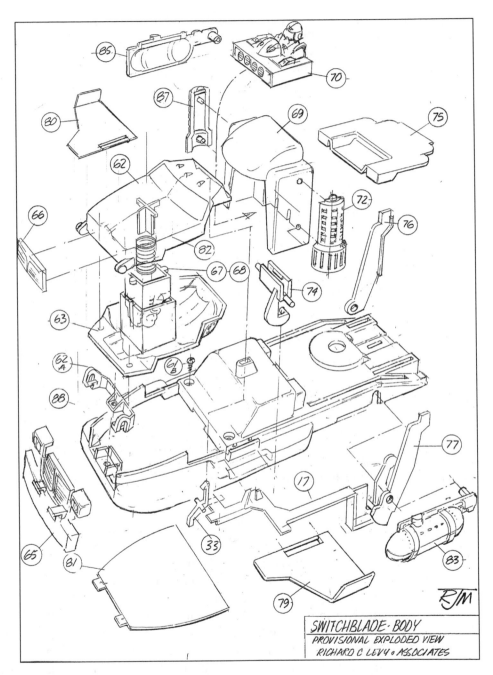

Exploded view of the production version of the Switchblade transforming body.

Figure 4.14

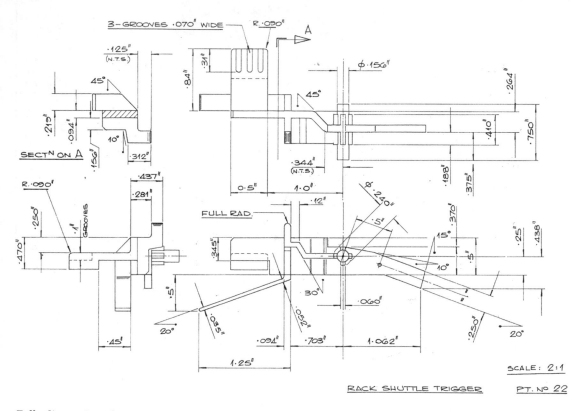

Fully dimensioned engineering drawing of the "Rack Shuttle Trigger" for Switchblade. (This releases the spring-loaded chassis during transformation, either when activated automatically by the timing mechanism or externally by the manual override button.) Courtesy of Peter Hall.

and reliability are essential to minimize rejects at the end of the production line and consumer returns. Ease of assembly with the minimum number of parts also contributes to a lower unit cost and increases reliability. This can be achieved by combining two or more parts into one by maximizing the potential of the injection-molding process (see Figures 4.5 and 4.7, showing the one-piece molded chassis members incorporating the side frame with all bearing mountings, screw bosses, and integrally molded styling features). This process of value engineering should become second nature to the designer through every step of the development to the final design of each component (Figure 4.14).

The line of draw and split line of every injection-molded part must be established, and as I mentioned earlier, it helps if the designer is "thinking molding" from the earliest sketches (Figure 4.15). The split line, or parting

Figure 4.15

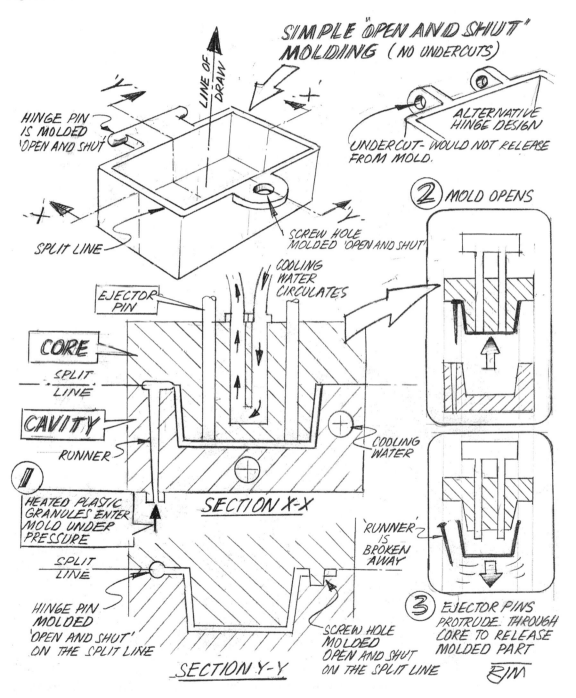

Sketch showing basic injection-molding principles.

line, is the dividing surface between the two halves of the mold, if the mold is "open and shut."

General Assembly Drawing

A general assembly (GA) drawing (Figure 4.16) is a scale drawing to lay out all the components and check basic clearances for the moving parts such as cams and linkages. This drawing is not fully dimensioned but is the master reference as the design evolves and develops. My partner on these ventures, Peter Hall, and I prefer to work on paper, for transfer to CAD as the design progresses. Many designers begin their designs by solid modeling on the computer—all a matter of personal preference.

For an interactive or robotic toy, liaison continues with the electronic development team to coordinate the sequence of animated functions (Figures 4.17 and 4.18), location of PCBs, sensor, speaker, microphone, and so on.

The motor and gearing must be selected to provide sufficient torque for the system with minimum current draw. The object of this exercise is to fine-tune and "balance" the system by matching the reduction gear ratio with the motor torque and RPM until the motor is running at maximum efficiency under full load. Mabuchi of Japan is a leading supplier of miniature DC motors and provides sample motors with specification sheets featuring various windings and brushes.

Prototype Models

The prototype builders will refer to the GA drawing to build a model to test and evaluate the mechanism. At this stage some components will be solid-modeled using Pro/ENGINEER, Unigraphics (Unigraphics Solutions, Inc.), or a similar application and NC (numerically controlled) milling used as an alternative to hand-fabricating or machining by hand-operated milling machines, lathes, and so on. Performance will be evaluated every step of the way, such as how much current the motor is drawing under load. If it is outside the parameter set for battery life, then the mechanism must be analyzed to identify any excessive friction or inefficiencies in bearings, gearing, cams, and so on and fine-tuned, or in some cases areas must be redesigned to improve the efficiency. The fine-tuning could involve opening up a bearing by a few thousandths of an inch, or checking meshing gears for a tight spot caused by a lack of concentricity not obvious to the naked eye but revealed by precise measurement.

Figure 4.16

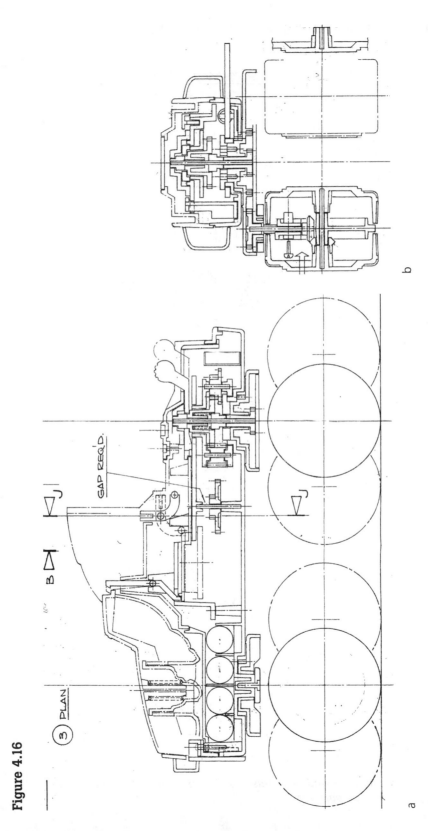

Part of a general assembly drawing for Switchblade (drawn conventionally on the drawing board): (a) side elevation; (b) cross section. Courtesy of Peter Hall.

Figure 4.17

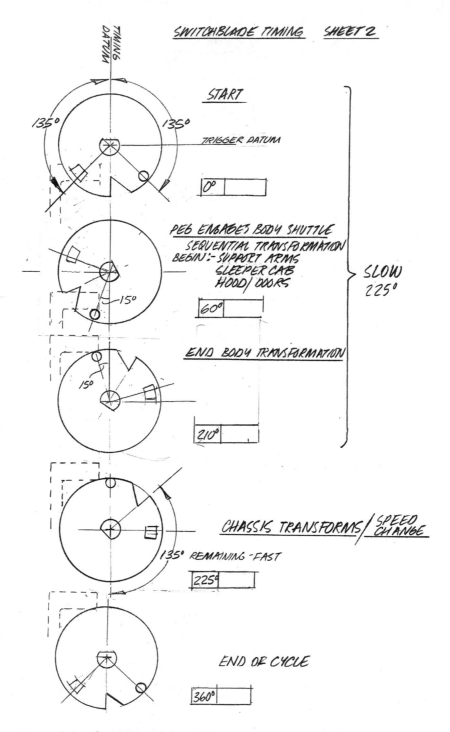

Determining the timing of chassis/body transformation and automatic speed change (part one).

Figure 4.18

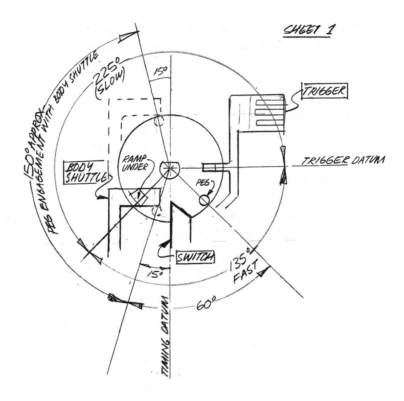

PROPOSAL FOR INITIAL TIMING SET UP

60° 'DWELL' - SLOW
150° BODY TRANSFORMATION - SLOW
15° 'DWELL' - SLOW
135° IN-LINE - FAST

CHASSIS TRANSFORMATION SHOULD OCCUR IMMEDIATELY
FOLLOWING HOOD LATCH RELEASE - ADJUST 15° 'DWELL'
TO SUIT.

*Determining the timing of chassis/body transformation and automatic
speed change (part two).*

More Brainstorming

Feedback from the model shop as the prototype progresses is discussed, and
modifications are incorporated. Another important rule for the designer:
Listen! Design solutions to seemingly insolvable problems can come from
anyone on the project, up and down the chain. And do not make believe it
was your idea! Give the credit where it is due and the whole team will feel

good about it, willing to contribute whenever possible. Make senior management aware of individual efforts and achievements of individuals, too often taken for granted.

Design Drawings

Work continues on solid modeling, combining aesthetics and the mechanical components. The mechanism must fit within the confines of the styling of the product, whether it is a doll, a robot, vehicle, creature, or whatever. This is all the more challenging if you are working on a product licensed by, for example, Star Wars or Disney, and aesthetic and functional approval must be gained from the licensor at each progressive step.

The designer's responsibility is to follow through with every detail and persuade the engineers just how important this particular facial feature is, maybe a slightly turned-up nose or a subtle change of angle at the corner of a mouth, creating an undercut in the tool. The designer needs to determine how serious the problem is and make a judgment: Compromise to eliminate the undercut, or insist that the design remains as is. It helps tremendously if the engineers realize that the designer is fully aware of the impact this will have on tooling. The designer should take the time to explain why the feature is so important to justify the need for the revision.

The mechanism, motor, gearing, battery box, and all components and systems will be created as subassemblies and imported into the main assembly. If it is an interactive product, the PCBs and sensors and so on will be located in the assembly, and the designer will work in continual close collaboration with the electronic team.

Prototype Model (Looks Like/Works Like)

Depending on the resources available and impending deadlines for the release of files and drawings for tooling, this will be built using a combination of rapid prototyping, NC milling, and fabrication by hand. It is also often more efficient to modify an existing part by hand than to create a new part from the revised database.

Modifications and adjustments made by the prototype builders must be analyzed and a design solution reverse-engineered into the database. Good communication and a constant flow of information *in both directions* are essential for the development to progress smoothly and efficiently. If the design team dictates ignoring such feedback, those very points will invariably come back to haunt later on, causing delays or even redesigns.

Figure 4.19

Seven-year-old Andrew testing a prototype of a transforming power wrench for a construction system.

Child-Testing

We have not mentioned those very important little people lately. They are, after all, the genuine unbiased experts in the business of toys. The basic research should have been conducted with early breadboard models and prototypes. It is reassuring to all, if time permits, to revisit the kids with the latest prototype while the opportunity exists to make changes before committing to tooling (Figure 4.19; see also Color Plate). It's not too late if a handle is too hard to turn or a switch awkward to operate. One slight problem: the prototype has cost thousands, if not tens of thousands, of dollars to produce. The uninhibited testing "to destruction" cannot take place until the first samples are assembled from the injection-molded parts.

Revisions

Any findings will be discussed within the design team, and proposals will be presented to marketing and management. Any of the changes that require further proving and evaluation will be built into the prototype and retested.

Formal Presentation to Marketing and Management

This process varies from company to company, but it is always important to keep senior management fully informed of progress (or the lack thereof) and, in particular, of any design changes that may have a significant impact on aesthetics, cost, or performance.

If the product is being manufactured under license, from Lucas Film or Disney, for example, then the designs and models have to be submitted for approval every step of the way, with appropriate modifications incorporated into the design.

Database

As the design is finalized, the work on the database intensifies, both in the main assembly (Figures 4.20 and 4.21; see also Color Plates) and the individual part drawings. The database solid-modeled on the computer is the modern equivalent of what used to happen on the drawing board. The challenge is to make everything fit inside the available space and avoid interference between the components. This is particularly complex when designing a mechanism involving cams and levers, as all potential configurations and relationships between components must be checked for interference, and modifications made as necessary. This is an ongoing process, as often more than one design engineer is involved, each working on different parts of the toy, and all efforts must be coordinated with good liaison and communication. Upon completion each component will be imported from the workstation where it was created into the workstation with the main assembly. Here each part will be assembled and checked for compatibility, function, and dimensional accuracy.

Metal parts, such as battery contacts, shafts, springs, and so on, will be solid-modeled and imported into the assembly, constantly checking and modifying fits and function. The purchased parts such as motors and electronic components are also solid-modeled and assembled into the database when the specifications have been finalized. Even the self-tapping screws must be added to the database to check for alignment of screw bosses and clearance holes. Interference between the screw head and other components must be checked, something that could very easily be overlooked and show up much later as a problem.

Bill of Materials (Parts List) Tool Plan

Each part is named, designated by a number, and arranged into groups according to material, process, or purchased part. In the case of the injection-

Figure 4.20

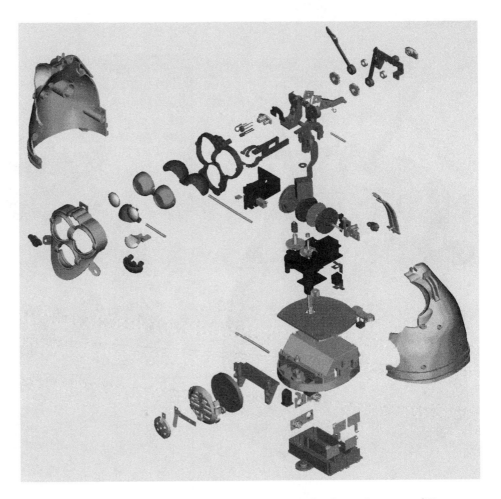

Exploded assembly of Furby from the Pro/ENGINEER database. Courtesy of Tiger Electronics.

molded parts, they are arranged in groups according to the material, for example, ABS, styrene (body shells, housings, etc.) or delrin (gears, cams, levers, etc.). A preliminary tool layout is developed that groups parts into "family molds."

Rapid Prototyping (Stereolithography)

This was a subject for science-fiction writers and pure fantasy until relatively recently. What? Grow complex parts from a computer file? In a word, yes! The files for each component are emailed or sent by Zip drive to the facility, where the data controls the *x, y, z* coordinates to build the part. There are a

Figure 4.21

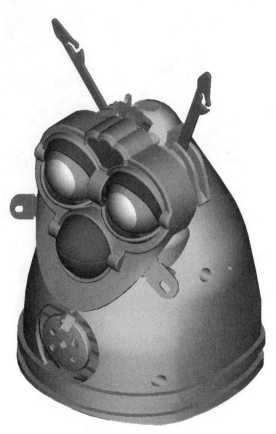

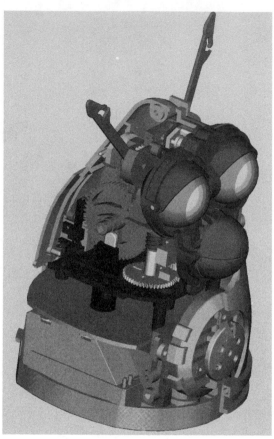

a   b

Two views of an assembly of Furby, (b) with the shell removed. Courtesy of Tiger Electronics.

few different systems available. Stereolithography (SLA) is extremely accurate but produces a somewhat brittle material. SLS produces a glass-filled nylon, giving durability and the ability to machine and glue to build the parts into a working model. Some processes direct a laser to fuse the material, either a powder (selective laser sintering [SLS]) or a liquid (SLA), while others (fuse deposition modeling [FDM]) function more like a three-dimensional printer. The parts are available in a matter of hours, cutting down development time dramatically.

SLA is useful as a reference for toolmakers, an opportunity to see an actual part rather than having to visualize from drawings. This is also the first opportunity for the design team to work with physical components, testing fits and tolerances and generally getting the feel of the assembly sequence.

This is often the time for an unwelcome shock, with the discovery of an interference between two moving parts that did not show up on the database. A solution must be found, with minimum impact on the surrounding parts. More revisions.

Revisions to Database

Revisions, revisions, revisions. Detail, detail, detail. The key to a successful design is following through on *every* detail, every hunch, every problem or potential problem. In the olden days, as my 10-year-old son refers to just about everything predating his birth, all the design drawings were prepared on the drawing board with pen and ink. This process has been replaced almost entirely by computer-aided design. Meticulous and diligent attention to revisions is important in both disciplines. It's not much good if you find the perfect answer to that interference problem but the solution is not communicated to the toolmaker in Hong Kong. And what about that part adjacent to it, connected by two screw bosses that have to be shortened by 0.75 mm? Driving home later the same day, staring at the rod light, you are suddenly reminded that the infrared emitter will now interfere with the sensor cover because the whole assembly has moved forward by 0.75 mm. Find a scrap of paper to scribble a note before the light changes or the vital information vanishes from your mind forever.

One always fears the discovery of the fatal flaw, just as the design is completed and put to bed. Such situations demand more than the usual amount of ingenuity to solve, often bordering on the impossible: the clutch that will not slip under any circumstances, the cam profile mysteriously developing a tight spot that somehow was never in evidence during all the earlier prototypes.

Eventually all the bugs are ironed out, at least for the time being.

Tooling Check Model

The tooling check model is a model made strictly to the dimensions in the database—no "tweaking" or adjusting allowed unless documented. This is a proving model to ensure that the design is sound, ensuring the minimum of debugging or progression later. All the parts with a mechanical function will be CNC milled, if the budget allows, to provide a close simulation to the injection-molded part. This means that the part will be accurately machined, controlled by the dimensions in the database, from a solid block of the same material specified for production. Allowance will be made for the fact that the flow lines created as the material flows under pressure into the mold will not be present in the machined part. This will influence the strength and flexibility of the component, in much the same way as grain structure influences the strength and stability of a piece of wood.

Any adjustments to the design or fine-tuning for optimum performance must be thoroughly documented and incorporated into the design.

What? More revisions?! Yes, and there will probably be even more, as those small, relatively insignificant issues from a few months ago loom large with time running out.

Time! I have not mentioned the schedule lately. Always that deadline for each step, and a need to find a way to make up that week lost earlier for whatever reason. No thanks are handed out for the perfect design completed a month late, completely missing the delivery dates for a major client.

Final Release of Database for Toolmaking

The tooling package is sent to Hong Kong and then mainland China or wherever tooling and production are scheduled to take place. This package usually consists of engineering drawings and/or the database, together with a tooling reference model or a set of SLAs for visual reference. It is ideally accompanied by at least one member of the design team to talk through the finer points of the design and debate any issues arising from the handoff.

Preliminary releases precede the final fully checked release, and care must be taken to ensure that the vendor works only to the latest files. The preliminary release enables the toolmaker to begin ordering steel, finalize the tool layout, and begin roughing out the cavities. Invariably a few early files will slip through the cracks, to be caught at the next step.

Several weeks, or a few months for the larger projects, are required for the tooling, when an impression or cavity for each plastic part is cut into the mold: two halves for the simple "open and shut" mold, or multiple shutoffs and sliding cores for the more complex parts. The sliding core (also referred to as side action) allows an undercut in the mold by retracting before the mold opens. Shutoffs are more complex split lines in the tool allowing for the molding of intricate features and diverse shapes.

This is often the quiet time in the schedule for the design team, relieved that tooling is finally underway, reflecting on the months leading up to this point, and eagerly awaiting first shots.

Mold Design

For the injection-molded parts, allowance must be made for shrinkage. Each plastic material has a specified shrink rate, for example, 2 percent. The cavity cut into the tool is made 2 percent larger, so that as the material cools the final size and shape are correct. Care must be taken at the product design stage to avoid thick sections causing distortion and unsightly sinking on the surface. A consistent wall thickness throughout the component helps to avoid these problems. The mold designer has to decide where to feed the mold to ensure a good flow of material to all extremities. The location of parting line and shutoffs will be finalized, and also the placement of sliding cores mentioned in the previous step. Ejector pins must be incorporated to eject the component from the cavity when the mold opens, and waterways run through the tool to circulate cooling water.

Good mold design (see Figure 4.15) and adherence to the highest standards in toolmaking will make a major contribution to the quality of the final molded parts, while maintaining a fast cycle time and a long life, perhaps producing a million or more moldings. The cycle time is the time taken for the mold to close, for the heated plastic granules to be injected under pressure into the cavity, cooling time, for the mold to open, for the molded parts to be ejected, and the mold to close, ready to repeat the cycle. You have probably observed on cheap imported items the results of sloppy or inaccurate toolmaking, such as "flash," the thin band of plastic squeezed out around a poorly finished parting line.

First Shots from Production Tooling

Everything stops when the box arrives. A hush descends as the increasing numbers press forward for a first glimpse. The last piece of tape is wrenched free and a plastic ziplock bag hoisted triumphantly for all to see. The decorum is short-lived! The horde descends to enthusiastically examine moldings and attempt to offer mating parts together. "It fits!" comes an excited voice from somewhere in the midst as two pieces are assembled. The first glimpse tells a lot; the quality and feel confirm. The room grows quiet, only the sound of the rustling of plastic bags and grunts of approval or dissatisfaction. The verdict is in moments later . . . *They are good!* A few minor problems are detected at first glance, maybe something totally unexpected in the form of an internal rib thoughtfully inserted for strength (but why didn't they ask us first?). But it was a good idea, so we will allow it to stay. Invariably something will be misinterpreted, hopefully nothing major with an easy fix.

Debug or Progression

The factory will meanwhile be fitting parts together and offering suggestions for adjustments. The design team will also develop a list of modifications to the tools based upon building a sample from the moldings, carefully documenting all the changes made to the parts by removing or adding material, opening up undersized holes, and bushing (filling) and redrilling oversized holes. Particular attention is paid to bearings for shafts and critically located parts requiring carefully maintained tolerances. A general tolerance is usually designated for the part, for example, ±0.25 mm. This means there could be a variation in size of 0.5 mm. But a hole forming the bearing for a gear could have a tolerance of ±0.05 mm, an allowable variation of only 0.10 mm. Only the critical dimensions have the tight tolerances, as it would be impractical and costly to insist that the entire part be controlled to an unnecessary degree of accuracy.

The information is passed back to the factory as a series of notes with sketches (Figures 4.22 and 4.23) and if necessary a revised file from the database. The tools are modified by removing steel if the part is undersized or welding and machining back if the area is oversized. The intention is to go into first shots "steel safe," meaning the injection-molded part will be undersized and the tool more easily corrected by removing steel, testing with another shot, and repeating the exercise until the molded part is within tolerance.

Revisions to the Database

It is essential to reverse-engineer all of the modifications arising from first shots into the database, revising each component and checking in the assembly to verify the change. This ensures that the database is a dependable reference for the continued checking of dimensions as the latest molded parts are received from the modified tools.

Preproduction Samples

Now work is well advanced in the factory setting up the production line and testing and developing the various jigs and fixtures needed during the assembly, for example, a mask for mask spraying the paint on a localized area of a component, or a fixture to hold a body shell while components are located inside and screwed into position. A few complete toys are assembled as a training exercise and to enable production engineers to further evaluate and time the assembly sequence, looking for improvements. Now we will find out just how good our "foolproof" design is! Even at this stage the production engineers could pass back some recommendations to contribute to an easier assembly and save time.

Quality control personnel will also monitor this process and finalize the plans for checking and sampling products as they roll off the assembly line.

Figure 4.22

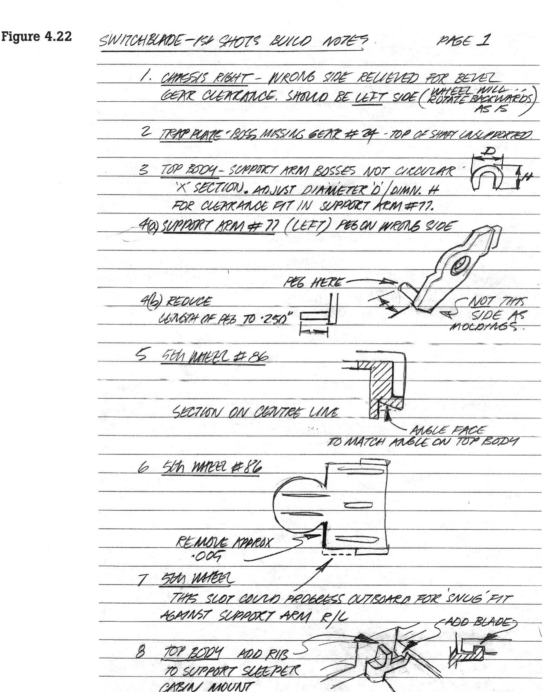

An example page of notes for tooling progression during debug, typical of many pages of revisions and modifications (one page out of seven communicating 46 points requiring action).

Figure 4.23

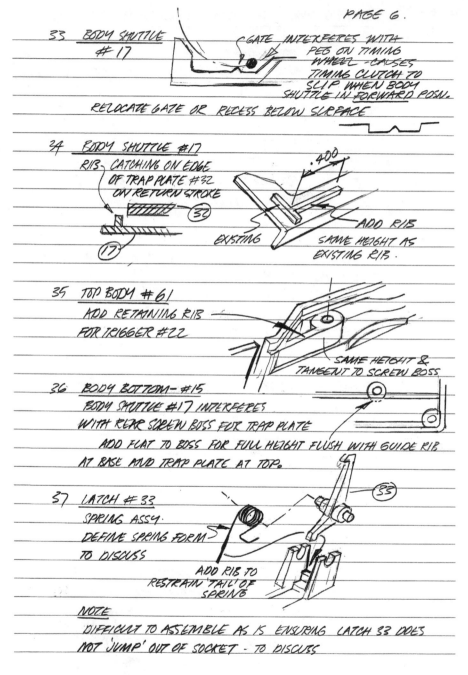

PAGE 6.

33   BODY SHUTTLE #17

GATE INTERFERES WITH PEG ON TIMING WHEEL - CAUSES TIMING CLUTCH TO SLIP WHEN BODY SHUTTLE IN FORWARD POSN.

RELOCATE GATE OR RECESS BELOW SURFACE

34   BODY SHUTTLE #17

RIB CATCHING ON EDGE OF TRAP PLATE #32 ON RETURN STROKE

.400

EXISTING   ADD RIB SAME HEIGHT AS EXISTING RIB.

35   TOP BODY #61

ADD RETAINING RIB FOR TRIGGER #22

SAME HEIGHT & TANGENT TO SCREW BOSS

36   BODY BOTTOM - #15

BODY SHUTTLE #17 INTERFERES WITH REAR SCREW BOSS FOR TRAP PLATE

ADD FLAT TO BOSS FOR FULL HEIGHT FLUSH WITH GUIDE RIB AT BASE AND TRAP PLATE AT TOP.

37   LATCH #33

SPRING ASSY.

DEFINE SPRING FORM

TO DISCUSS

ADD RIB TO RESTRAIN 'TAIL' OF SPRING

NOTE

DIFFICULT TO ASSEMBLE AS IS ENSURING LATCH 33 DOES NOT 'JUMP' OUT OF SOCKET - TO DISCUSS

Another example page of notes for tooling progression during debug.

Performance tests will be devised to check representative samples from batches coming off the line.

Testing

Now is an opportunity to test to destruction, with drop tests, crushing tests, pull tests, small parts test, electrical safety tests, battery life, flammability tests, and so on. The tests depend on the recommended age for the product and are defined in great detail by international and U.S. toy safety standards. Any failures or potential failures will be reported back to the design team to investigate and implement a solution.

Revisions to Tools

If the proposed change has no impact on the performance, safety, or reliability of the product, then the design change would be incorporated into the database and the revised file released for a change to the tool. More moldings are produced for final checking and in preparation for the trial run.

Trial Run

Now a few hundred products are assembled under the watchful eye of the production engineers, and passed along to quality control for testing. If all is well . . .

Production Start!

The news reaches the design team, and samples are eagerly awaited. Of course, everyone wants one, in a box, for their collection (Figures 4.24 and 4.25). This is regarded as a real trophy, especially by anyone fortunate enough to be a recipient.

Rumors abound a couple of weeks later of sightings at a toy store nearby, only to find upon investigation an empty shelf if the product in question happens to be a Furby! But it is satisfying all the same to be associated with a successful product flying off the shelves. And by the way, most toy manufacturers do not "create" shortages leading up to Christmas. If demand exceeds supply, every effort is made to make additional injection-molding tools, set up more production lines, work more shifts in the factories, and even air-freight product to shorten delivery times.

Figure 4.24

Switchblade box artwork.

4.4   The Hardest Part of the Process

The hardest part of the process is working to deadlines. There is never enough time. Yet, on the other hand, if there is too much time, the adrenaline is not flowing and it is often too easy to lose focus, leading to an inevitable rush to cross the finish line on time! So timing is everything.

I am constantly reminded of the adage "There is never enough time to do it right, but always enough time to do it twice"—a situation to be avoided if at all possible, but one I often find myself in, particularly when working with unproven state-of the-art computer-based technologies. It is always worth exploring, but it is essential to have a fall-back plan on a parallel track if you are working to a tight schedule.

As a freelance inventor/designer, it is also difficult to get the commitment from a company to sign an agreement and spend money to invest in the development of a new concept. This is the all-important first step, followed by the continued responsibility of all concerned to stay focused and committed all the way through to production.

Figure 4.25

More Switchblade box artwork.

Third, again as a freelance inventor/designer, it can also be very hard to maintain one's level of enthusiasm as the FedEx "body bags" return, containing the rejected concepts from manufacturers. You must stay focused on the next presentation and treat each new project as the potential "big one."

4.5   The Most Difficult Dreams to Make Real

The most difficult task I've had was the Furby mechanical development, due to the short lead time and the complexity and precision of the system. Very rarely had any of us worked to such close tolerances on a toy product—tolerances more usually associated with high-precision industrial products or clock-making! Solid modeling and rapid prototyping were employed to provide components for proving models, while simultaneously refining the mechanical interface of the control system with the electronic team in California. Many disciplines were involved, often on parallel tracks, all needing coordination to cross the finish line together: electromechanical mechanism design involving a motor, gearing, cams, and clutches; sculpting; plush and soft goods for the fur; incorporation of the electronic package with PCB, chip, and sensors; and so on. This was the most challenging of any project I had worked on in 28 years, and was made possible by the talents and enthusiasm of the people on the team.

Baby Grows (Playmates) presented the challenge of developing a simple mechanism with maximum effect (Figure 4.26). As I have mentioned earlier, it is relatively easy to develop a complex mechanism, perhaps with multiple motors and an impressive array of cams, gears, levers, and linkages. Let us assume it functions very well, but what about the cost and reliability? Probably way over the top of expectations. Then the real work of "value engineering" must begin, as I described earlier in this chapter—simplification without compromise (Figure 4.27). Baby Grows was a formidable challenge in this respect: The torso, legs, arms, and neck all had to grow simultaneously but by different amounts to maintain the correct proportions, and finally as a toddler, teeth had to come through, all for $24.99!

Switchblade was a variable geometry vehicle, capable of transforming while in motion from a conventional big rig truck into a futuristic in-line vehicle. It required the development of a complex mechanism featuring automated variable geometry, a timing and control system, and the need for stability during transformation. This was more complex due to the number of functions and the various control options. The challenge here was to integrate the mechanical systems into a single reliable and robust unit.

I mention "robust" because breakaway panels of bodywork were designed to "explode" and safely detach upon impact when the vehicle crashed, and

Figure 4.26

Baby Grows box artwork. Courtesy of Playmates Toys Inc.

Figure 4.27

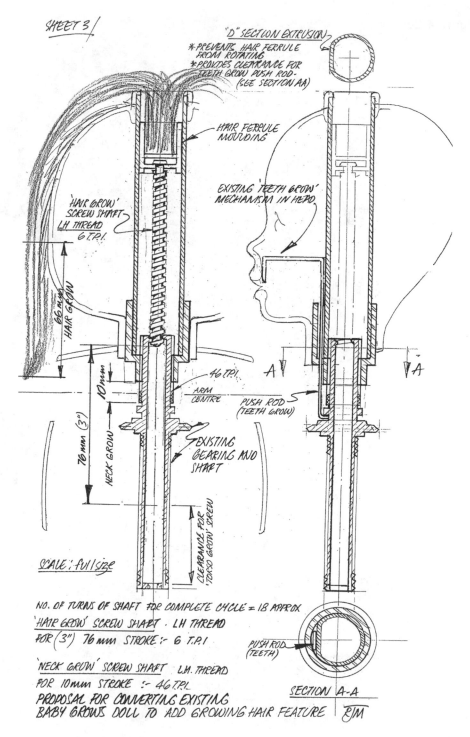

SHEET 3/

"D" SECTION EXTRUSION
* PREVENTS HAIR FERRULE FROM ROTATING
* PROVIDES CLEARANCE FOR TEETH GROW PUSH ROD.
(SEE SECTION AA)

HAIR FERRULE MOULDING

EXISTING 'TEETH GROW' MECHANISM IN HEAD.

'HAIR GROW' SCREW SHAFT LH THREAD 6 T.P.I.

66 mm HAIR GROW

10 mm
NECK GROW

76 mm (3")

46 T.P.I.

ARM CENTRE

PUSH ROD (TEETH GROW)

EXISTING GEARING AND SHAFT

A   A

CLEARANCE FOR 'TORSO GROW' SCREW

SCALE: full size

NO. OF TURNS OF SHAFT FOR COMPLETE CYCLE = 18 APPROX
'HAIR GROW' SCREW SHAFT · LH THREAD
FOR (3") 76 mm STROKE :- 6 T.P.I.

'NECK GROW' SCREW SHAFT · LH THREAD
FOR 10mm STROKE :- 46 T.P.I.

PROPOSAL FOR CONVERTING EXISTING
BABY GROWS DOLL TO ADD GROWING HAIR FEATURE

PUSH ROD (TEETH)

SECTION A-A   RJM

Design proposal for Baby Grows head mechanism.

Figure 4.28

18+
MONTHS
MOIS
MONATE

LL-100

Playboot. This is the home of the "MATCHBOX" family, complete with five family figures and play accessories.

La Botte. Voici la maison de la famille "MATCHBOX" avec ses 5 habitants et pleins d'accessoires.

Hausschuh. Das Haus der "MATCHBOX" Familie. Komplett mit fünf Figuren und viel Spielzubehör.

Matchbox Live-n-Learn Playboot.

then be easily reassembled to repeat the action over and over. Manual override controls were incorporated to allow this electrically powered toy to be played with when batteries were not available, a feature introduced by the design team to extend the play value and reduce the frustration factor.

4.6   Favorite Project

The Live-n-Learn Matchbox preschool range was my favorite project (see Figure 4.1). This was an opportunity to work with a small but highly talented team to develop from scratch a line of toys to compete with Fisher Price, Playskool, and so on. I particularly enjoyed the creative freedom and the camaraderie within the team. In a period of eight years over 30 products went into production, from simple push-along vehicles to printing toys and Build-a-Truck, a construction toy featuring a unique wrench and building method. The Playboot environment was the most successful, with over 2 million sold (Figure 4.28).

4.7   The Drama of Toy Design and the Mundane

Furby provided the most drama for me. A high-profile project of this order included massive media coverage, particularly during the introduction and lead up to Christmas 1998. In a period dominated by licensing and company acquisitions, here was the proverbial "bolt from the blue" created by independent inventors and licensed to Tiger Electronics. I was contracted to redesign the prototype for production, beginning with a small team and eventually working with a highly talented group at Hasbro in Rhode Island after the Hasbro acquisition of Tiger.

Drama also came in the form of tracking Furby on the Internet—instant response to a product still in development. Late in 1997, punching "FURBY" into the Internet search engine AltaVista would yield something under 400 sites, such as Mr. and Mrs. Furby and family living peacefully in a remote corner of Australia. Try now, and 48,000 plus sites will appear! Previously consumer feedback would take the form of a few letters to the customer relations department or some calls to the 800 number. There was never anything on this scale, and the design team received much valuable feedback by monitoring consumer response on the bulletin boards and chat sites featuring kids of all ages, from 6 to 66. (Don't miss the "Furby Autopsy" site, an incredibly detailed internal examination and analysis, with photographs.)

Furby was also a contender for "favorite project."

This was my introduction to working on interactive robotic projects, but I was drawing on all my previous 27 years' experience in the industry, in particular, the transforming mechanisms such as Switchblade (Figure 4.12) and Baby Grows (Figure 4.27).

At the time of writing, some 21 months later, I am still involved, working on the third generation of Furby and related interactive and robotic projects.

As for the mundane, the endless checking of details during the development process and following through to production and beyond would be high on the list, as would those countless instances working late into the night to meet a deadline. And did I mention costing and scheduling?

When people I have just met socially casually inquire, "And what do you do?" I reply, "Design toys." Following the pause and the raised eyebrows, the response is usually something like "Oh, what fun!" All I will say here is, I cannot guarantee your safety following such a reply. . . . Certainly, there is an element of fun buried in there somewhere, and it is definitely more illuminating than designing grommets (apologies to all you grommet designers out there). If you have managed to successfully navigate your way through this chapter, you will realize by now that designing and developing a toy, and in particular those of the robotic or interactive variety, involves challenges and frustrations rivaling any creative process.

4.8   Product Development and the Toy Industry: What Do You Need to Learn?

There are three main areas that need to be considered—robotics, product development, and the toy industry:

1. *Robotics:* Assuming there is an electronic team on the project, they would have to develop an understanding of the interface between the electronic control system and the mechanism. Typically there is a mechanical team and an electronic design team involved with robotic projects. A good basic understanding of electromechanical mechanisms would be a minimum requirement. As a member of the mechanical team, some knowledge of electronics and electrical engineering would be an advantage. They would be responsible for the mechanical design and development, and would have to learn about, and be capable of applying, the principles of levers, cams, motors, gearing, and so on.

2. *Product development:* Eventually they should know everything and more included in this chapter. Familiarity with basic manufacturing principles would be a minimum requirement, and the ability to apply those principles successfully during the transition from the first "looks like/works like" prototype to full production specifications within cost, time, and performance parameters.

3. *Toy industry:* If they are inventing and developing new concepts, they should become familiar with all the latest trends in all the categories they will be working in, from plush to interactive, diecast to dolls. The toy industry is evolutionary and in a constant state of change. Go to the toy fair in New York and also the international toy fairs if possible, read the trade press, visit toy stores, and talk to and play with kids to get the latest from the real experts.

4.9   The Next Five Years

The electronic and interactive categories will continue to expand and prices will fall as features multiply, keeping pace with technology. There will be more "realistic" dolls, robotic toys, pets, dinosaurs, vehicles, and so on. As computing power and screen resolution increase, the possibilities for hand-held electronic games will be endless. The interactive game divisions of the larger companies have expanded dramatically over the past few years, but CD ROM and Internet games are unlikely to replace traditional games completely. Hasbro Interactive has more software titles for popular games than any other company.

Robotics is firmly established in the construction category, for example, LEGO Mindstorms and Robotix from Learning Curves. Both these systems provide incredible opportunities for creativity straight out of the box, from basic programming to designing and building robotic vehicles, creatures, and so on.

There will always be traditional toys, but even their level of sophistication is rising, with built-in sounds, lights, remote control, and other very affordable enhancements.

Taking a look at the toy manufacturers, the landscape has changed dramatically over the past decade. Hasbro and Mattel have been aggressively acquiring the remaining medium and large companies, in most cases to gain ownership of a successful toy line or trademark. Fisher-Price (preschool), Tyco (radio-controlled vehicles), and Matchbox (diecast cars) are now owned by Mattel. Hasbro already owned Kenner (dolls, action figures, and vehicles), Milton Bradley (games), Parker Brothers (games), Playskool (preschool), and Tonka (trucks) and went on to acquire more recently Tiger Electronics (Furby, handheld electronic games, including Star Wars licenses), Oddzon (Kooshballs, etc.), Cap Toys (novelty candy and assorted action toys), Laramie (Super Soaker water guns), and Galoob (MicroMachines and Star Wars licenses).

These mergers have not been taking place only in the United States. Many companies around the globe have also been absorbed in this feeding frenzy. This also inevitably means that the parent company takes control of the creative process, eliminating much of the individual creative flair and restricting direct access by the inventing community in many cases.

There used to be a joke going around a few years ago that eventually there would be one retailer, Toys R Us, and one manufacturer, either Hasbro or Mattel, depending on who won the battle of the giants. It has almost happened! Fortunately the specialty stores are gaining in popularity as the consumer is prepared to pay a little more in exchange for some expert advice, and Mattel failed in its bid to acquire Hasbro a couple of years ago.

Licensing has also changed the face of the business over recent years, some would say on a scale that is detrimental. Many companies tend to play it safe by using a Star Wars or Disney or whatever license, often as a substitute for any real creativity, which is perceived as higher risk. This may be another cycle that could go full circle during the next five years, with a return to a more healthy balance of innovation and licensing.

The business will undoubtedly continue to flourish, continually reinventing itself in the year 2000 and beyond by emulating and exploiting the developments in the real world as it has done successfully for the past century, with robotic toys leading the charge.

Part II

Innovative Approaches to Using Robots for Education

The New Robotics
The Educators' Challenge

 **Allison Druin**

University of Maryland, Institute for Advanced Computer Studies, College of Education, Human Development Department

Technology and Education

> *Wut I want to bee [sic]*
> Wen I gro up I want to make tecknologee like my mom.
> She ses tecknologee is a noo thing to help peepl bee smart.
> It makes hard things esee and fun to doo.
> Sins I want to help peepl I want to make tecknologee like my mom.
>
> *(Druin, researcher notes 1997)*

These are the words of a six-year-old child. Between the spelling errors are some interesting ideas that reflect how many of us see the role of technology in our society. As this young person tells us, "tecknologee" is a good thing; it can "help peepl." Since this child is the daughter of a friend of mine who also happens to be a computer scientist and researcher, this optimistic opinion is not too surprising. But there are other children in this world, equally enamored with technology, who have not grown up with the same mom. One eight-year-old child from an inner city school asked, "How can I do what you're doing when I grow up? I didn't know you could do something fun." This question was asked of the founders of the KISS Institute for Practical Robotics. As the authors further discuss in Chapter 7, this child had never seen a robot before their visit, and he had never thought about any particular career path for himself. Being introduced to robots sparked this student's curiosity.

While there are many examples in this book that describe a passion for technology that can lead to learning, we need to remember that not every person in every part of our society is instantly overcome with joy for the newest, neatest, and never-to-be-forgotten technology. "As early as 1633,

London workers tore down the mechanical sawmills that threatened their livelihood. . . . The most publicized example came in 1811, when machine wreckers calling themselves Luddites destroyed textile machines in Nottingham" (Toffler 1980).

Some people reveal their dislike or fear of new technologies in less violent or drastic actions. For example, some people uncomfortable with new ways can replicate the old ways by using new technology. It is a *safe* way to sneak up on change. We see a great deal of this occurring in the world of education. Some teachers, who have little experience with new technologies in their classroom, have been known to force-fit new technologies to well-worn curricula. I recently met one middle-school teacher who, for the most part, only allowed her students to use LEGO Mindstorms when they were learning about gears, motors, and machines. The rest of the school year, the Mindstorms box remained hidden because "that was no way to teach math."

But this is not unique to the world of education. This symptom of replicating the old ways by using new technology can be seen, for example, in the evolution of the printing industry (Bolter 1991):

> The early printers tried to make their books identical to fine manuscripts: They used the same thick letterforms, the same ligatures, the same abbreviations and the same layout on the page. It took a few generations for printers to realize that their new technology made possible a different writing space; that the page could be more readable, with thinner letters, fewer abbreviations, and less ink.

Today we are seeing this same shift in thought and practice within the world of education. Many educators have come to embrace these changes and see the power of what technology can bring to learning. One high-school teacher in California, described in Chapter 7, explained:

> Robotics motivates students to make plans, to accomplish, to look forward, to achieve and to feel good about themselves, in some cases for the first time in their lives. The robotics class itself is set up to allow students to feel comfortable with the new and sometimes very complicated concepts that robotics brings with it. To build an autonomous robot, students must learn the basic concepts of mechanics, engineering and "Interactive C" computer programming. They must also learn the skills of effective communication, teamwork and problem solving.

New robotic technologies can engage students in exciting paths to learning. Unfortunately these new technologies do not come free. Many educators in low-income areas are still fighting tight school budgets that leave little room to purchase new technologies. I met one such educator from Philadelphia a few years ago. He wrote me this email (Druin, personal correspondence, 1996):

> Dear Allison Druin,
>
> . . . In the most deprived elementary school in the most deprived neighborhood of Philadelphia, what would be the single most and next most important statements I could make to business contributors as to how, specifically, say 10 computers might help the children in this school. What would be the essential, rock bottom fundamentals to be mindful of to prevent this from being just one more failure in attempting to assist economically and culturally deprived children . . .

I received this email approximately 15 minutes before I was to speak at a computer science seminar on Computers and Society. My topic was to be the role of technology in today's educational environments. When I read this email, I tossed my notes in the trash, printed out the email, and ran to the seminar. After some initial introductions, the seminar began with my reading the email aloud. I then asked the students, "What should I suggest to this man who emailed me?" What followed was a fascinating discussion on everything from how using technology could offer better jobs for young people in the future; to how students could learn about science, math, and technology; to how technology could help learners become better community participants. As students were tossing these ideas out for discussion, I realized that, surprisingly, their ideas reminded me of Herbert Kliebard's description of the ideas behind recent history's curriculum reform movements in the United States (Kliebard 1995). Thanks to this simple question of how to convince people to give computers to a school, college students were considering the basic reasons behind offering our children education.

Here was yet another instance where technology was prompting us to ask hard questions about what we do as a society and why we do it. Seymour Papert, best known for his research at MIT with children and the development of the Logo programming language, has said, "One could even argue that the principal contribution to education made thus far by the computer presence has been to force us to think through issues that themselves have nothing to do with computers" (Papert 1985).

Technology's Impact on Educational Goals

The addition of technology in the classroom has asked us as a society to reexamine our existing educational goals. It has asked us to stop and question what our true hopes may be for our children today and tomorrow. In doing so, we must ask, do our tools support these goals? If they don't, do we change the tools that we have? Do we change the goals we have? Do we change both?

As new educational standards and guidelines come pouring forth from governments around the world, the question for many educators is how to support curriculum guidelines yet take advantage of new creative tools. Alan Kay, vice president at the Walt Disney Company and father of the personal computer, highlights this dilemma with a story (Kay 1996):

> Suppose it were music that the nation is concerned about. Our parents are worried their children won't succeed in life unless they are musicians. Our musical test scores are the lowest in the world. After much hue and cry, [government] comes up with a technological solution: "By the year 2000 we will put a piano in every classroom!" But there are no funds to hire musicians, so we will retrain the existing teachers for two weeks every summer. That should solve the problem! But we know that nothing much will happen here because any musician will tell you, the music is not in the piano! What music there is, is inside each and everyone of us.

Kay points out that the existence of technology will not solve all of our problems. Instead, what may matter most is the creative ways in which we use those tools. Technology may be a powerful tool for problem-solving, and problem-solving may be a very important educational goal, but it is the *content* of that experience that is critical. This has been described as a "problem-centered" approach to learning. Priscilla Norton, a teacher educator at George Mason University who focuses on integrating technology in schools, has explained (Norton 1992):

> A problem-centered curriculum in the disciplines places a solution to a real-world problem of interest at the center of the learning experience. . . . Students' ability to solve the problem, to present their solution, and to revise their solutions in light of additional information become the goals. Placing the problem at the center emphasizes the students' doing rather than their mastery of discrete pieces of information and skills.

It seems that people learn when there is a driving want or desire to do so. Better grades, a higher-paying job, and the novelty of using new technologies may not necessarily be the only reasons why students want to learn more. I believe the desire for learning has to do with an animating idea or an engaging project. New technologies enable students of all ages to pursue richer, far more complex learning experiences. With robots, students can truly be scientists, engineers, designers, and builders. It is much easier to really *be* a scientist if you have more than paper and pencil at your disposal.

When I think back to the email question from that Philadelphia educator, I realize my reply to him had a great deal to do with problem-centered learning. I suggested that if he wanted to convince the outside community to give his school technology, he should first decide what he actually wanted to do with the donation. I explained that technology can be a very powerful tool, but not for the sake of teaching just about technology. I believe technology is an extremely important tool for exploring music, art, math, science, and more. I suggested to my emailer if he could explain what amazing things his students were going to do with the technology, he stood a much better chance of receiving a donation. I went on to suggest that education is an interactive process, and the more tools that can support this interactivity between student and student, student and teacher, and student and the world, the more exciting and meaningful the learning process could be.

Using Robots for Education

I believe that our chapter authors might agree with me. Each chapter in Part II describes exciting ways that new robotic technologies have been used to engage students in learning. Some of these chapters describe this learning in classroom environments, and some describe alternative learning environments such as summer camps, industry research labs, and religious school programs.

In Chapter 5, authors from the Kennedy Krieger School describe their classroom experiences with learners who are challenged socially, cognitively, and/or physically. They explain that building robots is a way to reach out to children who have difficulty learning in traditional ways. Robotic materials can offer a wonderful alternative to text-based materials because robotic technologies are extremely flexible for a classroom of special learners. In Chapter 6, authors from the MIT Media Lab describe how robots can be used to ask children and parents to think about ethics and values. Just as robotics might be used to teach math or science concepts, it can be used to make the study of values less abstract and more real to children and their parents. In Chapter 7, authors from the KISS Institute for Practical Robotics discuss how robotics can be a part of new classroom challenges in math and science. The authors share how the Botball contest challenges students to design, build, and program a small mobile robot to compete against other robots. In doing so, teamwork, engineering principles, math skills, and much more are learned. In Chapter 8, authors from Xerox PARC and Gunn High School describe how students have the opportunity to partner with industry professionals in a robot contest called FIRST. This learning experience, again, teaches much more than traditional robotics. As with the Botball contest, FIRST can influence attitudes, not just in relation to learning advanced concepts, but also in relation to future career paths. And finally in Chapter 9, authors from the University of South Florida and Carnegie Mellon University describe a robotics camp that brings students together to explore robotics while they learn about locomotion, animals, perception, behaviors, and much more. Students explore creatively and develop confidence in a wide variety of areas.

All of these chapters describe diverse approaches to using robots in educational ways. Although the educational settings might be different, and the subject matter varied, all of the authors describe the use of robotics as a tool for learning diverse knowledge. The purpose is not to teach children to become extraordinary robotics experts, but to engage, excite, and compel them to learn, among other things, about values, communication, teamwork, science, and math. All of these chapters describe students as problem-solvers, explorers, and builders. It is inspiring to hear how these new robotic technologies can make learning more concrete and physically active. In all cases, authors describe how traditional educational environments are transformed into constructivist, problem-centered learning experiences. These new technologies have changed what we once thought possible in education. Conversely, these educational experiences ask us to reconsider, challenge, and change the educational technologies we make in the future.

Closing Thoughts

William Doll, a postmodern curriculum theorist, has explained that "A matrix has no beginning and no ending; it does have boundaries and it has points of intersection or foci. So, too, a curriculum modeled on a matrix is non-linear and non-sequential but bounded and filled with foci and webs of meaning. The richer the curriculum, the more points of intersection, the more connections constructed, the deeper the meaning" (Doll 1993).

I believe the thoughts of Doll suggest important educational goals for our future. Thanks to the promises of new educational technologies, we can work towards rich learning experiences with "more points of intersection . . . more connections constructed, and . . . deeper . . . meaning" (Doll 1993). This is the educators' challenge in the years to come.

References

Bolter, J. D. 1991. *Writing Space: The Computer, Hypertext and the History of Writing.* Hillside, NJ: Laurence Erlbaum Associates.

Doll, W. E. 1993. *A Post-Modern Perspective in Curriculum.* Advances in Contemporary Education Thought series, 9. New York: Teachers College Press.

Kay, A. 1996. Revealing the elephant: The use and misuse of computers in education. *Educom Review* 31(4):22–28.

Kliebard, H. 1995. *The Struggle for the American Curriculum: 1893–1958.* Second edition. New York: Routledge.

Norton, P. 1992. When technology meets subject-matter disciplines in education. Part 3: Incorporating the computer as method. *Educational Technology* 32(8):35–44.

Papert, S. 1985. Computer criticism vs. technocratic thinking. *Proceedings of LOGO'85, Theoretical Papers,* pp. 51–53.

Toffler, A. 1980. *The Third Wave.* New York: Bantam Books.

Chapter Five

Teaching Diverse Learners Using Robotics

Gabrielle Miller
Kennedy Krieger Institute

Robin Church
Kennedy Krieger Institute

Mark Trexler
Kennedy Krieger Institute

Abstract

This chapter will focus on the use of robotics as a means to address the needs of diverse learners who, increasingly, are included in general education classrooms. The chapter begins with a brief description of the nature of inclusive classrooms and the characteristics of individuals with diverse learning needs, particularly students with learning disabilities. Suggestions are offered in this chapter for the use of robotics to support diverse learners in the areas of content acquisition, reducing social barriers, and beginning the process of workforce preparation. The chapter also briefly discusses the impact of school reform on the expectations for all students to be skilled in critical thinking and problem-solving skills necessary to be prepared to enter the workforce of the 21st century. Finally, student-based projects will be described to illustrate ways that robotics can be used with diverse learners.

5.1   Introduction

In every classroom there are students with diverse abilities who demonstrate a variety of levels of achievement. Some students excel with whatever curriculum or instructional materials that are used, while others struggle and progress slowly despite the best instruction available. Students with mild and moderate disabilities struggle and progress slowly more frequently than other students and require more creative instructional models to achieve academically.

Churton, Cranston-Gingras, and Blair (1998) offer a description of the basic principles of teaching students with diverse learning abilities (see Figure 5.1). While elements of all these principles are contained in this chapter, several emerge as critical to the successful use of robotics for students with diverse learning needs, specifically that (1) experiential learning helps students understand and interpret concepts, (2) cooperative learning facilitates appropriate social interactions, (3) inquiry methods encourage independent thinking and problem-solving, and (4) effective instruction uses a variety of strategies to facilitate learning (Churton, Cranston-Gingras, and Blair 1998).

Students with learning disabilities comprise over half of all students receiving special education services and can be found in every classroom in America. The federal government has recognized the characteristics of students with learning disabilities as follows:

- The individual has a disorder in one or more of the basic psychological processes (these include memory, auditory perception, visual perception, oral language, and thinking).

Figure 5.1

PRINCIPLES OF TEACHING DIVERSE LEARNERS

That all children can and do learn and that teachers encourage learning by understanding the teaching-learning process.

That children's learning is influenced by their environment and that certain conditions do influence a child's ability to learn.

That experiential learning and practice help the child to understand and interpret concepts.

That diversity among children should be celebrated and their strengths used in teaching all children.

That cooperative learning and instruction help children to grasp concepts and interact with peers and other teachers.

That successful teaching should result in children being less dependent on school and family and developing the skills to become independent learners.

That effective instruction is student–centered, focusing on children's strengths and utilizing a variety of strategies to facilitate learning.

That knowledge is effectively developed through well planned and appropriate instruction based on the identified needs of children.

That the use of inquiry methods encourage children to think independently and arrive at appropriate conclusions.

That teaching children from a holistic perspective allows for familiar and collaborative associations and addresses the diverse abilities of children.

That the teaching-learning process is facilitated through appropriate classroom management that creates an environment conducive to learning.

Principles of teaching diverse learners. Adapted from Churton, Cranston-Gingras, and Blair (1998).

- The individual has difficulty learning (specifically in basic reading or decoding, reading comprehension, writing, speaking, listening, and mathematics—either reasoning or calculating).

- The problem is not due to other causes such as limited intelligence, motor impairment, sensory impairment, emotional disorder, economic or cultural disadvantage.

- A severe discrepancy exists between the individual's measured capacity to learn and his or her actual achievement.

There is growing concern for the extreme difficulty these students experience in mastering academic material, even with a normal capacity for doing so (Lerner 1997). Many of these students are an enigma to educators because, while they have normal intelligence, they lack the language-processing skills required to read, write, and spell accurately. Some struggle with mathematics and spatial relationships, while others present a picture of total disorganization and are unable to focus their attention on the task at hand. Many prominent thinkers throughout history, including Hans Christian Andersen, Leonardo da Vinci, Auguste Rodin, Thomas Edison, Nelson D. Rockefeller, Winston Churchill, and Albert Einstein, have had learning disabilities and participated in an educational system that failed to recognize their needs or accommodate them effectively. It is precisely these students for whom experiential, cooperative, and creative instruction is most needed.

5.2   Problems Faced by Students with Learning Difficulties

Before a discussion about the use of robotics with students with disabilities can be meaningful, some explanation of common characteristics shared by diverse learners is necessary. Students diagnosed with disabilities exhibit a variety of learning and behavioral traits. As a result, the variation in the characteristics of individuals with learning difficulties is broad, making generalizations about these learners impossible. With this in mind, a brief discussion of the most common problems faced by students with learning disabilities follows.

Disorders of Attention

Students with these difficulties cannot focus on the learning task and cannot distinguish between important and extraneous stimuli. Therefore, everything going on around them seems of equal interest, and they may miss much of the content while they are directing their attention to background noise instead of what the teacher is saying. In addition they may exhibit hyperactive and impulsive behaviors.

Poor Motor Abilities

Students with learning and behavioral problems may have difficulty with gross or fine motor skills. Limitations in motor skills may manifest themselves in poor general coordination, episodes of "clumsiness," difficulty with spatial organization, and difficulty with paper/pencil tasks.

Information-Processing Problems

Students with learning deficits often have difficulty processing auditory or visual information. Problems at the phonologic level (or the sounds of language) will prevent the acquisition of reading skills, while deficits at the symbolic level affect the ability to recognize letters and affect reading and writing skills. Others may have difficulty with short-term memory and experience difficulty following oral directions.

Lack of Cognitive Strategies for Learning

Many students with disabilities do not know how to go about learning. They lack the metacognitive strategies for planning, organizing, and executing a plan of action. They are not active participants in the learning process and depend on others to provide the structure that they cannot bring to bear on the task at hand.

Oral Language Deficits

Basic underlying language disorders are common to students with learning and behavior problems. This can manifest itself in difficulty with listening comprehension (receptive language), general language development, speaking (expressive language), using language for social communication (pragmatic language), or in the development of concepts.

Reading Deficits

About 80 percent of students with learning disabilities have difficulty with reading (Lerner 1997). These problems can occur while learning the sound/symbol correspondence necessary to decode words or while learning a basic sight vocabulary for words that are not phonetically regular. Other students will have difficulties in comprehending what they read.

Written Language Difficulties

Writing involves the integration of many complex language skills. Students with learning disabilities can have difficulty organizing their thoughts logically and putting them down on paper while coordinating the tasks of spelling, punctuation, and handwriting.

Deficits in Mathematics

Problems in this area involve difficulties with quantitative thinking and spatial organization. Students may have deficits in computation, reasoning, or in understanding and using concepts of time and space.

Inappropriate Social Behavior

Many students with learning problems have difficulties making and keeping friends. Their social interactions are often immature and impulsive. They lack the appropriate social skills necessary for cooperative relationships.

The number of students with learning disabilities who participate in general education classrooms is increasing, in large part as a result of the movement to include students with diverse needs in the mainstream. With the inclusion movement changing the way in which services are delivered, the need for collaboration and coordination becomes critical. Simultaneously, school reform movements have resulted in a trend toward increasing the academic standards for all students. The challenge these two movements present for educators who work with students who have diverse learning needs is significant. Educators must identify new instructional frameworks within which to teach content, critical thinking, and problem-solving skills.

5.3   Robotics and Content Acquisition: A Rationale

An instructor's ability to create a learning environment that meets the needs of all learners is based, to a large extent, on an understanding of the strengths and weaknesses of the learners. With a clear understanding of student learning needs, an instructor can make sound judgments about everything from classroom management style to the arrangement of the desks.

Some of the most important judgments to be made in any learning environment relate to the instructional materials. When an instructor has a clear understanding of the content and learner needs, the selection and use of materials is relatively straightforward. When, however, there is a great deal of diversity in the learning styles of individuals in a classroom, the task of identifying appropriate instructional materials can become a significant challenge. Instructors who select materials based on learner needs often find it necessary to incorporate more than one set of materials during one class, which, in turn, adds to the classroom management demands. Conversely, limited consideration of student learning needs and/or limited resources can also affect material selection. When only one set of materials is available for use with a group of diverse learners, particularly if those materials are text-based, it restricts the teaching to the mean ability level of the class rather than recognizing (and accommodating for) individuals at both ends of the learning curve. Students with disabilities who receive instruction that is aimed at the mean ability level of the group typically fail to achieve positive academic outcomes (Wagner and Blackorby 1996).

The need to incorporate instructional materials that can effectively support learners with a wide range of abilities is clear. However, when, as some estimates have suggested, there can be as many as five different instructional levels within one classroom (Fuchs and Fuchs 1994), finding materials that are effective with a wide range of learners can be extremely difficult. Adding to the challenge is the fact that the majority of materials, particularly for older students, are text-based. As instruction becomes more content-based, students must have access to material—whether print or electronic media—that they can interact with independently to gather information and to produce products that, in turn, will demonstrate understanding of the material.

The ability to acquire and demonstrate knowledge of complex content, however, is not always a function of the ability to independently interact with text-based materials. There are a significant number of students, most notably those diagnosed with learning disabilities, who have average or above-average intelligence levels and the ability to acquire and demonstrate complex understanding of content, but have difficulty interacting with text-based classroom materials as a means to acquire and/or demonstrate knowledge.

The implication is not that the need to independently interact with text-based materials should be eliminated, but rather that teachers who are working with a diverse group of learners must insure that instructional materials offer options for all learners. Materials that offer learning options will encourage students' involvement with the material, rather than with the means to understand/communicate the material. Such materials are often more likely to engage students because involvement with the content is not a function of the reading or writing skill of the student.

One of the few types of instructional materials that can be used to support learners of all age and ability groups is robotics. Robotic materials offer a unique alternative to text-based materials because the same set of robotic materials can be used to create very different instructional experiences for students within the same class. That is, robotics can be used to create instructional (and assessment) experiences that are academically rigorous for some students, while for others they can be adapted to provide structure and support.

There is also a significant amount of diversity in the robotic materials available for classroom use. Some robotic materials require the construction of originally designed components, while others provide premanufactured (typically plastic) pieces that can be assembled to create original objects.

The system the authors have found to lend itself to the widest range of content and learner needs is the LEGO DACTA system, which uses premanufactured plastic pieces (bricks) to allow the user to construct virtually any object. Although the majority of the components in a LEGO system are rectangular bricks, elements such as wheels, axles, pulleys, and gears can be combined to create objects that demonstrate specific concepts and incorporate mobility into the object(s) created. A related software environment, LEGO Engineer (LEGO Group 1993), through which projects can be developed and controlled, offers a means for all students to practice design and programming principles.

Most recently, the development of the LEGO Programmable Brick, also known as the RCX, has significantly expanded the creative and programming options for users. The RCX is a small battery-powered microcomputer. Through the use of a software program developed by National Instruments called ROBOLAB, students can create and download a program into the RCX. Once downloaded, a desktop computer is no longer needed to run the LEGO program, thereby helping to overcome the logistical problems of too few computers in a classroom. And, because the programs are downloaded via an infrared transmitter rather than wires, students have the option of creating a wider range of projects and programs.

Robotic materials, such as LEGO systems, are most traditionally used to demonstrate physical science and/or engineering concepts. For example, using LEGO elements to create a model of a simple machine that uses a lever or a pulley is a common project. However, robotic materials also have instructional applications across other content areas that are often overlooked. A social studies class, for example, might gain a greater understanding of how American settlers built sod homes during the period of westward expansion if they were to use LEGO elements to try to build a sod home into the side of a model hill. Robotics might also be used to help students in a math class understand the difference between area and perimeter or any number of geometric concepts.

Another advantage to using robotic materials in a content area is the amount of flexibility they offer in terms of instruction and assessment. During instruction, robotic materials can easily be used with students who exhibit a wide range of ability levels, supporting differentiation and the use of cognitive learning theories, such as constructivism, that have been demonstrated to be effective with students who have disabilities (Mercer, Jordan, and Miller 1996). For example, an instructor who is working with a group that is learning about vehicles may have students who clearly understand the relationship of axles to wheels and are ready to move on to new material, in the same class with other students who are experiencing difficulty understanding how wheels and axles work together. Using the same set of robotic instructional materials, an instructor might easily create activities in which some students continue to explore the relationship between axles and wheels while other students complete an activity designed to determine the effect of the location of axles and wheels on a vehicle's stability.

In terms of assessment, the fact that most robotic systems require the user to construct objects creates opportunities to assess the critical thinking skills needed for object construction as well as the critical thinking skills necessary to synthesize content and form. The opportunity to use nontextual materials to evaluate student understanding provides opportunities for all students to demonstrate understanding of content whether they are able to independently interact with text or not.

Using robotics with diverse learners increases the means of instructors to insure that all students benefit from instruction. As with any other instructional material, however, without thoughtful consideration of how robotics will be incorporated into instruction, its successful use is unlikely.

5.4 Factors Contributing to the Successful Use of Robotics with Diverse Learners

Working with students who have diverse learning needs, particularly those with disabilities, is one of the most challenging aspects of teaching. Not surprisingly, as individuals begin to understand the degree of complexity involved in meeting the needs of diverse learners, there is a (sometimes frantic) search for simple solutions. Invariably this search leads to two conclusions. The first is that there are no strategies that always work for all students with disabilities. The second is that the answer to meeting the needs of diverse learners almost always lies in a teacher's ability to develop problem-solving strategies. That is, the students, their learning needs, and the classroom climate are in a constant state of change. Universal solutions, therefore, are impossible. However, effective teachers know how to prevent, recognize, and solve problems. They also know the learners, the content, the daily changes in classroom climate, and the most effective way to structure their interactions with students.

Similarly, there is no standard formula for using instructional materials, such as robotic materials, with diverse learners. There are, however, factors the authors have found to contribute to the successful use of robotics with diverse learners. A description of the five that the authors have found to contribute to the successful use of robotics with diverse learners follows.

Clear Focus

Clearly defining the purpose for which robotic materials are incorporated into a lesson is perhaps the most important element of a successful experience with robotics in a classroom of diverse learners. There can be any number of purposes to incorporate robotics into a lesson that may or may not directly relate to content acquisition. No matter what the purpose, it is important to clearly define what students should learn by the end of the lesson and how robotics will assist learners to achieve that objective. It is also important that the purpose be realistic given the constraints of time, class size, and student skills.

Once that objective is clearly defined, it is equally important to insure that students understand the objective. Students who clearly understand the instructional expectations are more likely to be meaningfully involved with the material and benefit from instructional activities (Rosenberg, O'Shea, and O'Shea 1991). However, it is important to remember, particularly when working with a group of diverse learners, that not all students can efficiently process information that is presented in only one format and that objectives must be communicated using more than one modality. Although it can be time-consuming initially, when instructional objectives are presented verbally, in writing, and with a graphic representation, the likelihood that all learners (particularly those who are inefficient learners) will achieve desired outcomes will be increased (Joyce and Weil 1978). Students who clearly understand objectives and expectations are more likely to remain focused and benefit from robotics in the classroom (Good and Brophy 1978; Smith and Lucasson 1995; Smith et al. 1998).

Content Creativity

As previously noted, although robotic materials seem to lend themselves best to use in science or technology classrooms, there are innumerable ways to integrate robotics and traditional content. Robotic projects can either be infused into content-based instruction or content-based instruction can be infused into robotic projects. In either case, finding ways to do so is not always obvious and requires both knowledge of the content and creativity on the part of the instructor. The diversity and flexibility of robotic materials can provide the means to incorporate tangible instructional materials in lessons where they might not otherwise have been used. For example, preliminary data demonstrate that when secondary foreign language students use physical representations of objects to create stories to learn/practice vocabulary, they are more likely to demonstrate vocabulary and usage skills at a higher level than peers using text-based materials (Niellsen 1996). This research might be the basis for the use of robotics in a foreign language program. That is, rather than using existing objects to encourage students to practice and use a foreign language, incorporating robotics would offer the means to have students create object(s) around which vocabulary/conversational skills could be developed.

Similarly, enhancing assignments that already incorporate robotic themes could also offer a way to incorporate robotics across a variety of content areas. A writing assignment in which students must write the directions for an imaginary robot to complete an assigned task offers an effective means for students to practice technical writing and sequencing skills (Miller 1989). Adding a physical robotic component, however, might not only support those students who have difficulty organizing thoughts to write sequentially but might also offer opportunities for highly able students to add a level of complexity that could significantly enrich the project. Planning for and creating a robot offers numerous opportunities to incorporate technical and creative writing activities as well as complete research projects related to robots. Writing assignments describing the planning of the robot, describing the characteristics of the robot, and sequentially describing the tasks intended for the robot might also easily be incorporated into the project.

An added component to such an exercise, given the use of a LEGO system, might be the incorporation of the LEGO Programmable Brick (or RCX) into the robot, allowing students to program the robot to complete the task(s) described in the writing. Incorporating the RCX would not only offer the opportunity to practice programming skills, but might also complete a technical writing assignment that describes the logic behind the program and the efficacy of the robot's functioning, and identifies areas for improvement/enhancement.

Another way to incorporate robotics into a content area is to consider how the content might be used in an authentic (or real-life) situation. In addition to stimulating creative ways to incorporate robotics into instruction, the use of authentic situations has been linked to increased student learning and generalization (Poteet, Choate, and Stewart 1996).

Creating a classroom minieconomy in which students are required to develop and sell products using a school-based currency is an example of an authentic situation in which students could use robotics. Objects sold in their minieconomy might easily be created with robotic materials. Rather than have students complete a theoretical exercise on economies, all aspects of planning the development, production, marketing, and sales of robotic-based products and/or related services could be incorporated into the project.

Cross-content authentic instruction can also be supported through the use of robotics. A collaborative planning effort by the English, math, social science, and science teachers, for example, might result in a project that requires a seventh-grade class to solve a particular problem. Students might be given a scenario in which a town is experiencing rock slides from a nearby mountain that are causing severe damage to the town's drawbridge. Students, grouped in heterogeneous "contracting teams," could be charged with proposing a new design for the bridge. Requirements that the design is technically sound as well as aesthetically pleasing could easily be incorporated into the project along with opportunities for teams to "interact" with townspeople by presenting and defending a model of their proposed design. As an alternative to a two-dimensional drawing of the proposed drawbridge, robotics offers a way for students to create the model using familiar materials and interact with the bridge (i.e., test the strength of the bridge, reconfigure the elements of the bridge, etc.) with relative ease. The ability to interact with elements of the bridge also offers an opportunity for students to enhance their understanding of the basic engineering principles necessary to create a bridge. A project such as this one provides an opportunity for robotics to act as a link between content areas.

Thus, creatively using robotics relates not only to its use within a content area, such as building sod houses or creating minieconomies in social studies, but also between content areas. Although opportunities to incorporate robotics are not always apparent, with creative thought robotic instructional materials can easily be incorporated into a variety of content-based situations.

Cautious Constructivism

There is a significant amount of professional literature detailing the cognitive structures believed to be at the heart of content acquisition (e.g., Harris and Graham 1996; Pressley et al. 1996). One of the most widely recognized cognitive theories proposes that learners acquire content more meaningfully when they are provided with the opportunity to independently construct meaning from authentic problems. That is, constructivist theory proposes that in order to facilitate content acquisition, an instructor must provide opportunities for learners to construct knowledge by interacting directly with the content, most typically through the solution of an authentic problem (Harris and Graham 1994). Interaction with the content offers students the opportunity to acquire knowledge from personal interaction and is thought to support the independent development of cognitive structures necessary for content acquisition. When students are actively involved in learning, they are more likely to independently acquire knowledge, more likely to be responsible for their own learning, and ultimately be better prepared to generalize those skills into new settings (Harris and Graham 1996; Pressley et al. 1996).

Alone, however, constructivist teaching practices are not enough to insure that all learners can derive educational benefit (Deshler, Ellis, and Lenz 1996; Harris and Graham 1994). Among the most common characteristics of inefficient learners (typically those with learning disabilities) is an inability to independently generate the cognitive structures necessary for content acquisition (Deshler, Ellis, and Lenz 1996). That is, although inefficient learners gain information from opportunities to interact with instructional materials, these same individuals often have difficulty organizing and/or using the information they may have gained. In fact, without specific ongoing support, constructivist instructional practices increase the likelihood that inefficient learners will practice errors, be unable to identify attributes necessary to make the correct inferences from information gathered, and fall short of having the means to acquire and organize new content (Moore, Reith, and Ebeling 1996).

That is not to suggest that constructivist teaching practices hold no promise for inefficient learners. It is important for students with disabilities to have the opportunity to interact with material and to make inferences relative to the project being completed. However, it is also important to insure that students can distinguish important content from irrelevant details and ultimately gain the desired information. Thus, students with disabilities need constructivist practices that include frequent purposeful interaction with the instructor. Instructor techniques such as modeling, guided thinking/questioning, and think-aloud strategies have been shown to benefit students with disabilities and are necessary for them to derive educational benefit from constructivist learning practices (Harris and Graham 1996; Harris and Pressley 1991; Moore, Reith, and Ebeling 1996; Pressley et al. 1996).

Controlling the Chaos

Without thoughtful consideration of classroom management and materials management, using robotics with a group of diverse learners can present significant classroom and materials management challenges. It is important, particularly for distractible learners, to insure that materials are well organized and that activities in the classroom are focused and purposeful.

In terms of classroom management, as previously noted, it is important to begin by insuring that objectives and expectations are presented in a way that is clear to all students (Good and Brophy 1978). It is also important for the teacher to consider the readiness of the students to deal effectively with manipulatives (in this case, LEGO elements helping students learn a particular concept) necessary for robotic instruction. Offering independent access to robotic elements to students (or groups of students) who have difficulty regulating their behavior would, in all likelihood, be counterproductive to content acquisition. All students should have the opportunity to interact independently with robotic materials and, ideally, receive direct instruction in materials management. Also, students experiencing behavioral difficulties might be invited to participate in a teacher-managed classroom demonstration, rather than offered opportunities to work with robotic materials independently. Then, as students demonstrate understanding of behavioral limits and become more familiar with the use of robotic elements in the classroom, opportunities for students to interact independently with materials can be increased.

Another important aspect of controlling the chaos relates to materials management, particularly since students with disabilities typically experience difficulty with materials organization. The elements of a robotics system (such as the LEGO system) are also small, very numerous, and can be a challenge to organize. Although organization of materials seems relatively unimportant, it should be remembered that valuable instructional time is often wasted in ineffective instructional material management (Rosenberg, O'Shea, and O'Shea 1991; Smith et al. 1998). In this case, searching through piles of elements to find the pieces necessary to complete a project has a negative effect not only on instructional time but also on the student's interest level and willingness to participate in the project. When, however, the student looking for pieces has a disability, instructional time lost can increase and student willingness to participate in the project is likely to decrease. Developing a routine in which students categorize components during noninstructional time can yield significant benefits relative to time and classroom management.

Drawing Conclusions

The first, and most obvious, conclusions relate to whether students were able to successfully acquire content. These conclusions are most typically drawn at the end of an instructional unit and are most commonly based on objective assessments. Performance-based assessments have been advocated as a means to determine not only a student's understanding of the content but a student's ability to apply the content (e.g., Fuchs and Fuchs 1994; McLaughlin and Warren 1992). An advantage to the use of robotic instructional materials is the opportunity to maintain ongoing evaluation of student understanding based on a student's performance. Without relying on objective measures, a teacher can make a clear determination of the level of understanding of each student, gain insights into student thinking patterns, and have the opportunity to make ongoing adjustments to instruction based on a performance assessment.

With thoughtful implementation, robotics can offer a powerful instructional tool to teachers working with groups of diverse learners. Much of the decisions relative to its use, however, are a function of the specific characteristics of the learners and the classroom environment. With thoughtful planning, robotics can be a very effective tool to support learning and motivation for all students.

 ## 5.5   Using Robotics to Address Social Barriers

Improving academic achievement for any group of students is not exclusively a function of instructional methods. Social interactions and social networks can have a significant effect on the ability of students to achieve the academic goals and objectives set for the group (Pomplun 1997). When there is a great deal of diversity between members of a group, particularly academic diversity, social barriers can evolve that not only affect instruction but can affect students' willingness to seek support from others (Wenz-Gross and Siperstein 1997). The ability to work with others is not just a secondary social skill. It has been recognized as a critical skill needed by all workers to be prepared to enter the workforce of the 21st century (U.S. Department of Labor 1991; Wagner and Blackorby 1996). Thus, there is a need to insure that all students have opportunities to participate in activities that reduce social barriers and offer opportunities to benefit, both academically and socially, from instruction.

Role of Social Interactions

There is wide recognition in professional literature regarding the role of social interactions in academic achievement, particularly with regard to academically diverse groups of students (e.g., Fad, Ross, and Boston 1995; Fuchs and Fuchs 1994; Malmgren 1998). Much of the literature can be characterized as efforts to understand the nature of the interactions between diverse groups of learners (typically those with and without disabilities) (e.g., Jackson, Enright, and Murdock 1987; McIntosh, Vaughn, and Zaragosa 1991; Zaragosa, Vaughn, and McIntosh 1991). Although reactions to students with disabilities by students without disabilities have not always been categorized as positive, it is widely recognized that academic opportunities for students with and without disabilities to participate in cooperative learning activities can yield positive results for all (Slavin 1986; Slavin, Madden, and Leavey 1984; Slavin, Madden, and Stevens 1989/1990) Further, researchers who have focused specifically on the interaction of students with disabilities within cooperative learning groups have found that both the nature of the task and the frequency of participation affect academic achievement. For example, Pomplun (1997) found that when heterogeneous groups are presented with nonroutine open-ended tasks, their frequency of participation increases. Pomplun also cites research by Cohen (1994) that suggests that academic gains of heterogeneous groups were best predicted by the number of task-related interactions within a group. Thus, although opportunities for students to interact in heterogeneous groups are important, the nature and the frequency of the interactions are equally important, particularly with regard to academic performance.

These research studies validate the need to insure that when students who participate in diverse classrooms are grouped for learning activities, careful consideration is paid to both the nature of the task and the characteristics of the learner. Although research data (Cohen 1994) suggest that participation levels increase when groups are presented with open-ended tasks, it is important to insure that the task demands are appropriate to the cognitive skills of all students. Balancing (open-ended) task demands with the cognitive skills of group members is essential to maximize the social interactions and academic achievement of all students (Harris and Graham 1996; Pressley et al. 1996).

Identifying learning tasks that maximize the contributions of all members in a heterogeneous group can be difficult. When, for example, groups are asked to work toward solving a problem that has a correct or incorrect answer, interactions between group members are typically characterized by information flowing from the highly able students to the less able students (Pomplun 1997; Wenz-Gross and Siperstein 1997). Group problem-solving activities that include components that offer structure as well as more than one correct solution are likely to support participation by all students and improve the likelihood of academic gain.

Robotic materials offer a unique medium around which projects that encourage social interactions might be developed. Incorporating a robotic set of materials, particularly the LEGO system, presents students with a construction system familiar to virtually all children, creating a common frame of reference for group members. The LEGO system is also one that provides a means for students to assemble and disassemble component parts easily to demonstrate/test an idea. The ease of assembly adds another way to participate in that it makes showing, rather than describing, an idea an option for those who may have language deficits.

Perhaps the biggest support robotics, such as the LEGO system, can provide for social interactions is the variety of involvement it offers to students of varying abilities. Whether a student helps conceptualize a model, finds and constructs components collaboratively, or uses Lab VIEW software to create a program for the RCX brick, there are a variety of tangible ways students can participate in the solution to a problem. Being able to contribute tangibly also serves as a reminder that all students participated and that all students' efforts are important—a fact that is often lost to students when group activities require written solutions composed by one student.

Opportunities for students to practice collaborative social skills serve two important purposes. The first and most immediate purpose relates to content acquisition. Cooperative learning experiences are widely recognized as a means to support all learners and provide opportunities for students to become more directly involved with the content (Slavin 1986). In addition, collaborative problem-solving skills have been recognized as an essential skill for workers in the 21st century. In order to be able to collaborate successfully with others, students need opportunities to practice collaboration, and the related social skills, in a variety of ways. Incorporating robotic materials into collaborative problem-solving tasks offers a means for all students to tangibly participate, recognize the contributions of others, and feel a common sense of accomplishment that will work toward reducing social barriers between groups.

5.6   Incorporating Robotics into Workforce Preparation

The Secretary's Commission on Achieving Necessary Skills (SCANS) was formed by the U.S. Department of Labor to identify the workforce needs for the 21st century. The commission found that not only will there be an increasing need for highly skilled workers as the new century begins, but that schools are not adequately preparing students to meet the changing demands of the workplace (U.S. Department of Labor 1991, p. xiv). The SCANS report identified two areas of need. The first was a set of skills and competencies that all workers need to be successful in the world of work,

Figure 5.2

Workplace Know-How

Workplace Competencies—Effective workers can productively use

Resources They know how to allocate time, money, materials, space, and staff.

Interpersonal Skills They can work on teams, teach others, serve customers, lead, negotiate, and work well with people from culturally diverse backgrounds.

Information They can acquire and evaluate data, organize and maintain files, interpret and communicate, and use computers to process information.

Systems They understand social, organizational, and technological systems; they can monitor and correct performance; and they can design or improve systems.

Technology They can select equipment and tools, apply technology to specific tasks, and maintain and troubleshoot equipment.

Foundation Skills—Competent workers in the high-performance workplace need

Basic Skills Reading, writing, arithmetic and mathematics, speaking, and listening.

Thinking Skills The ability to learn, to reason, to think creatively, to make decisions, and to solve problems.

Personal Qualities Individual responsibility, self-esteem and self-management, sociability, and integrity.

SCANS competencies.

commonly known as the "SCANS competencies." The second finding of the SCANS committee was the need to change the way instruction is provided in schools. Specifically, the need to insure that students have opportunities to participate in activities that connect school to work is a reform essential to insure students are adequately prepared to enter the workforce. Figure 5.2 provides an overview of the SCANS report.

In 1994, Congress also recognized the need for systemic educational change to prepare all students to enter the workforce. The passage of the School to Work Opportunities Act (STWOA) provided funding enabling states to make changes to the educational system necessary to insure that all students are prepared to enter the workforce. Specifically, the STWOA reiterated the need to insure that all students understand the direct relationship between school and work through participating in school-based activities, work-based activities, and activities that connect school to work (U.S. Department of Education 1994).

The implications of the SCANS report and the STWOA are significant, particularly in an era of school reform. Schools are being asked to reevaluate existing models of instruction to incorporate opportunities for students to understand the relationship between school and work. Both the SCANS report and the STWOA recognize that one of the biggest barriers to insuring students understand the relationship between school and work relates to the misperception that academic rigor and work-based learning are a contradiction in terms. National and state school-reform movements such as Goals 2000 (Educate America Act of 1993) that focus on the need to raise academic standards make the assumption that improved academic skills directly generalize to workforce readiness. As a result, educators are under increasing pressure to focus exclusively on the need to improve student performance on standardized academic assessments.

The intent of the SCANS report, however, was to clearly communicate that, given the changing demands of the workplace, high academic performance is necessary but no longer sufficient to prepare anyone, with or without a college degree, to enter the workforce. All students need experiences that incorporate both academic rigor and work-based learning to be adequately prepared to enter the workforce.

Thus, the SCANS report argues that the perception held by many educators that improving student academic performance and offering work-based learning activities are separate responsibilities is erroneous. Indeed, work-based learning experiences that incorporate industry-based standards as an evaluative measure can be more rigorous, and are certainly more relevant, than experiences that train students to improve performance on standardized educational assessment measures (Benz, Yovanoff, and Doren 1997).

Educators not only need to recognize the relationship between work-based learning and academic rigor, but must begin to model that relationship to students by incorporating work-based learning experiences into curriculum offerings, not with the intent of completely replacing traditional activities, but as a means to enhance existing offerings and help students understand the relationship between school and work.

Robotics can be used to powerfully demonstrate the connection between school and work. The fact that robotic materials allow the user to understand concepts in an applied format allows the instructor to use the same instructional materials in a variety of ways, depending on the content and the instructional needs of the student. Robotic materials also offer a relatively straightforward means to incorporate performance-based assessments across content areas and ability groups. The flexibility of the materials (elements) also allows the instructor to incorporate work-based contexts into projects. If, for example, a middle-school social science teacher wanted his students to understand the role of assembly lines in industrialism, he might have students develop an assembly line to create a robotic product. The project offers the opportunity to build traditional academic skills by researching assembly lines and identifying the characteristics that made them so effective. The project also offers students the opportunity to plan and create an assembly line that, as in the world of work, must create a working product and meet criteria for speed, safety, and efficiency in order to be effective. By blending academic challenges with work-based challenges, a project such as this one offers the opportunity to (1) model/understand the relationship between school and work, (2) incorporate a variety of validated instructional and assessment methods, and (3) engage students in a motivating activity that can easily be modified to insure that all learners derive benefit.

As previously noted, a relatively new element of robotic systems is programmable interfaces, which allow the user to develop basic programming through the use of ROBOLAB software. In terms of the programming demands of ROBOLAB, the modified Lab VIEW environment in which ROBOLAB is embedded offers users a symbolic programming system. The advantage of such a system, particularly for groups of diverse learners, is that it allows an individual to focus on the logic behind a program and eliminates the need for an individual to learn a programming language to successfully write a program. The ability to focus on the logic of the program, rather than on the programming language, allows students of varying abilities to demonstrate logical thought in much the same way that eliminating textual demands allows individuals who are unable to independently manipulate written text to demonstrate content knowledge.

In addition, having students operate in a modified version of Lab VIEW offers the opportunity to develop competencies in a software environment that is very similar to software used in a wide variety of industrial manufacturing settings. Thus, incorporating programming with robotics offers a means to directly relate academic rigor with work-based learning. In this case, using Lab VIEW software not only offers students the opportunity to develop traditional academic skills but allows them to do so in a work-based context that gives them the chance to become familiar with a software environment that is actually used in industrial manufacturing applications.

In order to prepare a workforce that is capable of meeting the challenges of the next century, it is critical that educational reform efforts continue. It is, however, equally important to realize reform efforts that address academics alone will not prepare students to be successful members of the workforce. Students at all levels need to be held to high academic standards and also need to understand the importance of those academic skills in the environment in which they will be used. Opportunities for students to experience a variety of activities that blend school-based, work-based, and connecting activities with high academic standards are essential for students to leave school ready to enter the workforce.

The use of robotic materials offers educators an excellent way, using validated instructional and assessment methods, to consistently provide the learning experiences needed to meet the academic and work-based needs of students who have varying age and ability levels.

5.7   Robotics in the Classroom: Case Studies

As previously noted, much of the information presented in this chapter is based on experiences with students at the Kennedy Krieger School (KKS) in Baltimore, MD. Twice the recipient of a prestigious National Blue Ribbon Award for Excellence from the U.S. Department of Education, the Kennedy Krieger School serves as a model program for students with complex and multiple learning and behavior problems. The school is part of a larger developmental disabilities center, the Kennedy Krieger Institute, which is affiliated with the Johns Hopkins University and Medical Institution. Students are referred to the school directly by local school districts who have determined that, for many reasons, they cannot meet the individual special education and related needs of a particular student. Because of the unique population of students attending the school, a variety of related service professionals (i.e., social workers, occupational therapists, physical therapists, and speech/language pathologists) work in close collaboration with educators to provide meaningful instruction in a variety of classroom settings. Students at the Kennedy Krieger School receive instruction in a comprehensive curriculum including reading and language arts, science, social studies, math, art, music, physical education, technology, and a variety of special areas. Instruction is thematic, which lends itself well to cross-curricular planning, allowing teachers and clinicians the opportunity to work side by side in a classroom to meet the unique and multiple needs of the students.

These students, many of whom experienced a great deal of academic failure before attending KKS, have not only excelled using robotics in the classroom but have successfully competed in local technology-based contests. The successful experiences of these students demonstrate the efficacy of robotic instructional materials with students who have been diagnosed with moderate to severe disabilities, a group who are routinely excluded from participation in school-based technology training programs (Lombard, Hazelkorn, and Miller 1995).

The three case studies that follow are included to illustrate how robotics can be used to support all learners, especially those who have experienced failure. The first case study offers an example of a group project that required students who often have difficulty communicating to collaborate in the development of a LEGO Intelligent House. The second case study describes the experiences of two young men who found a creative outlet in robotics. Beginning with an existing LEGO predesigned project, the students synthesized a number of elements to create a project that significantly enhanced the project's original design. Finally, the power of robotics to attract students to technology is illustrated through the final case study. After watching a number of their peers successfully complete robotic projects, two young women, who had previously expressed no interest in participating in robotics, created a Tilt-a-Whirl model and discovered a brand-new area of interest.

Collaboration + Support = LEGO Intelligent House

Many of the students who attend KKS, as previously noted, have experienced a great deal of academic failure. It is not surprising, therefore, that most are reluctant to participate in cooperative learning activities and need social and instructional support to be able to do so. Thus, as the LEGO Intelligent House project began, an authentic design team collaboration model was used to support student interactions. Students received direct instruction in the roles of, and relationships between, members of the design team as well as collaboration strategies. Then, rather than having students address all the elements of the house as a single design team, students were divided into mini–design teams, based in part on student interests. One mini-team was responsible for programming, one for structures/electronics, and a third for architecture/landscaping. In addition, one student assumed the role of project manager and was responsible for coordinating the actions of each of the groups.

Before separating into mini–design teams, the entire design team participated in a guided discussion of the overall characteristics of the house. Discussion centered on whether the house would have features such as (1) a porch light, (2) moving garage door, (3) doorbell, (4) ceiling fan, (5) security system, and (6) elevator. Consensus was reached, in large part, based on hardware realities (such as the limited number of sensors available) and teacher guidance.

Students then separated into mini–design teams and began. Teachers maintained ongoing contact with all three groups, monitoring student progress and using questioning techniques to insure acquisition of necessary concepts. End-of-week reflection sessions were held to review progress

Figure 5.3

A team design project—the creation of an Intelligent House.

made during the week, identify (collaborative and design) challenges, and develop an action plan for the next week.

There were also a number of content areas infused into the project. For example, teams were required to research geographic regions of the country, identify the types of building materials typically found in those regions, and identify the implications of the region's climate on the design of the house. A great deal of vocabulary specific to design and home building was also incorporated into the project. Students had to refer to themselves and others in terms of the role they played in the project. They were required to use the actual component name, rather than a generic term like "thing" when completing a supply list or communicating with other members of the team. In addition, all written and verbal communications between teams had to demonstrate the best effort of students to model businesslike writing skills.

Students reported that specific design decisions were difficult throughout the project because as teacher-led discussions were minimized, not all students were able to demonstrate the communication skills necessary for consensus building and decision-making. However, with ongoing teacher involvement, students were able to successfully collaborate to create an Intelligent House with the added feature of a hidden control mechanism (RCX brick) in the bathroom (Figure 5.3, see also Color Plate).

Jack and Travis's Development of a Robotic Arm

Often, opportunities to use robotics to understand a particular scientific principle inspire students to create unique applications based on their learning. Two students in the middle school, both of whom were very interested in exploring the capabilities of the RCX, chose to construct a large gear train and power it with the RCX. Both were particularly interested in how fast a slow-moving axle was turning in the middle of the gear train. They decided

Figure 5.4

Meeting the challenges of robotics provides important opportunities for triumph.

to calculate the speed of the LEGO motor by determining the gear ratio between the two points and were motivated by the axle they had created to learn more about gears. Their understanding of gears led them to build a robotic arm that demonstrated what they had learned about gears. Then, after learning about the capabilities of the RCX brick, these students realized that they could attach the light sensor on the RCX brick to their robotic arm and use ROBOLAB to program the arm to sort LEGO bricks by color (Figure 5.4; see also Color Plate).

These students were able to synthesize form and function with programming to create an original project that reflected their growth in engineering and programming principles.

Girls and Technology

At any age or at any level there are relatively few females involved with technology. Although the reasons for the gender disparity are unclear, the number of female participants in technological programs or with technological interests is relatively small.

Similarly, the two girls who are the focus of this case study expressed a great deal of reluctance to get involved in technological projects of any kind.

Therefore, when the teacher came into the classroom at the midpoint of the school year to find the girls actively engaged in creating a LEGO Tilt-a-Whirl project, he was quite happily surprised. The girls reported no particular event that changed their minds about technology, only that they had seen everyone else participating successfully and finally decided to try a project on their own. They were able to follow the directions to create a Tilt-a-Whirl independently and were very proud of their completed project. The successful creation of the Tilt-a-Whirl significantly changed the attitudes of these two girls toward technology. Both now confidently create robotic projects and have begun to explore the possibilities of original projects and programming the RCX using ROBOLAB.

5.8 Conclusion

Although it is often overlooked, robotics offers tremendous potential as a means to support the learning of diverse groups of students. In the experience of the authors it has provided a way to address issues of content acquisition, socialization, and workforce development. We strongly believe that all students will need to demonstrate technological competence as they enter the workforce and that students with diverse learning needs can develop the skills necessary to demonstrate technological competence. Our experiences with robotics and students with disabilities can serve not only to demonstrate the efficacy of robotics as an instructional tool but also as a model for others helping diverse groups of learners to succeed.

5.9 References

Benz, M., P. Yovanoff, and B. Doren. 1997. School to work components that predict post-school success for students with and without disabilities. *Exceptional Children* 63(2):151–165.

Choate, J., and S. Evans. 1992. Authentic assessment of special learners: Problem or promise? *Preventing School Failure* 37(1):6–9.

Churton, M., A. Cranston-Gingras, and T. Blair. 1998. *Teaching Children with Diverse Abilities*. Boston: Allyn and Bacon.

Cohen, E. 1994. Restructuring the classroom: Conditions for productive small groups. *Review of Educational Research* 64(1):1–35.

Deshler, D., E. Ellis, and B. Lenz. 1996. *Teaching Adolescents with Learning Disabilities*. Second edition. Denver: Love Publishing.

Fad, K., M. Ross, and J. Boston. 1995. We're better together: Using cooperative learning to teach social skills to young children. *Teaching Exceptional Children* 27(4):28–35.

Fuchs, D., and L. Fuchs. 1994. Inclusive schools movement and the radicalization of special education reform. *Exceptional Children* 60:294–309.

Good, T., and J. Brophy. 1978. *Looking in Classrooms.* Second edition. New York: Harper and Row.

Harris, K., and S. Graham (eds.). 1994. Implications of constructivism for students with disabilities and students at risk: Issues and directions. Special Issue. *Journal of Special Education* 28(3).

Harris, K., and S. Graham. 1996. Constructivism and students with special needs: Issues in the classroom. *Learning Disabilities Research and Practice* 100(3):134–137.

Harris, K., and M. Pressley. 1991. The nature of cognitive strategy instruction: Interactive strategy construction. *Exceptional Children* 57:392–405.

Jackson, S., R. Enright, and J. Murdock. 1987. Social perception problems in learning disabled youth: Developmental lag versus perceptual deficit. *Journal of Learning Disabilities* 20(6):361–364.

Joyce, B., and M. Weil. 1978. *Models of Teaching.* Boston: Allyn and Bacon.

LEGO Group. 1993. LEGO Engineer [Computer Software]. Enfield, CT: Lego Group.

Lerner, J. 1997. *Learning Disabilities: Theories, Diagnosis, and Teaching Strategies.* Seventh edition. Boston: Houghton Mifflin Co.

Lombard, R., M. Hazelkorn, and R. Miller. 1995. Special populations and tech prep. A national study of state policies and practices. *Career Development for Exceptional Individuals* 18(2):145–156.

Malmgren, K. 1998. Cooperative learning as an academic intervention for students with mild disabilities. *Focus on Exceptional Children* 31(4).

McIntosh, R., S. Vaughn, and N. Zaragosa. 1991. Review of social interventions for students with learning disabilities. *Journal of Learning Disabilities* 24(8):451–458.

McLauglin, M., and S. Warren. 1992. Outcome assessment for students with disabilities. Will it be accountability or continued failure? *Preventing School Failure* 36(4):29–33.

Mercer, C., L. Jordan, and L. Miller. 1996. Constructivist math instruction for diverse learners. *Learning Disabilities Research and Practice* 11(3):147–156.

Miller, J. 1989. Using Imaginary Robots to Improve Sequential Thinking and Writing Skills of Middle School Students. Unpublished manuscript.

Moore, P., H. Reith, and M. Ebeling. 1996. Considerations in teaching higher order thinking skills to students with mild disabilities. In E. Meyen, G. Verguson, and R. Whelan (eds.), *Strategies for Teaching Exceptional Children in Inclusive Settings,* Denver: Love Publishing, pp. 101–119.

Niellsen, G. 1996. The Effect of Student-Created Manipulatives on the Vocabulary and Usage Skills of Secondary Students Learning Japanese. Manuscript in preparation.

Pomplun, M. 1997. When students with disabilities participate in cooperative groups. *Exceptional Children* 63(2):183–193.

Color Plates

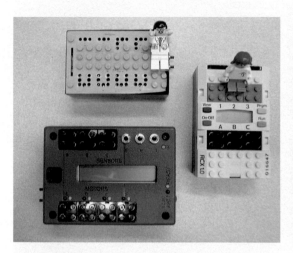

Figure 1.1 *Progression of Programmable Bricks. Counterclockwise from upper left: MIT Logo Brick (1987), MIT Red Brick (1995), LEGO RCX Brick (1998).*

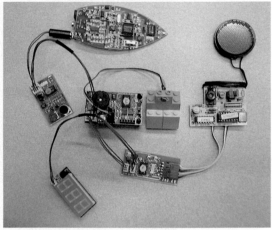

Figure 1.4 *Cricket with bus devices. At center is the "Blue Dot" version of the MIT Cricket with a simple light sensor to its immediate right. Arranged around, from top clockwise, are bus devices: MIDI Boat music synthesizer, Polaroid ultrasonic distance sensor, three-digit numeric LED display, and sound sensor.*

Figure 3.10 *Using the PETS robot at the University of Maryland.*

Figure 3.11 *Two members of the University of Maryland intergenerational design team off to do usability testing for the PETS robot.*

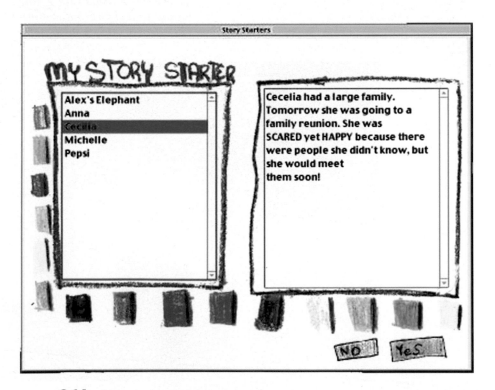

Figure 3.14 *The Story Starter screen from the PETS robot.*

Figure 4.19 *Seven-year-old Andrew testing a prototype of a transforming power wrench for a construction system.*

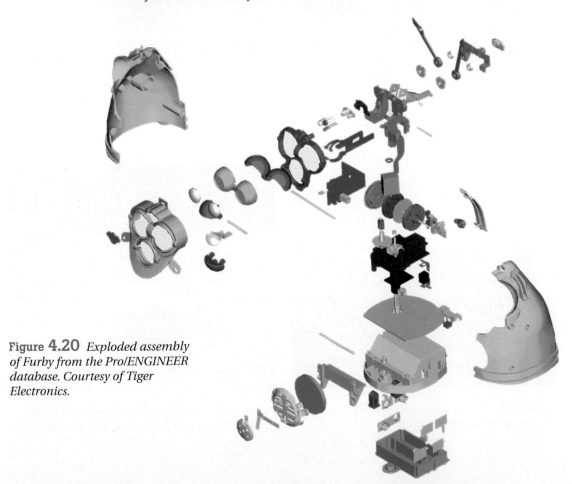

Figure 4.20 *Exploded assembly of Furby from the Pro/ENGINEER database. Courtesy of Tiger Electronics.*

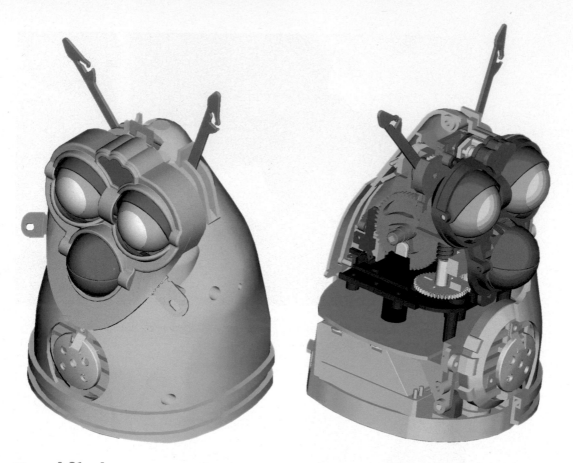

Figure 4.21a, b *Two views of an assembly of Furby, (b) with the shell removed. Courtesy of Tiger Electronics.*

Figure 5.3 *A team design project—the creation of an Intelligent House.*

Figure 5.4 *Meeting the challenges of robotics provides important opportunities for triumph.*

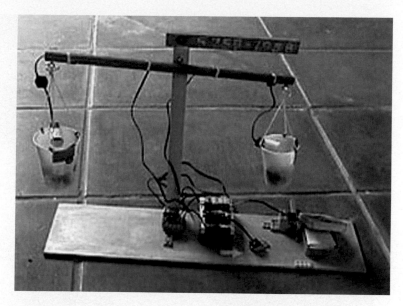

Figure **6.1** *The scale project.*

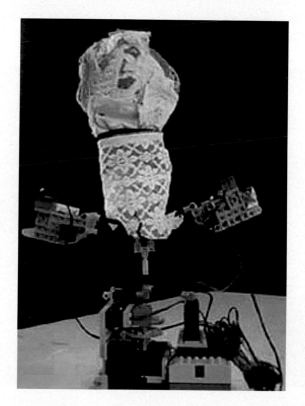

Figure **6.9** *The giving and receiving project.*

Figure 7.4 *A fifth grader fine-tunes her team's robot during a KISS Institute Robotics in Residence program at Nysmith Elementary School in Reston, Virginia.*

Figure 8.4 *As an engineering skill demonstration, the FIRST Robotics Competition provides intense excitement as robots sometimes must resort to brute strength to score points.*

Figure 8.9 *For part of the FIRST Robotics Competition, students create a 30-second animation of their robot. To prepare, Gunn High School students gathered in a garage over the summer and trained to become proficient at illustration and modeling software. This is one frame from the 1998 entry for the Autodesk Award for Excellence in Engineering Creativity and Communication.*

Figure 9.4 *A Robocamper mimicking gaits in an after-lunch relay race.*

Figure 9.7 *Two Robocampers with their soda-can-carrying robot.*

Figure 9.8 *Two Robocampers constructing a mobile manipulator.*

Poteet, J., J. Choate, and S. Stewart. 1996. Performance assessment and special education: Practices and prospects. In E. Meyen, G. Verguson, and R. Whelan (eds.), *Strategies for Teaching Exceptional Children in Inclusive Settings*, Denver: Love Publishing, pp. 234–235.

Pressley, M., K. Hogan, R. Wharton-McDonald, J. Mistretta, and S. Ettenberger. 1996. The challenges of instructional scaffolding: Instruction that supports student thinking. *Learning Disabilities Research and Practice* 11(3):138–146.

Rosenberg, M., L. O'Shea, and D. O'Shea. 1991. *Student Teacher to Master Teacher: A Handbook for Preservice and Beginning Teachers of Students with Mild and Moderate Handicaps*. New York: McMillan.

Slavin, R. 1986. Learning together: Cooperative groups and peer tutoring produce significant academic gains. *American Educator* (Summer):1–7.

Slavin, R., N. Madden, and M. Leavey. 1984. Effects of cooperative learning and individualized instruction on mainstreamed students. *Exceptional Children* 50(5): 434–443.

Slavin, R., N. Madden, and R. Stevens. 1989/1990. Cooperative learning models for the 3R's. *Educational Leadership* (Dec/Jan):22–28

Smith, D., and R. Lucasson. 1995. *Introduction to Special Education: Teaching in an Age of Challenge*. Second edition. Boston: Allyn and Bacon.

Smith, T., E. Polloway, J. Patton, and C. Dowdy. 1998. *Teaching Students with Special Needs in Inclusive Settings*. Boston: Allyn and Bacon.

Stainback, W., and S. Stainback (eds.). 1992. *Controversial Issues Confronting Special Education: Divergent Perspectives*. Boston: Allyn and Bacon

U.S. Department of Education. 1994. School to Work Opportunities Act of 1994. Pub.L., No. 103-239 [On-line]. Available: *www.stw.ed.gov/factsht/act.htm*.

U.S. Department of Labor. 1991. The Secretary's Commission on Achieving Necessary Skills: What Work Requires of Schools. Washington, DC: U.S. Government Printing Office. ERIC Document Reproduction Service No. ED 332 054.

Wagner, M., and J. Blackorby. 1996. Transition from high school to work or college: How special education students fare. *The Future of Children: Special Education for Students with Disabilities* 6(1):103–120.

Wenz-Gross, M., and G. Siperstein. 1997. The importance of social support in the adjustment of children with learning problems. *Exceptional Children* 63(2): 183–193.

Zaragosa, N., S. Vaughn, and R. McIntosh. 1991. Social skills interventions and children with behavior problems: A review. *Behavior Disorders* 16(4):260–275.

Kid's View

   ## My Robot

By Alex Kruskal, age 7

I think a robot is a thing that helps you do more than just play and all those nice things. It can help you with your homework if you don't understand things, like a word that you don't know. And it tells you what the word means if it's a hard word and you don't know it. So it helps you. And it can help you do other things that are hard. So, if it's hard to put on sun lotion and you can't reach all the way or figure out a way to put it on, then the robot does it with soft hands so it won't scratch you. It has soft hands, not crabby or furry hands.

If I had a robot, this is what I would want my robot to do. My robot would cook lots of food for me. I could put something in the robot's mouth. The robot would heat it up, in its stomach and in the back, it would open a tray and put the bags of food on it. A little thing would come out in the back and it would be flat and it would be for a plate. And the robot would cook the food, and it would put it on the plate that is on the tray. The ears of the robot would be the switches that you use to pick the time. If it's string beans, you would be able to put a couple at a time in the square hole of the robot's mouth. Then you'd put in more and more string beans and the robot would close its mouth when you say "Done." And when you say "Open," the robot opens its mouth. The feet say if you want the oven or the microwave. Animal parts, all kinds of different stuff, and different shapes should go on a robot.

Making a robot is like playing around with a friend, but you're playing around with stuff to make the robot really good. It's not like games, where you don't make anything. With a robot, you make it yourself. Even if you make a game yourself, making a robot is different because you have to do all the planning. With a robot, you make the whole thing, and you need to learn how to make it.

You should make a robot for kids and make it so it's strong so it doesn't break. It would take lots of time to make the robot because you keep making it better and better. But it's fun to do it over and over again because you get more interesting things every time. Even things that haven't been invented before.

Chapter Six

Technological Prayers

Parents and Children Exploring Robotics and Values

Marina Umaschi Bers
MIT Media Laboratory

Claudia Urrea
MIT Media Laboratory

Abstract

"Con-science" is a research program that explores how learning about technology and values can be integrated through the design of an interactive robotic contraption. In this chapter we present a first pilot experience conducted in a Jewish community school in Buenos Aires, Argentina, with parents and children during the Jewish High Holidays. We describe the goals of the project as well as the robotics technology and the constructionist methodology used. We also present the learning process that took place during the workshop and the final robotic projects that were produced and shared with the community as creative prayers. Con-science is an attempt to engage a community in building and programming artifacts to explore values and identity as a constructive and active process.

6.1 Introduction

> From the moment we enter school or church, education chops us into pieces:
> it teaches us to divorce soul from body and mind from heart.
>
> —*Eduardo Galeano, "Celebration of the Marriage of Heart and Mind"*

When children are young they ask all sorts of questions: "Why is the sky blue?" "Where does God live?" "How do cars work?" "Why do people fight?" The curiosity of the child does not make a distinction between disciplines. Children are little humanists, little engineers, little theologians, and little scientists at the same time. As time goes by, school compartmentalizes children's curiosity into the curriculum. This is particularly striking in the case of technology and values, two areas that are hardly integrated in traditional education.

On the one hand, learning and teaching about values happens in public schools through character formation or moral education (Kohlberg 1982), or in parochial schools in religion classes. When values are integrated with other disciplines, it is usually with social sciences or philosophy (Lipman 1988). On the other hand, learning about technology (Ritchie 1995) is easily integrated with math and sciences. Values and technology rarely meet in traditional schools. However, they are both present in the lives and concerns of children.

In this chapter we present an attempt to integrate learning about technology and values in a hands-on way, by involving families, as well as teachers, in the design and programming of robotic creations that represent their most cherished values. This attempt is the core of an ongoing research program at the MIT Media Laboratory, which we call Con-science. This term is the English version of the Spanish *conciencia,* formed from the prefix *con,* meaning "with" and *ciencia,* "science." *Conciencia,* as a whole, means consciousness or ethical awareness. We chose the name "Con-science" to highlight our educational vision of integrating values with the scientific and technological areas.

The premise of Con-science is that a holistic learning experience should respect and leverage children's curiosity as well as include the possibility to pursue both the technical and the moral questions in an integrated way. We believe that parents' involvement in this type of exploration about values is essential because values are too important to be the sole responsibility of schools. The workshops held within the Con-science program have four pillars: (1) a design-based constructionist approach to learning, (2) the use of new technologies, such as the LEGO Mindstorms robotic kit, to transform the designs into self-behaving mechanical artifacts, (3) the creation of narratives to complement the physical artifacts, and (4) the engagement of both parents and children, learning together while building and programming artifacts that reflect their sense of identity and the values they live by.

This chapter tells the story of a first pilot workshop conducted in the Arlene Fern Jewish Community School in Buenos Aires, Argentina, during the Jewish High Holidays. We describe why we chose that particular site and dates, the workshop methodology, the participants, the technology used, the learning processes, the final projects shared with the community as creative prayers, and the future directions for the Con-science research program.

6.2   Pilot Experience

The first pilot workshop of the Con-science research program took place in the Arlene Fern Jewish Community School in Buenos Aires, Argentina, during September 1998. The workshop had 25 participants: nine families (in pairs of one parent and his or her fourth or fifth grader), one child with developmental problems who came along with his special education teacher, and five adults (two teachers and three mothers who came alone because their kids were still too young to participate). Children were granted special permission from the school principal to miss a week of classes and participate full-time in the workshop. Parents made a big effort to attend the workshop by taking time off from work.

The timing of the workshop was carefully selected to overlap with the Jewish High Holidays, a period of 10 days in which the community gathers to celebrate the Jewish New Year and the Day of Atonement. In this context, children's curriculum focuses especially on the values of these festivities, the most holy in the Jewish calendar. To hold a workshop during these holidays was very meaningful because of the spiritual work of reflection and forgiveness that takes place both in the school and the community. The workshop was a first step towards forming a community of parents, children, and teachers who would later integrate this approach to values and technology into the school's curriculum and make it available to a wider audience. In the future, the MIT team would only be external consultants. For instance, since the first Con-science workshop was conducted, other workshops in the same spirit have been organized in the school by former participants in the first experience.

6.3   Site

The Arlene Fern Jewish Community School has certain characteristics that made it a unique pilot site for starting our research program. Perhaps the most salient is that it is a value-centered learning environment, which emphasizes the importance of "being" in addition to "knowing." The school's mission is to educate not only the children, but also the family and the community. The school is based on a liberal Jewish world view; however, its approach to universal values and its search for meaning and spiritual growth, while rejecting dogmas and certainties, applies to broader religious and cultural traditions.

The school was funded in 1995 by Rabbi Sergio Bergman as part of the Emanu-El community, the only Reform synagogue in Argentina. Today it has approximately 400 students and 100 teachers. It includes kindergarten and elementary school with a trilingual program in Spanish, English, and Hebrew. It is a private school, but, in accordance with its ideological social action position, it gives full scholarships and half scholarships to those in need. Children with special needs and developmental problems are welcomed and integrated into the classroom, with the constant tutoring of special education teachers.

During the Jewish High Holidays the school organizes activities for the whole family. For example, they engage in creative prayers by writing, dramatizing, or drawing their own prayers about meaningful contemporary themes. Usually there is an open house in which the creative prayers are shared with the community. This provided an excellent opportunity to present the process and results of the Con-science workshop to the community.

One of the key elements in deciding on the pilot site was the fact that there were already established contacts with the school and its founder and spiritual leader, Rabbi Sergio Bergman. One of the authors of this chapter, Marina Umaschi Bers, who is from Buenos Aires, has worked closely with

Rabbi Bergman for many years. Rabbi Bergman has also participated in several other activities related to values, education, and technology organized by MIT (Bers and Bergman 1998), as well as in the 2B1 gathering that took place at the MIT Media Lab in the summer of 1997. This conference was aimed at creating a network of people doing interesting educational projects in developing countries. As a follow-up to this gathering, a group of parents of the school created a self-directed after-school Logo group, which has been actively engaging families in the design of computer games to teach about Jewish values and festivities. This group formed the nucleus of parents who participated in the experience described in this chapter.

6.4 Motivation

Motivating the Con-science research project is the underlying philosophy of constructionism (Papert 1980). It asserts that learners are likely to construct new ideas when they are building artifacts that they can reflect upon and share with others in their learning community. Constructionism is not only a theory of learning, but also a theory of education. Therefore, it takes an interventionist perspective and concerns itself with the design of learning environments (Harel 1991; Hooper 1993; Cavallo 1999) and construction toolkits to support children to make epistemological and personal connections (Resnick, Bruckman, and Martin 1996).

Some of these construction toolkits, like SAGE (Bers and Cassell 1998) or Zora (Bers 1999) are purposefully designed to support children's exploration of their identity and values, while experimenting with powerful computational ideas. Other construction toolkits are designed for a broader range of content areas and can be used for different purposes, like the Programmable Brick (Martin 1999), and its successor, the Cricket, described at length in Chapter 1. This technology is a tiny, portable computer embedded inside a LEGO brick. People can build all sorts of artifacts as well as program them to interact with the world through sensors and motors. Traditionally the research experiences that would use this technology involve the integration of robotics, engineering, and programming with disciplines such as math and sciences. For example, the Beyond Black Boxes project (Resnick et al. 1999) develops computational tools and projects that allow children to create their own scientific instruments and become engaged in scientific inquiry not only through observing and measuring but also through designing and building.

In the same design spirit, the Con-science research program seeks to develop tools and methodologies to help both children and parents learn together about technology and explore their values. In the next section we present the research methodology, including evaluation techniques, and the technology used in this first pilot workshop in the Arlene Fern Jewish Community School.

6.5   Methodology and Evaluation

We worked with a project-based immersing methodology. By "project-based" learning, we mean that learners were asked to choose a project that they would like to work on for the whole duration of the workshop. They were involved in all aspects of the project. They chose the values to explore, decided the materials to use, managed the resources and time frame, resolved the technological challenges (both in terms of programming and mechanics), created a narrative around the final project, and presented it to the other members of the community through creative prayers.

By "immersing" learning, we refer to the notion that learners immersed themselves in the learning process by having a lot of time devoted to play and to explore their ideas in depth. For example, in this particular workshop, we worked with parents and children during five days, eight hours a day. During that time, participants could try many ideas and had enough time to iterate through different versions of a same idea. Each participant was asked to keep a design notebook to document the project progress as well as ideas and difficulties. We created a workshop website to collectively document the experience. A machine was dedicated to function as a local Web server. People were encouraged to add their own thoughts and descriptions in Spanish. Each night, we would translate into English, then edit and organize the different Web pages. Since this was the first pilot workshop within the Con-science research program, documentation was very important to allow future experiences and comparative studies.

To evaluate this workshop, we used a qualitative approach that included interviews with participants; observations of interpersonal relations, use of the new technology, changes in ways of approaching problems and thinking about conflicting issues; compilation of the personal design notebooks, annotations in the website, posters, and wish cards created by the participants for the open houses; and, finally, presentation of the final projects and creative prayers to the community. The workshop was videotaped, both to document the experience and to facilitate observation and analysis of certain key moments throughout the process.

During the workshop, we observed people deeply engaged in discussions about values, and we also noticed some changes of attitude on what was right or wrong within the work environment. For example, at the beginning of the experience, most of the participants, both children and adults, rushed to collect as many motors and sensors as possible, without taking into consideration their real needs. By the end of the workshop we observed that people started to share limited technological resources as well as ideas and programming strategies without a top-down intervention.

6.6 Technology: Hardware and Software

The technology we used during the workshop is called the LEGO Mindstorms Robotics Invention System. The set contains an average of 700 LEGO pieces, the Mindstorms RCX or tiny computer embedded in a LEGO brick, an infrared transmitter for sending programs to the Mindstorms RCX, the Mindstorms software, light and touch sensors, motors, and a building guide. The Mindstorms RCX has been under development for almost 12 years. It is the result of the collaboration between LEGO and a group at the MIT Media Lab led by Fred Martin. The Mindstorms RCX is an autonomous microcomputer that can be programmed using a PC. It uses sensors to take data from the environment, process information, and power motors and light sources to turn on and off.

During the first day of the workshop we experienced what became a constant problem: the infrared communication between the Mindstorms RCX and the computer was affected by the intensity of light in the room and by interference with other bricks nearby. The operational system of the RCX, Firmware, which needs to be downloaded before usage, was getting corrupted. While some kids complained ("Someone is putting programs in my brick") as if it were a conspiracy, others started to invent their own ways to get around the problem. They hid the bricks from each other, put them under the table, or covered them with a piece of paper in order to avoid interference.

The RCX software is an icon-based programming language, loosely based on Logo. It allows users to drag and drop graphical blocks of code that represent commands such as left and right turns, reverse direction, motor speed, and motor power; sensor watchers that trigger actions; and control structures to build routines. Users can drag the icons together into a stack, in a similar way to assembling physical LEGO bricks, and arrange them in logical order to produce new behaviors for a robotic construction. This graphical environment became an easy-to-use tool that facilitated the programming task for the novice children and parents. Yet, some parents who were experienced programmers found the environment frustrating and limiting. Some examples of things difficult to implement with the Mindstorms software are "OR" and "AND" conditions, which require elaborate programming solutions using other elements of the language.

6.7 Process: The Con-Science Workshop Day by Day

As we mentioned earlier, we created a Web-based journal documenting the pilot experience. In order to convey the spirit of the workshop, this section is composed of short excerpts from it. The full text and pictures can be accessed at *http://el.www.media.mit.edu/projects/con-science/*.

First Day: Becoming Familiar with the Technology

Participants gathered to start the activities. Each one introduced him- or herself. We explained the workshop's goals, talked about previous experiences with the technology, and showed some videos. The first activity of the day was designed to help people become familiar with the Mindstorms RCX, the sensors and motors, and the programming language. They were asked to start a motor or initiate a routine when a touch sensor was pressed. The groups spontaneously started to build little contraptions in order to learn the programming aspect. Most of the groups built vehicles that could move and respond to a sensor's stimulus. Only one of the groups used the gears to build a pulley for an elevator, and not a car or truck.

In the afternoon the task was to build kinetic sculptures using not only LEGO pieces, but also art materials. The goal of the activity was to push their thinking in different directions, other than building cars and trucks. It took some time, but people came up with merry-go-rounds, flowers that open up to the light, dancing dolls, cargo transporters, and sweeping robots.

By the end of the day, the groups presented their projects. Some of the children appreciated the fact that there were other materials than LEGO, but others complained about the difficulties of plugging motors and sensors in the right places. Marcia (all names of workshop participants have been changed to protect subjects' anonymity), a nine-year-old girl, was very happy because she was able to spend a long time with her father without him getting upset at her. With a big smile she said, "Parents are great when they do not get upset," and intentionally, and for the first time in the workshop, geared the conversation from technological issues to social ones.

Second Day: Starting the Final Projects

In the morning every group presented the details of the programs they implemented for their projects. The goal was to create common ground for the groups by sharing problems and programming tips with each other. Since some of the youngest kids were very confused, we decided to organize

Figure 6.1

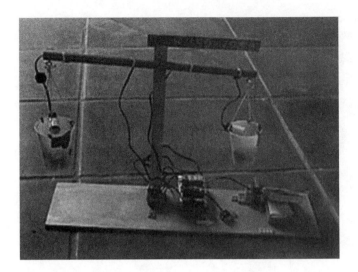

The scale project.

a theatrical improvisation to help them understand the different programming blocks and the control flow. Some kids pretended to be commands that
turn motors on and off, and others played as sensor watchers that trigger
actions and as control structures, such as "repeat forever," or "wait until."

After this exercise, we made the first attempt to integrate values and technology. As a first step we showed them a project we had built that integrated
them. This project, called "the scale," is an example of transforming an
abstract value, such as the "balance between the good and bad actions of the
previous year," into a concrete artifact that responds to people's interactions.
The scale had two buckets on each side, one for good actions and another for
bad actions (see Figure 6.1 [see also Color Plate]). Volunteers were asked to
write on a piece of paper an action from that year. They hid the paper in a little wooden cube and put it in the corresponding side of the scale. Light sensors were used to detect when new actions were placed in any of the two
buckets. A program detected the event and kept count of the number of
actions in each side. After a participant finished putting his or her actions in
the corresponding buckets, a touch sensor had to be pressed. This started a
sound that qualified the balance of the year, either positive or negative.
Finally, a motor-driven contraption opened a small box that offered a poetic
message for reflection.

This example was a concrete introduction to our goal of integrating technology and values. Rabbi Bergman led an activity to explore the values of the
Jewish High Holidays. During a long discussion, people suggested a list of relevant values such as forgiveness, friendship, celebration, memory, balance,
and judgment, among others. We made cards with each of the proposed

Figure 6.2

Mother and children in the workshop.

values. When the groups started to select the materials to use for their final projects (e.g., sensors, motors, cardboard), they also chose one or more of the cards with the values that they wanted to explore.

During the afternoon, the groups worked on the design of their final projects (see Figure 6.2). They discussed different ideas and used their design notebooks to do quick prototypes. At the end of the day each group gave a progress report and described the project they wanted to build by the end of the week. Most of the parents found it very easy to integrate the chosen values into their technical design. Some of the kids complained that the activity was not as fun as some earlier ones because they had to think hard before adding new pieces to their contraptions. "Yesterday every piece I found I could fit into my project. Now it is more serious, and I can't put any piece anywhere. I have to think about the overall meaning of the project," said Marco, a 10-year-old boy who was very excited by the engineering aspects of the activity.

Third Day: Working Hard

The groups exchanged ideas and suggestions about their projects. Juan and Enrique, fathers who are engineers, helped other groups to improve their projects by building stronger structures. The more advanced groups started to prepare for the next day's open house for the schoolchildren, teachers, and staff. For example, Miguel, an architect and father of a nine-year-old boy, drew a complex model of the Star of David that his son was building with LEGO. Ema, a special education teacher, made a big poster with the

Figure 6.3

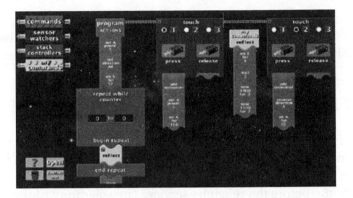

The Mindstorms RCX programming environment.

control flow of her group's project. Rabbi Bergman brought the shofar, a sheep horn blown during the High Holidays, so kids could compare its sound to the melody they were programming in the computer.

A group of people working on a conveyor belt that transported actions had a hard time finishing their project. At first we thought that the problem was caused by some logical error in their program, but later we learned that it was due to the limitations of the programming environment. They wanted a motor to run after either a first or a second condition was detected. As we mentioned before, "OR" and "AND" statements are difficult to implement using the Mindstorms software, but finally, with some collaborative effort from the group and ourselves, they implemented a complicated solution using a counter (see Figure 6.3).

Fourth Day: The School Open House

The school open house had two goals: (1) to show to the rest of the school what the Con-science workshop was about and (2) to be a rehearsal for Friday's creative prayer, in which project demonstrations were going to be given for the wider community.

During the school open house most of the parents decided to pass to their kids the task of showing their projects to their peers. Juan, the father of a nine-year-old, was surprised to observe his daughter explain in full detail the programming aspects of their project, since he previously thought that she wasn't fully understanding. The open house lasted two hours, during which the young visitors asked lots of questions.

The workshop participants were very proud to show their projects to their classmates and assumed a pedagogic role while explaining how sensors, motors, and Mindstorms bricks worked. Children who seemed very dependent on their parents during the workshop were completely on their own during the open house, and parents that were very involved during the workshop relaxed during the open house and let their children take the lead.

Fifth Day: Evaluating and Preparing for the Creative Prayer

During the last day of the workshop we had two tasks in front of us: to evaluate the experience with parents and children and to prepare for the creative prayer open house on Friday. The creative prayer was going to happen in the synagogue before the religious service. The solemnity of the space and the sacredness of the day, the most important Sabbath of the year, made it a very big event.

As a way to evaluate the experience we decided to write a collective prayer to thank for all the new things we learned and experimented with during the workshop. One by one, the participants went to the blackboard and wrote their contributions. Later we transcribed it into a big poster to hang in the temple, and we made photocopies to hand out to the visitors with their prayer books. The collective prayer read as follows: "We, the participants of the LEGO-Logo workshop, give thanks because: We had the possibility to experiment, to work, and to share new materials with classmates, our parents, and people whom we didn't know before. We were creative and we could build projects that express what we believe, feel, and live by. We played with materials that opened up many new possibilities. We shared in community and we were able to create while playing."

Besides the collective prayer, every group prepared a blessing or good wish card to emphasize the value that they worked on in their projects. The idea was to hand them out to the visitors as if they were business cards. For example, the group who chose the value "give and receive" wrote: "We wish that in this New Year you have many opportunities to give good moments and receive lots of love." Many groups accompanied the text with drawings made on the computer.

Sixth Day: The Creative Prayer Open House

The open house for the community was held in the synagogue as a creative prayer. We installed the computers, the projects, and the posters in one of the corners of the synagogue. An hour before the religious service, we invited the community members to walk around, ask questions, play with the projects, and talk with the presenters (see Figure 6.4). The blessings or good wish cards were very successful and were distributed nonstop. The group of

Figure 6.4

The creative prayer open house.

parents that started to work with Logo MicroWorlds a year before also showed their projects. Even though the number of visitors kept growing, the open house ended with Rabbi Bergman inviting everyone to sit down to continue with the traditional religious service. During the sermon, he referred to the learning experience that took place during the workshop and connected the act of creation in which everyone was involved with our role as partners in the creation of the world.

6.8   Projects

In this section we describe some of the projects built by parents and children. We group the projects into three different categories according to the way in which the technology was used to explore values: (1) technology to represent symbols, (2) technology to represent values, and (3) technology to evoke reflection and conversation. Projects in the first category, technology to represent symbols, treated values in a shallow way. People created artifacts that resembled the Jewish symbols without deeper exploration of the nature of the values represented by these symbols. Projects in the second category, technology to represent values, involved both artifacts and stories that made the chosen value more explicit. Projects in the third category, technology to evoke reflection and conversation, treated values in a more elaborate way and provided an opportunity for others to engage in experiencing the complexity of the chosen values and participate in thoughtful discussion.

This taxonomy of different ways of using the technology to explore values was not in our mind before the workshop. It resulted as we analyzed and compared the different projects and learning experiences.

Technology to Represent Symbols

Every tradition has symbols that reinforce a sense of group identity. The Jewish tradition is particularly rich in these symbols, which are usually associated with a festivity or a ritual. To recognize and distinguish the symbols of a tradition is one of the first steps towards building knowledge about the tradition and eventually identifying with it. Often symbols are used by educators as a way to give concrete shape to abstract values. However, a rich educational experience can't be limited to learning about symbols. Symbols should be a gateway to deeper explorations of the values and sociocultural practices of a tradition.

During the workshops several groups used the technology to create symbols. For example, Michael, a 10-year-old boy, said: "We built a 'Maguen David,' Star of David, as a symbol of our Jewish people and we programmed it to turn forever like the wheel of life and have flashing lights resembling candles welcoming the New Year. We also reproduced the sound of the shofar. It has three different tones that are supposed to awake us for reflection and atonement." Michael's group chose the value "awakening" or "call for reflection." They designed their project by anchoring it to traditional symbols. The construction of the star was done in a very careful way out of LEGO pieces and flashing lights (see Figure 6.5). The center of the star was connected to a platform that moved with a motor. They used a touch sensor to launch and stop their program, which had three basic jobs: turn the motor on, turn the lights on and off, and play the sound of the shofar.

A second project in this category was built by Paul and Ariel, father and nine-year-old son, who chose the apples and honey that symbolize the wish to start a sweet New Year. In every Jewish home, during the first dinner of the New Year, there is a plate with apples to dip in honey. When talking about his project, Paul said, "We built a crane that transports apples from one place to the other in order to prepare them to celebrate Rosh Hashanah (New Year)." Paul and Ariel were very intrigued by the idea of building a complex carlike artifact (see Figure 6.6). When showing their project to others, they would explain the details of its mechanics and program and would very often forget to make the connection with the chosen value "sweetness." The crane car was built with the Mindstorms RCX as a remote control connected with touch sensors. They used three touch sensors. The first sensor moved the crane, so when the sensor was pressed, the program started the motor to

Figure 6.5

The Star of David project.

Figure 6.6

The crane and the apples representing a sweet New Year.

make it move forward, and if pressed again, it changed the direction to make it move backward. The second and third sensors were used to control the pallets. When the crane reached the platform of apples, one of the sensors had to be pressed in order to open the pallets, then the other sensor in order to close the pallets and pick an apple to transport to the honey plate.

The examples presented above show how certain groups used the technology to create projects that represent Jewish symbols. Although they started to connect these symbols with their meanings, they did not explore in depth the relationship between the values and the symbols.

Figure 6.7

The friendship project, its poster, and its creators.

Technology to Represent Values

Some people created projects that used the technology to represent values not only as a symbol, but also as the theme. For example, a group chose the value "friendship" and created a puppet theater. The theater had a curtain that opened to show the performance of two LEGO dolls hugging after a fight (see Figure 6.7). Marcia, nine years old, created a story about the girl's situation and the connection with some of the values of the High Holidays, such as Teshuva, or response. "This project tells the story of two girls that after a fight give each other a hug and become best friends," explained Marcia. "This project talks about the Teshuva that allows us to repair our mistakes. The friends did Teshuva and became friends again with a big hug." Marcia built the dolls with LEGO bricks, attached colorful strings as hair, and placed motors in the arms to swing back and forth, simulating a hug.

The friendship project used technology as well as storytelling. Since the chosen value was the main element of this project, the group seemed to have the need to tell a story to reinforce the interpretation of the value. They wrote the story in the good wish card that was handed out to visitors during the open houses. Telling a coherent story around the robotic creation was as important as getting the mechanics and the programming right. They used technology to represent a value as a powerful idea that needs to be supported by both a behaving artifact and a compelling story.

Figure 6.8

The giving and receiving project and the group who built it.

Technology to Evoke Reflection and Conversation

Some groups used the technology to design an engaging activity for others to experience their own interpretation of the chosen value. For example, one group chose the value "giving and receiving." Juan, one of the fathers in the group, said: "We talked a lot about giving and we found out that giving is, at the same time, receiving. So through our project we wanted to show that when we give something we do not exactly know what we are receiving but we always receive something back." Pattie, Juan's eight-year-old daughter, explained this idea with a concrete example: "We made a doll with two yellow hands and every time you give her a present in her hand, she turns around and gives you something back with her other hand. But you don't know what she is giving you. There are smiles, flowers, and hugs in her second hand and you can receive anything." (See Figures 6.8 and 6.9; Figure 6.9, Color Plate only.) The first component of the giving and receiving project was the head of the doll, built out of art materials they glued and colored in an artistic way. The body consisted of a geared mechanism, which provided strong motion to the rest of the doll, and a motor attached to a rotation sensor to keep track of the turns. Both hands had light sensors and light sources. They used the light source to make the light more constant, so the small changes in the light reading were easy to detect. They wrote a program that detected a new object in the receiving hand, made the doll turn to offer a gift with the giving hand, and waited to turn back after it detected the taking of

Figure 6.10

The action-transporting conveyor belt and the group.

a gift. This was a very complex project both in terms of technology and mechanics as well as in the conceptualization of the value they chose. The group spent a long time conceiving a design that would actually represent the notion of giving and receiving. They found the doll and her two hands a very appealing one.

Another example of the creation of projects that evoked reflection and conversation is the case of Paula and her 10-year-old son, Matias. With the help of two other moms, they created a conveyor belt contraption that transports the actions of the previous year (see Figure 6.10). Paula explained how they came up with the idea: "During the High Holidays we think about the actions in our everyday life. It is the time to think, reflect, and become conscious about our past deeds, so we can choose to continue with the good deeds or to rectify the actions that we believed were wrong." This idea gave birth to the conveyor belt. The machine was designed to carry actions until a reflection point, where the users could spend the needed time to decide about their positive or negative significance. An action considered good was transferred to a good container, and an action considered bad was taken back, meaning that people had to amend it. The mechanics consisted of a structure to hold the belt, which was made out of rubber bands, a motor located in the starting point of the contraption to move the belt, and two touch sensors to select between good and bad actions. Actions were foam rubber cubes wrapped in color papers and labeled with a name, such as "helping," "being selfish," and "sharing." A program was created to start the motor for a given number of seconds and wait for the sensor input to take the actions to the next stage. If the sensor for good actions was pressed, the program started the motor in the same direction to go forward. If the sensor for bad actions was pressed, the program made the motor move in the opposite direction, taking back the action to the staring point.

For the two groups presented above, it was very important to have users of their projects not only learn the value of reflection, but also experience it by reflecting about their own actions. During the open houses they were very careful to explain both the complex mechanical structure and the state of mind into which they wanted the users to be drawn.

6.9 Technology and Values

Why robotics and values? Aren't writing, reading, drama, and storytelling powerful and easier ways to approach issues concerning values? Isn't robotics a field of computer sciences and engineering concerned with the creation of devices that can move and react to sensory input? What is the connection between these two realms? There is a long tradition in the use of humanistic tools, such as storytelling, for humanistic purposes, like values education. And there is also a more recent tradition of using scientific tools, such as robotics, for learning about math, sciences, and mechanics. However, our approach is about the integration of both the soft and hard sciences, and their tools.

Learners have different interests and strengths. Some are naturally inclined towards the humanities, while others prefer technology. Within Con-science both technology and values are integrated to support diverse learners. On the one hand, we noted that those interested in values, but not in technology, ended up mastering the technology due to their high motivation to build an artifact that expressed their values. On the other hand, we noticed that people who initially only wanted to work with the technology also ended up exploring values by the need to choose a project theme.

Interest in Values Supports Learning about Technology

Let us go back to Marcia's project on friendship. She had a hard time building the mechanics for the movement of the doll's arms, as well as writing the program to control the hug. Her dolls looked as if they were hitting each other instead of hugging. When showing the project to the young visitors, one of the youngest ones complained, "This is not about friendship! The dolls are not hugging but slapping each other." The young boy was referring to the fact that both arms wouldn't move up at the same speed and wouldn't reach the same altitude. Marcia tried to convince him that he was wrong and created a complicated story about a new type of hug. But the young boy wouldn't give up and invited his friends to give their opinion. After engaging in a long discussion about what friendship is, everyone agreed that the project wasn't about friendship but about fighting. Marcia wasn't happy. The next day she talked with the other group members, and they all agreed that there were two possible solutions. She must either change the story and the value conveyed by the project or work harder on the programming. Despite the fact that Marcia said that she hated programming, she chose to do it because friendship was a very important value for her. She debugged her program and played with the mechanics until she came up with a movement that looked very much like a hug.

Marcia's story is about how the technology was used to engage a child in a high-intensity intellectual effort. Marcia's friendship theater, and the fact that it wasn't working as expected, generated an in-depth discussion about value issues such as what friendship means. In a normal class situation this philosophical discussion would have been initiated by the teacher (e.g., the teacher telling a story about friendship and asking kids to comment on it), or at a very high personal cost (e.g., if there was a fight in the classroom and the conflict needed to be resolved). The presence of the social interaction with the visitors during the open house also established the scope of the project, which in a normal setting is given by the teachers. The personal attachment that Marcia had to the value she chose motivated her to work harder to debug her program. Given Marcia's preferences, it would have been easier for her to change the theme around her project than to fix the programming. Yet she benefited from learning to find a solution with the technology.

Interest in Technology Supports Learning about Values

During the open house for the community, Matias presented the conveyor belt that transports actions. When playing with the contraption, one of the adult visitors pressed the "good action" touch sensor and observed the action block move forward very slowly on the belt. He commented: "I see, the good actions take more time. Since they are good, they should last longer." Although this deep reflection about values was triggered by the performance of the technology, this wasn't the original reason why Matias's contraption performed in that way. The belt structure was divided in two parts because the rubber bands were not long enough to cover the whole area. They were slightly different in length, which affected the speed in which the actions traveled on the belt. Before the visitor's comment, Matias explained the difference in speed only in technical terms, but afterwards he became interested in this new way of explaining why good actions travel slower than bad actions.

This incident shows an example of ways in which the richness of the learning environment encourages people to explore new areas. The comment made by the visitor raised for Matias the issue of how actions happen in real life. During the workshop Matias showed more interest in the technology than in the values aspect of his project. Building a tangible artifact to share with others, however, helped him to reflect about the experience in a different way. During the creative prayer in the last open house, Matias demonstrated his project by explaining how the value he had chosen with his group was conveyed and implemented in the project and how the technology worked.

6.10 Learning Families

During the workshop, parents and children were faced with many challenges. Some were technological and others personal. Most of the participants were not used to spending long hours working together with members of their families, as partners, on a project that involved new skills and new materials. The traditional role of the parent as "know-it-all" and the child as the learner were disrupted. Although in some cases, parents still knew more than their children did (for example, in the case of parents with engineering and computer training), in general children were more familiar and confident with the work. For example, most of the boys were very familiar with the LEGO bricks, and most of the children had an easier experience learning and doing the programming.

According to their own idiosyncrasies and family dynamics, they accepted the challenge with courage and found their own ways of interacting. For example, a father and his 11-year-old daughter, Carolyn, spent a lot of time discussing the goals and implementation of the project as if they were two adults in a work meeting. Their relationship was as equals. Sometimes they would take turns in trying out different technical options, while at other times they would debug together. In our opinion, this group did not manage to make a final project that reflected the complexity of the underlying thought processes and serious debates, but the real value was in the process through which they conceived and implemented their project.

Other families couldn't work as equals. Either the child or the parent took a dominant role at different times. For example, the 10-year-old Michael, while working on the computer programming for the Star of David, would ask his dad to bring him water and cookies because he was too busy to interrupt.

In his opinion, his father wasn't able to help him with the programming. In a similar way, his dad, an architect, would build the complex star out of LEGO bricks and would ask Michael to find for him the needed pieces, without letting him intervene in the design. With the exception of two fathers who were engineers and a mom who was a computer scientist, it was common for kids, particularly boys, to take over the programmer's role. For example, Miguel proudly wrote in the website that his mom couldn't figure out how to program the Mindstorms brick but he managed to master it without much effort. The truth is that his mom tried to learn the programming environment, but every time she would get close to the computer Miguel would take over.

6.11   Conclusions

Issues regarding values and education are controversial: Whose values are to be taught? How to avoid indoctrination without ending up with a relativistic perspective? These questions do not have easy answers, and some people have chosen to avoid them by rejecting moral education in public schools. In religious schools like the Arlene Fern, most of these issues are resolved by the fact that there is a shared agreement about the values cherished within the community between all the parties involved in the educational process. Schools of this sort are up-front about their concern with the students' development of a lifestyle, a mindset, and a behavior system within a certain moral landscape.

Even though indoctrination is not an issue in this type of education, two questions still remain. First, how can the teaching and learning about values be made into a concrete, hands-on activity? Instructionism, the educational approach that proposes that information needs to be transferred from the teacher to the learner, is not always an effective model (Papert 1993). Constructionism seems to be more appealing due to the personal investment of the learner, the emphasis on making artifacts to make ideas concrete, and the ability to test them in the world. By constructing an external object to reflect upon, people also construct internal knowledge. Constructionism, however, needs materials in order to construct. The richer the materials, the more potential the learning experience has for the participants.

Storytelling and storywriting have been the traditional materials for values education. When these activities are augmented by new technologies, such as the Internet, they offer new possibilities. For example, Kaleidostories is a Web-based narrative environment that supports children's expression by offering them the tools to create role models and stories conveying values. Every child participating in the experience is represented by a figure in the kaleidoscope. Its color and shape change according to how many role models and values are shared between the logged user and the other participants. Children can send messages to each other and engage in discussion about similarities and differences (Bers 1998). Although tools of this sort are explicitly designed to help children explore their values and seem to fit naturally with the goal of integrating values and technology, robotic construction kits, as shown in this chapter, can also be very powerful tools. They precipitate discussion about values as well as provide material to build concrete artifacts representing a chosen abstract value.

The second question regarding values in education has to do with how to involve the family in the learning process. Values are not something that we hold only when we are in school. Values are part of one's entire life and need to be understood in the context of who we are (e.g., our identity). Therefore, value education should engage the family. In the Con-science program we involve both children and parents. They worked together on robotic projects that gave physicality and dynamism to abstract values cherished during the Jewish High Holidays. Parents and children shared a space to talk about values in a concrete way and to engage in a different type of relationship. Despite their differences in age and experiences, both parents and children were faced with the challenge to gain new insights about technology and values in an integrated way.

During the workshop we observed that both parents and children were gaining technological and moral fluency. The term *technological fluency* refers to the ability to use and apply technology in a fluent way, effortlessly and smoothly, as one does with language (Papert and Resnick 1995). In the case of the Con-science program, people were able to use the technology in a creative way to make projects that represent their most cherished values. According to their initial familiarity with programming and building, they became technologically fluent in different ways.

By *moral fluency* we imply the ability to be fluent regarding issues in which there is a right and wrong, responsibilities and consequences, and different points of views and alternatives to choose. This is the basis for developing a sense of responsibility for the actions that we take in the world, creating an awareness of the connection between who we are, our identity, and what we consider most worthy, our values. For example, during the workshop, participants engaged in thoughtful discussion about the nature and contradictions of the act of giving and receiving, and the different points of view about what friendship is.

Despite the success of the workshop in terms of motivating these discussions, we believe that moral fluency, as well technological fluency, takes time to achieve and requires hard work. But once acquired, they have an impact in ways of thinking as well as behaving. The passage from the moral thought to the moral deed is a very hard task, and we cannot claim that the workshop participants accomplished it. If some of them showed signs, it is probably due to the value-centered environment they are engaged in throughout the year, and not only during our workshop. The behaviors that participants exhibited, particularly the children, served as indicators for the school of the successes and failures of its mission.

We hope that this first pilot workshop within the Con-science research program can serve as a seed that will give birth to other projects with similar goals. Our plan is to work with different secular and religious groups concerned with bringing technology and values together, and to be able to do longitudinal and comparative studies between the types of projects and values chosen by different populations. Hopefully our research will contribute to envisioning an education that doesn't chop us into pieces, as the initial quote by Galeano pointed out, by divorcing soul from body, mind from heart, and technology from values.

6.12 Acknowledgments

We thank Rabbi Bergman for his profound commitment to this workshop and for making it possible, and the principal and teachers from the Arlene Fern Jewish Community School for supporting this project. We are very grateful to the families and the teachers who participated in this workshop, and who are still teaching others what they learned with us. We are also grateful to our advisor, Prof. Seymour Papert, for supporting this innovative experience and to Prof. Mitchel Resnick, Dr. Fred Martin, and Jacqueline Karaaslanian for helping us with diverse aspects of this project. We also thank the members of the Epistemology and Learning Group and the LEGO Group for their sponsorship.

6.13 References

Bers, M. 1998. A constructionist approach to values through on-line narrative tools. *Proceedings of ICLS 98.* Charlottesville, VA: AACE, pp. 49–55.

Bers, M. 1999. Zora: A graphical multi-user environment to share stories about the self. *Proceedings of CSCL '99.* Charlottesville, VA: AACE.

Bers, M., and S. Bergman. 1998. A constructionist perspective on values: A response to postmodern fragmented identity. In *Identity, formation, dignity: The impacts of*

Artificial Intelligence upon Jewish and Christian Understandings of Personhood at *www.media.mit.edu/~marinau/BB-values.html.* Cambridge, MA: MIT.

Bers, M., and J. Cassell. 1998. Interactive storytelling systems for children: Using technology to explore language and identity. *Journal of Interactive Learning Research* 9(2):183–215.

Cavallo, D. 1999. Project Lighthouse in Thailand: Guiding pathways to powerful learning. In *Logo Philosophy and Implementation.* Montreal, Quebec: Logo Computer Systems, Inc.

Harel, I. 1991. *Children Designers: Interdisciplinary Constructions for Learning and Knowing Mathematics in a Computer-Rich School.* Norwood, NJ: Ablex.

Hooper, P. 1993. They have their own thoughts: A story of constructionist learning in an alternative African-centered community school. In Y. Kafai and M. Resnick (eds.), *Constructionism in Practice,* Hillsdale, NJ: Lawrence Erlbaum Associates.

Kohlberg, L. 1982. The just community approach to moral education in theory and in practice. *International Conference on Moral Education.* Fribourg, Switzerland.

Lipman, M. 1988. *Philosophy Goes to School.* Philadelphia: Temple University Press.

Martin, F. 1999. *el.www.media.mit.edu/groups/el/projects/programmable-brick/*

Papert, S. 1980. *Mindstorms: Children, Computers and Powerful Ideas.* New York: Basic Books.

Papert, S. 1993. *The Children's Machine: Rethinking School in the Age of the Computer.* New York: Basic Books.

Papert, S., and M. Resnick. 1995. Technological fluency and the representation of knowledge. Proposal to the National Science Foundation. MIT Media Laboratory. Cambridge, MA.

Resnick, M., R. Berg, M. Eisenberg, and S. Turkle. 1999. *Beyond Black Boxes: Bringing Transparency and Aesthetics Back to Scientific Instruments.* To be published in *Journal of Learning Sciences.*

Resnick, M., A. Bruckman, and F. Martin. 1996. Pianos not stereos: Creating computational construction kits. *Interactions* 3(6)40–50.

Ritchie, R. 1995. *Primary Design and Technology: A Process for Learning.* London: David Fulton Publishers.

Kid's View

   ## Robot Recipe

By Hanne Olsen, age 11

Hello, my name is Hanne. We made a robot with kids and adults. Sometimes making a robot was hard, and at times it was pretty easy. The times that it was hard was when you sat and worked long and hard on something and it was not good enough. Or when you have to spend a really long time on something but you want to get up and run around, so you hurry and mess up. Sometimes it is easy when you get to sit around and the other kids have to work. Also it is easy when you have to sew the fur that we put over the robot so it looks more like an animal. As I said before, it can be easy and hard.

Making robots can compare to other things that kids do in their daily lives. It can be kind of like schoolwork or projects where you have to do a good job. Also making robots is like projects because in the end, if you do a good job, you get rewards and it all pays off. It can also be like housework because housework is tedious! But everything in the end pays off.

I think that a robot is a piece of machinery that can be helpful around the house or in factories. It can also be fun to play with or watch. Robots can be hard to use but mostly they are fun. If any kid wants to make a robot, they should have some things in mind. First, they might not want to have a robot that does housework or homework because what would you do if it broke or you lost it? Of course you would buy a new one but that would take a while and what would you do in the meantime? That's why robots shouldn't do chores.

Chapter Seven

"So That's What Pi Is For!" and Other Educational Epiphanies from Hands-on Robotics

David P. Miller
KISS Institute for Practical Robotics

Cathryne Stein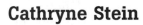
KISS Institute for Practical Robotics

Abstract

Children learn about their world and its technology by playing. Modern toys with closed construction do not offer children the opportunities they need to explore, take things apart, and figure out how it all works. There are few chances to experience the creative side of the technology that we all take for granted.

Robotics is a prime opportunity to "play" with technology. While playing, children also learn; their robotic experiences cover a wide range of disciplines. In this chapter we will describe several educational programs based on robotics that accomplish specific educational goals. The programs (and goals) are described in detail, and the wide-ranging effects on students and educators are documented as well.

7.1 Who Will Build the Machines? (Modern Toys Are Too Modern)

When I (DM) was about six, I received a battery-operated car of some sort for a birthday present. After playing with it for a couple hours, I did what I did with most of my toys, I tried to take it apart. But something was wrong—my screwdriver just wouldn't work on the screws at the bottom of the car. My trusty slotted screwdriver had never failed me before, but these screws had two slots (like a "+") and the slots didn't cut all the way across the screw head. Fifteen minutes later I was frustrated and upset. Later that afternoon, my parents introduced me to the exciting world of Phillips screws and screwdrivers. With these new tools I was able to take the car apart, and in a matter of hours learn about, and unintentionally destroy, the mechanisms used to transfer the power from the DC motor to the wheels.

Those of us who grew up before the widespread use of integrated circuits have certain advantages over children who grow up playing with modern toys. With rare exceptions, toys produced prior to 1975 were mechanical— any electronic aspects to the toy were usually just standard linear DC circuits. By looking and touching, one could trace out the control system of a toy with your finger. There were very few toys that could not be broken down to their component parts and then put back together with a set of screwdrivers and pliers.

As a result, those of us with an engineering inclination could easily get quite a bit of insight as to how things worked, just by taking things apart and seeing what happened when you made changes. Experimentation, while not always intended by the manufacturer or encouraged by the parents, was nonetheless a readily accessible option to most children.

That is no longer the case.

Microelectronics allows toys and other devices to exist that would otherwise be impractical or impossible to create. It has changed the way almost everything is made. These changes, combined with changes in product liability, have created a generation of toys in which custom integrated circuits are used in place of a more straightforward cam and switch, plastic welded boxes are used where a box lid and four screws might have done the job, and software and microprocessors are used on toys where in previous years children simply made motor sounds with their mouths.

These changes are not all for the good. In working with thousands of children in grades K–12 (approximate ages of 5–18), we have found that there is a basic lack of understanding of how one uses simple machines in ordinary devices. Many school-aged children have no understanding of what a gear might be used for, and several students claim they have never seen one before. Basic mechanical connectivity is an unfamiliar concept. When we ask children to build a car out of LEGO Technic, they all know that they need a motor to turn the wheels, but very few see the connection between the spinning motor shaft and their desire to make those wheels turn.

Close to half the children we have worked with for the first time simply mount the motor somewhere near the part of the car they want to move, and assume that is enough to do the job. Sometimes they add gears, not connected to anything, for the simple reason that they know that real cars have gears between the motor and the wheels. But their placement of the motor and the gears is a strong indication that they really have no understanding of the underlying causality of why things work mechanically.

One could take some comfort in these developments if it turned out that children had an understanding of software or electronics that made up for their lack of understanding of the mechanical world. Unfortunately, this does not appear to be the case for most children. Computers and software have followed the same patterns as their mechanical counterparts. Prior to 1980, most computers had very distinguishable parts for the various functions that went on in the machine. As the technology has improved, the parts have gotten smaller and more integrated. It is now often easier to replace the entire machine than to fix a bad component.

In the past 10 years, software has met a similar fate. In the time of mainframes, and the early days of the personal computer, most software was open source, and the code itself was of a size that could be comprehended by an individual. Proprietary software and the massive increase in processor speed and memory have allowed applications and operating systems to grow to a size and complexity that is daunting to most everyone, and certainly not a situation that encourages novices to find out how things work.

The result is that many children today have little idea of how things work, and even fewer have any hands-on experience. This situation has been exacerbated by schools reducing or eliminating shop courses and even automobile maintenance courses. In most public schools, there is no place for students to get experience in designing, creating, or even working with machines. This should lead one to wonder: Who will create the next generation of machines in our future?

This was some of the motivation for the formation of KISS Institute for Practical Robotics. We wanted to create a program that would allow us to stimulate children's natural curiosity; give them exposure to mechanics, computers, and other relevant technology; and tie all of this in to what they were already learning during the rest of their school education. This last point is crucial—if exposure to robots does not increase a student's appreciation and motivation for the rest of their schoolwork, then it will serve as a distraction and eventually prove detrimental to their education.

Some indications of the success of KISS Institute programs in this regard are the increased levels of school attendance during and following KISS Institute programs and the insights and sudden understanding that many of our students experience as a result of participating in these programs. We will document some of these through the remainder of this chapter.

7.2 KIPR in Brief—Who We Are, What We Do, and How It All Started

KISS Institute for Practical Robotics (KIPR) is a not-for-profit robotics research and education organization, started in 1994. The name, including the well-known acronym KISS (Keep It Simple Stupid), was suggested by a friend after observing some of our first robots.

KISS Institute does both research and education, and our mission is twofold:

1. to use robotics in order to communicate the excitement, knowledge, and practical understanding of science, programming, math, and technical problem-solving to the public

2. to promote and carry out research and development in the practical use of robotics in order to benefit the general public

To accomplish our missions, KISS Institute has established several programs, each designed to bring robotics technology to a particular audience:

- K–12 robotics courses and programs for schools and community groups (described below)

- professional development courses for teachers, engineers, and scientists

- basic research in applied robotics, including educational and assistive robotic technology

- supporting research for government and industry in such fields as automated docking and precursors to planetary rovers

7.3   KISS Institute Educational Programs

To create the technologists of the future, KISS Institute has developed programs for students of all ages and levels of expertise.

The Botball Program

KISS Institute's Botball program is a national program aimed at getting middle- and high-school students excited about technology and learning about engineering and computer science. Botball puts robotics equipment into schools, and trains students and teachers in the use of that equipment. Botball is organized into spring regional tournaments and a national Botball tournament held at a professional conference during the summer.

So what exactly is Botball? The Botball program challenges students to design, build, and program (in C) a small mobile robot to compete in a highly charged double-elimination tournament that pits robot against robot in a game of skill, speed, and strategy. Students work in a team, and each team is given a specialized kit that contains a microcontroller, motors, sensors, lots of LEGOs, and plenty of other goodies.

In addition to the robotics tournament itself, as part of the Botball program students participate in an Internet research/website development competition. Students are given a specific robotics challenge. They must then use the Internet to do research, design a solution, and create a website—using whatever tools they wish—detailing their solution to the assignment.

Each regional Botball program kicks off with a hands-on tutorial for the lead teachers. This three-day tutorial covers basics in robotics and offers

Figure 7.1

Judges wait as teams make final preparations.

techniques in using this material to support current curricula. At the tutorial the teachers are given their team's robot kit to work with so that they can experience hands-on learning while a KISS Institute instructor is available. At this time, the particulars of that year's game challenge are fully described.

After the tutorial, teachers take their kit back to their teams, and the students have approximately six weeks to design, build, take apart (reconstruct, deconstruct, etc.), and program (debug, rewrite, argue with the hardware people) the robot.

No remote control is used in Botball whatsoever, and students must learn to program their robots in order to effectively compete. The robots must even be able to start themselves at the appropriate time and turn themselves off at the end of the match.

At the end of the six-week period students bring their robots, along with family, friends, teachers, cheering squads, and so on, to the regional Botball tournament. The tournament starts with seeding rounds in which robots compete unopposed, and after that, we run the head-to-head, double-elimination tournament and watch what happens. Professional roboticists and engineers observe each robot and judge the rounds (Figure 7.1).

Botball features student-built robots, and to help ensure that quality we do not allow any adults in the pit areas, except tournament officials. There is usually some grumbling about this; however, we have also been thanked many times for enforcing this rule, both because it is fair, and because it

Figure 7.2

Students show off their robots during the North Florida Botball Tournament at the University of North Florida.

allows teachers the freedom to enjoy the tournament without feeling the pressure to work with the team at every moment.

After the Botball tournament, we host an informal awards party with refreshments. Everyone is relaxed by this time, and there is an air of great conviviality and respect for one another's robots, or at least for attempts made. At this time we present awards for the Internet research/website development competition, and the robotics tournament. In addition to the top three places, we also give awards in such categories as Best Offense, Best Defense, Best Seeding Round, Best Looking, and other judges' picks. The winners are justifiably proud (Figure 7.2).

The Robotics in Residence Program

Botball typically involves high-school students, though several middle schools have also participated. In contrast the Robotics in Residence (or RinR) program is aimed primarily at the K–8 grade range.

The RinR program has been modeled on other successful residence programs used in many elementary schools throughout the country. As in the Artist in Residence or Author in Residence programs, in the Robotics in Residence program a trained roboticist spends several days at a school with

Figure 7.3

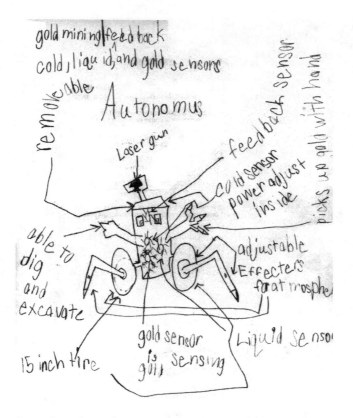

Second-grade student David Hughes designed a complex robot to mine gold. Note the obligatory laser gun, which will doubtless be a standard feature on future gold mining robots.

an agreed-upon number of contact hours for certain classes. In a typical RinR program, which lasts about a week or five school days, this KIPR robotics instructor will concentrate on a particular grade (e.g., fourth grade).

During the week the roboticist will give a series of assemblies reaching all the students in the school. Depending on the length of the residence and the size of the school, the roboticist may also give individual workshops in many of the classes. Younger students are often asked to do a paper design of a robot they would like to build (Figure 7.3). For the grade(s) on which the work is primarily focused, the KIPR instructor will normally have at least five contact hours with each student group (less than 30 students per group— usually a single classroom). During this intensive time period, the roboticist will direct the class in a robot-building project.

The students usually work in pairs and construct a simple robot system to meet the challenge. These robots usually have to be programmed, but depending on the age and abilities of the students, there are many types of challenges available, ranging from the students using a bar-code programming scheme, to selecting preprogrammed C modules and having the students stringing them together. Whatever the method used, the students end up designing and at least directing the programming of their robots (see Figure 7.4, Color Plate only). At the conclusion of the session, the students put on an exhibition for some of the grades that do not have an opportunity to do the building exercise.

Outreach

In addition to our Botball and Robotics in Residence programs, KISS Institute is involved in a variety of outreach programs, frequently to minority, economically disadvantaged, or underrepresented groups. One of our earliest programs was a collaboration with the University of Maryland College Park (UMD) that involved working with fifth graders from Randle Highlands Elementary School, an inner-city school in Washington, DC, with very limited resources. About 25 students spent the day at the Autonomous Mobile Robot Lab at UMD, where they worked with robotics instructors. They spent the day building and experimenting with robots, and taking miniworkshops on gears, system design, programming concepts, and other facets of robot creation.

The goal of "Robot Day" was to teach content, improve attitudes about science, technology, engineering, and math in general, and allow students to experience, through hands-on activity (see Figure 7.5), how and why we use the tools of science and math in the real world to do cool stuff. In addition, we tried to create an awareness of the fun and excitement associated with being on the creative side of technology.

Based on written and verbal feedback from the students, these goals were achieved for many of the participants. Several students wrote that they were now interested in teaching robotics as a career, and others agreed with Mia S., who said that she "would like to be a scientist and build things, like robots." On the other hand, we understand that robotics is not for everyone, and we were amused to note that in that evening's newscast that covered Robot Day, the reporters did manage to find the one girl who said that she might want to do robotics when she grew up if she "couldn't find a real job."

Of course a one-time event is not as likely to have as much impact as a continued course of study or a series of such events; however, we feel that these students at least were exposed to educational and career possibilities they may not have considered, and had a good time in the process.

Engineering outreach to young women and girls is a hot topic these days. Statistics indicate a declining female enrollment in computer science degree programs and engineering (with the exception of chemical engineering).

Figure 7.5

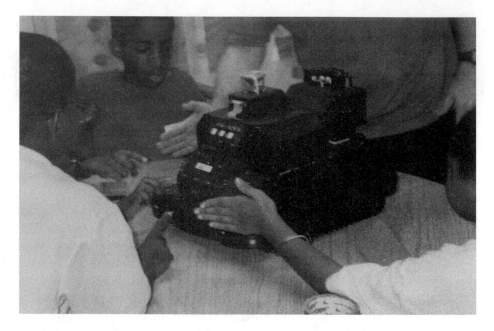

Robot Day: Students experiment with Scratchy, a robot at the Autonomous Mobile Robot Lab at the University of Maryland.

As one might suspect from these trends, the number of boys participating in Botball has been far larger than the number of girls. However, there have been a few all-girls teams—and much to the consternation of the many all-boys teams, they have performed exceptionally well, especially in the head-to-head competition. In a recent national tournament, the top two teams in the head-to-head competition were an all-boys and an all-girls team. In a stereotype-destroying strategy, the all-boys team's robot was thoughtful and had several strategies that allowed it to "be polite." The all-girls team's robot relied on raw speed and brute strength. In the end, well-designed brawn beat out well-designed brains, and the girls won.

Educational Goals

Both the RinR and the Botball programs have similar educational goals. In broad terms we are striving to

1. expose students to basic engineering principles

2. present an appealing application of various math skills

3. promote interest in science and math

4. initiate awareness and basic skills in computer programming

5. build problem-solving skills

6. encourage teamwork

7. motivate students in all areas of school

In the following sections we will delve deeper into each of these goals, illustrating them where appropriate with specific episodes from teachers or students.

Teaching basic engineering principles

In both the RinR and the Botball programs, students learn by doing. However, simply giving students a problem and expecting them to solve it when they are lacking the tools will teach them nothing but frustration.

Engineering relies on humanity's accumulated knowledge of science and math. Giving students this background, even during an intensive week of interaction, would be difficult, to say the least. Fortunately, while a working knowledge of the scientific and mathematical fundamentals on which engineering is based is beneficial, it is not necessary for these students to learn at this time (and is not well known by many practicing engineers).

Engineering, like many other professions, is learned by experience—primarily the experience of others who have come before. Engineering is in many ways the ultimate example of *case-based reasoning*. It is a discipline that is not only well illustrated but is best taught by example. This is especially true with robotics. Robots are a conglomeration of many types of basic systems: mechanical, electrical, control, engineering, and computer science. Well-designed robots also have some human factors and aesthetic engineering in them as well.

When we give a Botball teachers' tutorial, we do present the participants with one solution to that year's challenge. We spend a great deal of time developing this solution because it must have certain properties:

1. Each subsystem must be an example of good engineering.

2. The robot as a whole must solve the problem.

3. The robot must be robust and reliable.

4. The robot must solve the problem very badly.

5. There must not be a single obvious improvement to make to this robot to make it a good solution to the problem (numerous obvious improvements are acceptable).

Figure 7.6

Sixth-grade students designed and built this robot to snuff out a candle (photo by Tina Yalen).

The example hardware and software that we provide must contain properties that we would like the students to emulate in their robots. Therefore, everything has to work reliably. More than that, we want the students to take these systems apart and to be able to incorporate some of the pieces into their own designs. The subsystems should be good and useful examples; however, they will not be the most appropriate way of solving the particular aspect of the program for which they are being utilized. We make sure everyone realizes that we have chosen a non-optimal solution as an example in order to avoid having teams simply duplicate our design.

In addition to providing non-optimal examples of the solution, we also go through several exercises to create modules and subsystems that could prove useful in their solution. One goal of the training program is to leave the participants with the skills and experience to quickly create the necessary pieces that will enable them to build a robot that will solve the challenge. They will also have had some experience in integrating several of these modules together into a functioning system. They will then need to create a design and figure out how to integrate the pieces that they have selected into a functional robot. Usually during this process they will find that they must adapt some of the modules we gave them into wholly new structures—adding to their corpus of engineering solutions.

We use similar exercises during the RinR program. The main difference is that in the RinR, the exercises are more directed, and the resulting systems are usually simpler (though often there is a wider variety of modules since students may be working on different challenges during the RinR [Figure 7.6]).

Applying math to robotics

It is probably fair to say that K–12 students spend more time learning math than any other subject. It is probably also fair to say that for the majority of students, they have no idea why they are doing so other than the seemingly arbitrary requirements of their school's system.

Mathematics is greatly underappreciated by most people, and we believe the reasons are twofold: it is difficult for most people to do; and to many people math appears to have no practical use, with the exception of basic arithmetic (and even this, since the advent of the inexpensive electronic calculator, is no longer a convincing use for many people).

Most math texts contain page after page of "exercises"—most of which are abstract with no hint of possible uses. The exceptions, of course, are word problems, which are meant to tie math into the real world. Unfortunately, most word problems in math texts are so contrived as to only exacerbate the separation that most people feel between what they are learning and any real-world utility. Few of us have ever needed to calculate cousin Jane's age, knowing only that the digits of her age add up to her shoe size and that in 1990 she was twice the age of cousin Billy, whose age and shoe size sum to his IQ (he has large feet and is not very swift).

For students to care about math they must be able to apply it to something that they do care about. Homer Hickman and his friends decided to learn calculus so that they could design better rocket engines.[1] Over the last 40 years, the country has changed, and encouraging thousands of children to mix their own rocket fuel is probably not a good idea. However, robots are a less explosive solution to the same problem.

KIPR educational robots and robot kits use math in a variety of ways. Kids want their robots to move quickly, or they want to have them lift heavy objects. We give them all a standard set of motors—motors that are not particularly good at going fast or hauling heavy loads. We also give them lots of gears and teach them about speed-torque trade-offs. In many a second-grade class (approximate age of 7) several students will stare with awe and admiration at the one or two students who know their multiplication tables and can predict how may times a motor needs to turn to make the wheel on their robot turn once (without counting revolutions by hand).

When students have built their robot, they often want it to go somewhere in particular—this provides a great opportunity to teach them about dead reckoning. Students usually try to get a robot to run a particular course by using a series of timed moves—this tends to work very poorly. Friction, battery level, changes in the robot mass, and Murphy factors all make timed moves a very unreliable method of predicting the robot's position.

---

1. See *The Rocket Boys* by Homer Hickman.

In dead reckoning, a robot's position is calculated by measuring the distance traveled by the left and right side wheels (usually by using *encoders*). The robot's distance traveled is simply the average of the distance traveled by the left and right sides. The heading of the robot (in radians) at any time is simply a function of the difference between the distance traveled by the two sides modulo the separation between the left and right sides. In order to explain this to the student one needs to draw the robot making a turn and then show the circles that each side and the center of the robot would make if it drove in a circle. Students also need to calculate the circumference of the wheels, so they know how far it travels per wheel rotation. All of a sudden radii, circles, circumferences, and so on have utility—as one of our students suddenly loudly exclaimed, "So that's what pi is for!"

Promoting early interest in science and math, leading to potential career paths

"How can I do what you're doing when I grow up? I didn't know you could do something fun." This question came from a nine-year-old boy at Staunton Elementary School in southeast DC (an inner-city school). Further discussion indicated that he had never seen a robot before and had never thought about any particular career for when he grew up, much less working in technology.

When we explained to his fourth-grade class the importance of learning all the math and science you possibly could so that you could put it to use when you grew up, the general comments from the class expressed amused surprise that there was actually a use for all this "junk" they were supposed to learn in school.

Robots rank right up there with dinosaurs when it comes to grabbing the attention of elementary school students, and as previously discussed, robots are an excellent mode of teaching many content areas. Robots are also exceptionally effective at influencing attitudes, not just toward science and math but also toward career paths in technology and engineering. And when it comes to affecting lifelong attitudes, it's well known that the earlier you start, the more powerful the impact.

Several years ago we contacted Sunrise Valley Elementary School in Reston, Virginia, our local school. Our plan was to offer an after-school fifth/sixth-grade robotics class in order to get students prepared and interested in taking more science-, math-, and engineering-related classes in middle and high school (with the ultimate goal of creating a better world through creative and sensitive engineering, and a better society through enthusiastic, well-prepared, and productive citizens—but that's a whole different chapter in a some other book).

We distributed flyers to the fifth and sixth graders (ages 10–11), and the next day 30 registrations appeared: 29 boys and 1 girl.

This overwhelming imbalance highlighted an obvious need to reach out to girls, and this inspired immediate action on our part. We received permission to present short robot demos for second graders. During these demos (presented by CS), students were invited to push buttons, flip levers, and otherwise interact with a couple of real robots. We then distributed flyers to the second graders for an after-school robotics class. This time we had enough responses to form two classes, and about 40 percent of the registrants were girls.

Four years later when this group became sixth graders, we again offered a fifth/sixth-grade class. This time half the students who signed up were female. None of this resembles an actual scientific study (which we are developing); however, there was a fairly strong indication that when students had a fun experience with robots at an early age, they were much more likely to pursue that topic at a later point in their life. Presumably, the same effect would occur later in life, in that students would be more likely to choose college courses and/or career paths further down the line after having been exposed to fun experiences with robotics in middle and high school.

It is not enough to simply study robotics, however. Hands-on participation is crucial to the learning process, and vital to the "outreach" aspect of the program, particularly with female students. During an interview, one young woman from Wakefield High School in Arlington, Virginia, who participated in Botball, remarked that she was having much more fun than she expected to have in doing this project. In fact she admitted to having "signed up for Botball in order to avoid doing a science project, but then I discovered that I enjoyed it, and then I found out that I was actually *good* at it, which totally surprised me!"

The impact of early experiences cannot be overstated. Recently we received email from Anstes, a 12-year-old student who had taken after-school robotics classes four years earlier when she had been in second grade. She vividly remembered second-grade robotics as "a really fun experience" and went on to relate how that class had affected her attitude:

> I really got to see how math and science were used in real life. I finally saw math as something besides numbers. . . . Before then I hadn't really been interested in anything math or science related. But using your knowledge to program and work with robots seems really cool. Maybe I'll try it. . . . It really broadened my horizons.

Awareness and basic skills in computer programming

Most elementary and high schools now offer computer courses; however, these courses, for the most part, do not teach computer science or computer programming. Instead, these courses concentrate on basic skills such as keyboarding, and on using standard (or what some people would like to assume are standard) applications such as Microsoft Excel or Adobe PhotoShop. Some students come out of these courses believing that they know all there is to know about using computers. They see community college courses on using Netscape Navigator or similar applications and already feel superior.

Unfortunately, creating a spreadsheet in Excel or some similar exercise is now often (incorrectly) referred to as computer programming—and if this is what people think computer programming is, then we are not going to see any better applications in our lifetime. The ability to use applications is a fine thing, but it does not enable anyone to create original programs. In order to create new applications, control robots, or use computers in any new or creative ways, students must learn to use a computer language (such as C, Java, Perl, etc.) to write instructions that give a computer all the necessary steps it must follow in order to produce the desired results. This is what computer programming is.

Robots make the need for computer programming obvious. You've got a machine sitting on your desk. If you want it to do something, then you need to tell it how to do that from step one. Programming is the way to instruct a robot.

Robots also make programming more interesting. Programming tools such as IC allow students to interact with their robot on a line-by-line basis. This means that they need only type a few keystrokes—a single line of code— in order to get the robot to do something. By the time they've written a whole program, their robot is wandering around, doing things they may never have expected it to do. Most students find it amazing that so little programming is needed to make their robot do something interesting (at least to them).

In every case where we've had students with programming experience, they have expressed their preference for programming a robot over creating some artificial program (e.g., recipe manager, checkbook balancer, GPA calculator, etc.). The fact that we use in our robotics programs the same computing language that other classes have used for these more mundane applications makes it all the better. The students realize the utility of what they have already learned, and if they have not yet had those classes, they realize that robotics will make those classes so much easier. Finally, many high-school students, as they look through the pages of the local want ads for a summer job, quickly realize that the programming skills they are learning while making their robot run around, will also make them instantly employable.

Building problem-solving skills

The many types of challenges encountered by students and teachers of robotics are clearly quite diverse—mechanical, electronic, programming, human factors, and so on—all can present problems to be overcome at any stage of development. The excitement happens as people develop useful and inspired responses to deal with the inevitable obstacles in the creative process.

To illustrate just one example of problem-solving on the fly, the following is an excerpt from an essay written by a student from Langley High School in Virginia, who participated in the 1999 DC Regional Botball Tournament. This student's team (like many) came up with a design that outstripped their ability to implement (and test) in the allotted six weeks. But this team addressed their situation with some real-time problem-solving (and luck).

The Botball tournaments are often the first time the robots are tested in head-to-head competition. The changes and redesigns that are done in the pit in between matches are sometimes amazing. This essay was a spontaneous reaction to this student's experience and was not written for any class, nor was it solicited by us.

> I was so excited, I still don't know the name of the school where the tournament was held. But we got there after a thirty minute drive, entered and registered, found our team's table, and started setting up the computer we brought. Unluckily, our monitor power cable was missing! Though we had everything else working, without the cable we were just working blind! With still so much work yet to do, we absolutely had to use the computer. How could we do anything without a monitor power cable to make the monitor work? We knew we had to solve this problem, and through all this trouble, the work still needed to be done.
>
> While the others were still constructing the last parts of our super-complicatedly-designed robot, I tried to "communicate" with that computer blindly. By hitting the keyboard with imagination and some logic, I eventually opened the program up and was able to send commands to the board with my eyes closed. When the motor started turning, everybody was yelling excitedly. That moment was so cool!
>
> We basically had a lot of time to finish up our robot, because we were one of the very last teams in the seeding round. From sometime after eight to sometime around eleven, Josh, Mohammed, and Lynda worked pretty hard on the ball separator, while I got to fix my program after borrowing a cable from another school. Theoretically it was a perfect design. The robot should be able to grab balls, raise them, detect the color, put the right balls in a basket and put the wrong ones in something like a jail, and eventually dump the right balls into the goal. However, practically, it was very unstable due to the complexity.
>
> During the seeding round the robot worked unexpectedly badly on the game board. We thought it would at least move—something on its extra function

had a serious problem that prevented our entire robot from working properly. It was a very embarrassing moment. It was a good thing that the seeding round was just a single-player game, and was not counted into the score. So we still had time before our real competition began.

After lunch the climax of the day was about to begin. We knew definitely that our robot did not work at all, although we had perfect theories. After that crazy idea was accepted, we tore everything off in just several seconds. We really did not need theory at that moment, because all the sensors would mean nothing if other robots ran into us. In a combat, brain means nothing without muscle. We realized that we only needed something that runs and pushes. We decided to build a totally new robot that would be simple and strong.

Deconstruction and reconstruction was probably the most exciting moment of the day. Other teams around us were totally amazed by how crazy we were—tearing off our robot right before our game started. I tried to read Josh's expression. I knew that the now-destroyed design had kept him up after three in the morning for days. I couldn't figure out why he did not seem upset, nor could I understand my own feelings. I felt only excited when pressing one key to delete 95% of the code that had taken me weeks to write. We had never expected to win anyway, so taking this shot was nothing to worry about.

My hands were shaking, because time was still too short. Our first game was about to start, and we were only halfway there. I felt I had to handle so many things that four hands were not even enough. Then I could not see the robot. "Wh . . . wh . . . Where is our robot?" "Oh. Mike took it to the front," Mohammed replied. "WHAT? Wa . . . Wait! WHAT ARE THEY DOING WITH-OUT THE HANDY BOARD?" Holding the microcomputer board high, I yelled out loud. Without the board, the robot is just a combination of Lego pieces that every four-year-old kid knows how to make.

Nothing was set yet! Even the construction was not finished. I tried in my top speed to get the new code down on the board and take it to them. But that did not seem possible, and I was still too slow. I heard the game starting, and I heard a lot of noise. Then I found my team members jumping off the ground and yelling like madmen. "We won!" somebody said, maybe Lynda. Mohammed explained, "Our robot sits there and gets zero, and theirs got a negative point!" "What?

I was told later on that we had actually lost that game, because no score ends up being negative and the other team had the running robot. But still Mike did a great job bringing the half-done Lego pieces there, saving us from missing our turn and being kicked out of this contest.

The game format used double elimination, so whether we won or not, we got to play a second game. Before the second game started, we had our new robot ready. Lights on! Our robot ran forward at the very first second. Theirs started at the same moment, but was much slower.... We won after ninety seconds for having pushed two of our balls to their half of the board. "Yes! We did it!" All of us, including Mrs. Lindsey, were so proud of winning.

Still you can never rely on any brainless thing. Our next opponent was one of the three most advanced designs I saw in that day. Though they lost in a later game, I had to say they had the best way to deliver balls. This match started out the same as in our previous game, however, they positioned their robot at an angle at the very beginning, which avoided our evil strategy to have head-on collisions.

We pushed them back a little bit, trapped them with the long bumper, but they eventually escaped after twenty seconds. Because our "robot" knew nothing other than running forward, it stuck in the corner against the pipe edges. At the end they had three balls behind the line, while we had only two. We lost, but we lost happily.

Encouraging teamwork, camaraderie, and other socially useful characteristics

A quick glance through the headlines of any newspaper will reveal that many high-school students are taking part in antisocial (sometimes violently antisocial) behavior. Many of these kids are not engaged in normal school activities and instead are putting their sometimes extensive creative abilities into performing these antisocial acts.

One high-school teacher who participated in the 1999 Silicon Valley Botball program remarked that as she watched her team work together to create a complex, very concrete product, she saw this process bring out the best in everybody (although, admittedly, not at every moment). She commented that it was a shame that those youths who made bombs and planned shooting sprees did not have an outlet as challenging, fun, and inclusive as robotics to keep them productive and engaged instead of wasting their tenacity and intelligence on planning and carrying out violent acts.

This teacher went on to discuss the positive characteristics she had witnessed in the context of students building the robot and participating in the tournament. In that spirit, we want to mention some remarkable acts of sportsmanship we have witnessed on the part of the middle- and high-school students who have participated in this program.

Figure 7.7

Students prepare their robot for the DC Regional Botball Tournament at the Smithsonian Air and Space Museum.

Only one member of the Chantilly High School Botball team, from Chantilly, Virginia, was able to attend the DC Regional Tournament (Figure 7.7). This student arrived early, set up, and was extremely focused as he made his last-minute preparations.

At one point his robot was all set up on the table while he turned around to do some final programming. The light sensors on the robot must have picked up some stray bright light in the room because the robot, as it was programmed to do, suddenly lurched forward and sped straight ahead toward the light—straight ahead and off the edge of the table, crashing onto the floor.

Every head swiveled in that direction and a collective groan filled the room. Then there was a moment of silence. Everyone could imagine being in this person's place, and the thought of starting over with just an hour or less left before the seeding round was overwhelming. The luckless robot-builder stood in shock over the fallen robot. It was in pieces everywhere.

Very quietly, nine or ten individuals from several other schools walked over to this fellow and carefully began picking up the pieces. They worked together to rebuild the robot, even helping with the reprogramming as much as they could. When it came time for this young man's robot to perform, at least he had something to bring to the arena. His robot wouldn't move for its first try, but after he had had a bit more time to work with it, he was able to make it function somewhat, and the day was not lost.

Many people came over to us that day remarking on the extraordinary sportsmanship and camaraderie exhibited by those members of rival teams who helped this individual put his crashed robot back together. Adults were clearly moved by witnessing this spontaneously honorable and generous side of teenage behavior—a side that is not often shown in the media or acknowledged enough.

We frequently see this type of sportsmanship in Botball tournaments, although rarely in such extreme circumstances. The tension of problem-solving under pressure can work for good or ill, and we are delighted to see that in general the result has been a situation of empathy, cooperation, and honor.

One of the most unique and honorable approaches to Botball was displayed at the 1999 National Botball Tournament at AAAI in Orlando, Florida. The Menlo-Atherton team had designed an "attitude adjuster" into their robot so that they could quickly tweak it to either focus on simple point-scoring while ignoring the other robot, or they could program it to behave in a hostile and destructive manner toward their opponent's robot. Before each match, the Menlo-Atherton team took into account their opponent's strategy based on seeding rounds and previous performance, and they adjusted their robot's "attitude" accordingly. Thus, their robot simply ignored robots who were not aggressive, focusing on getting points instead, but when matched against a destructive robot they could easily give back as good as they got. In one round they accidentally employed the aggressive strategy against a passive robot—completely interrupting that robot's ability to score points, winning the round, and causing their opponents' robot some slight damage. At the end of the round they came over to their opponents and apologized profusely.

Motivating students with diverse skills and attitudes in all areas of school

One of the major benefits in using robots as tools for learning is that the topic attracts such a wide range of students. Robotics is just as appealing to students who, in the past, have been considered underachievers as it is to honors students. In fact one of our earliest tip-offs to this phenomenon was an experience that took place when we first started giving robot demos to elementary schools.

One of us (DM) gave a demo to a first-grade class in Arlington, Massachusetts, and noticed a young boy, Daniel, who asked numerous appropriate questions, also suggesting simple experiments in the process.

He and several other students worked together to set up the experiments, which were then run in the class. After the class his teacher was amazed by this child's contribution and informed us that this child was almost never engaged in what was going on, and furthermore tended to be a troublemaker and a bully. If robotics could motivate and engage a student like Daniel, we wondered which other students out there were just waiting for a robot to show up to arouse their interest and provoke their participation in class.

The following essay was sent to us by Jeneva Westendorf, a teacher at Foothill High School in California, who participates in the Silicon Valley Botball program. She not only illustrates how a well-run robotics project can attract and inspire all different kinds of students, but she also captures the impact it has made on individual lives.

> If someone had told me in December of 1997 that I would be working in the field of autonomous robots, I would have told them they were out of their minds. Yet, here I am 18 months later with 2 regional competitions, a full-year integrated science course, a summer school robotics program, an extended mentoring relationship with NASA/Ames Research and other business mentors. Several students have jobs with NASA, students have goals and dreams that they never dreamt of having. Our school and district of 11, soon to be 12, high schools in the East Side Union High School District now have an exciting future in science and technology.

> Foothill High School is a continuation high school with Santa Clara County support services for our students with physical, emotional, substance abuse, and juvenile justice issues. The students have been unsuccessful in a traditional high school setting, and have been unsuccessful in coping with the challenges of their neighborhood and family lives. Therefore, the positive impact that robotics has had has been very apparent in this setting. After competing in the 1998 regional Botball robotics tournament at NASA/Ames, my principal Tim McDonough asked me if I would be interested in teaching a full year course using KIPR's robot kits. Knowing the positive impact the competition experience had had on the 3 students that had participated in the Spring and Summer of 1998, I developed a one year course in robotics as part of the Integrated Science program. Flying, virtually, by the seat of my pants, I began a course in robotics.

> One of the students that was a participant in the 1998 Botball regional competition graduated and became my colleague after he was hired last summer by Foothill to assist me in developing curriculum for the robotics class. That student, Gary, is now a full time paraprofessional, working with students in our special education program "New Directions." He has been instrumental in motivating students, who otherwise would not have been particularly suc-

cessful with "traditional" teaching techniques, to produce in amazing ways using the KIPR LEGO Robotics Kits. He also served as mentor for one of the four teams we fielded in this year's 1999 Regional Competition. His team took 3rd place in the competition and won a $4,000.00 travel grant for our teams to compete in the national competition at the AAAI Conference in Orlando, Florida. Now, because of these opportunities, Gary has plans to attend San Jose City College in the fall of 1999 to begin studying for his B.A., and other students in this program have found success and are looking forward to the future.

One of these students (R___), who had had a very violent temper, had been abusing alcohol, and was anti-social in large group settings, is now learning to control his temper, look at his alcohol abuse, and to cope much better socially. To what do I attribute his success? I believe that his involvement in robotics and Gary's influence are what became the turning point for R___. R___ was able to cultivate his hidden engineering and mechanical talents. He quickly caught on to "Interactive C" programming as well. R___, himself, was amazed at his talents and the real JOY that he felt by discovering these talents was a real gift to him. To me, this is what being a teacher is all about, the joys and successes of one's students! Robotics sets the stage for students to experience continuous success. My experience has been that one success in this field leads to another and another and so on; Gary is an example. The LEGOs used in the kits further attract the kids to build, create, and program creations they would have never dreamt they could create. The compact size of the LEGOs motivates the students to give their creativity a try! The programming piece allows the students to tap talents in logic and math that they once were unable to recognize in any other way. Robotics is also a great introduction to the uses of Algebra, Geometry, Trigonometry and the science of Physics. It gives practical application to these disciplines so that they have more meaning and use for the students, therefore motivating them to want to learn these subjects, rather than learning them in isolation.

This is why I love robotics! Robotics is a tool for learning through experience and discovery. Students get to "own" their learning and the teacher becomes the facilitator of their learning. It's not the teacher's "stuff" that is being shoved down their throats, but it's theirs!!!!!!! When it's theirs it's everything to them and they become excited about their education! And this excites me and makes my job worthwhile. It also makes me feel like I'm making a major contribution to society as an educator. As a mentor of mine, Dr. Dorsey Davy, once said, "If you don't care who gets the credit, the job gets done!" In this case, the students get all the credit and the learning gets done. My students here at Foothill have experienced and are still experiencing this "discovery" learning. I have had a total of 32 students come through my robotics class this year. The maximum number of students that I take into class at a time is 16.

Of the original 16, nine are still with me, and of that original nine, six competed in the regional competition. All six of these students have plans to attend college. And of the total 32 students that have taken the class, all except two have plans and are on track to graduate from high school.

Robotics motivates students to make plans, to accomplish, to look forward, to achieve and to feel good about themselves, in some cases for the first time in their lives.

The robotics class itself is set up to allow students to feel comfortable with the new and sometimes very complicated concepts that robotics brings with it. To build an autonomous robot, students must learn the basic concepts of mechanics, engineering and "Interactive C" computer programming. They must also learn the skills of effective communication, teamwork and problem solving. They get to learn by making mistakes, in fact mistakes are essential to their learning. The students are not used to mistakes being "OK." Most of their lives they have been taught that mistakes are absolutely not "OK"! But, with robotics they learn that "tearing it down" and putting it back together is a must or the machine isn't going to work; mistakes then become more than "OK"!

7.4 Finishing Up

Robotics is one of the great integrating disciplines. Mechanical, electrical, and computer engineering are all used in obvious ways, as are physics and mathematics. New designs for "artificial muscles" and other new types of actuators are bringing chemical engineering into robotics as well. Applications of robotics for bridge and building inspection, and the increased use of "actively controlled structures" in new building projects, have caused civil engineering to become intimately involved in robotics. Control theories such as behavior control and cooperating robots use biological systems as their inspiration. Robotics in manufacturing has huge economic and social implications with a potential that is comparable to the advent of the industrial revolution. And as robots become more common, the aesthetics of the devices, along with the natural language interfaces, will have to be greatly improved. So robotics touches on almost every discipline.

Because of robotics' multidisciplinary nature, it would be possible to teach the entire K–12 curriculum using robotics as a framework. We are unaware of anyone doing that, but it's possible. A more acceptable approach is to teach general science using robotics as the overarching framework.

Several schools have created semester- or year-long courses built around Botball that they now use to teach general science. KISS Institute is working with them to standardize and publish these curricula. In the not-too-distant future you should be able to download these from the Internet.

Robotics is like a box of chocolates: you never know what you are going to get, but you know your hands are going to get dirty. So go out and build something, and remember to keep watching the Web!

7.5   Acknowledgments

The authors wish to thank Jeneva Westendorf, Elaine Chang, Terrance Reese, Peter Jaffe, Anstes Agnew, and Peter Hou for their contributions and ideas for this chapter. We also wish to thank the many teachers, sponsors, and students who have contributed so much to the success of these programs.

Kid's View

   ## The Robot We Made

By Lauren Sumida, age 8

We first started our team by making unmovable robots with art supplies: feathers, cups, clay, socks, markers, craftsticks, fluffballs, and LEGO bricks. Then we started on the robot named PETS (personal electronic teller of stories). Our robot looks like a combination of animals: a cow head, gray fur body, green duck mouth, dog paws, wings, duck feet and a fish tail. It sings songs, and it can move, and it can tell stories. I think a robot is an electronic person. Because it helps you. In our case, the robot my team made tells stories.

What other children should know about robots is to work hard, but have fun! A robot compared to doing other things is fun, but sometimes it is challenging. I was in the software group. The skeleton group worked on the skeleton of the robot. The skins and sensors group worked on what the outside should look like. We still have a few more things to do but we have a wonderful robot.

Chapter Eight

Eat, Sleep, Robotics

Mark Yim
Xerox Palo Alto Research Center

Mark D. Chow
Xerox Palo Alto Research Center

William L. Dunbar
Henry M. Gunn High School

Abstract

This chapter describes some of Gunn High School and Xerox Palo Alto Research Center's experiences over the past three years in the FIRST robotics competition. The goal of the competition is to inspire students to find the exciting aspects of engineering through teaming of schools with corporate sponsors. What appeared to the authors at first to be a challenging science project rapidly engulfed the team and their sponsors with the drama and excitement of a rock concert, a Super Bowl, and space program all rolled into one.

8.1   Introduction

Ben peered at the chain tensioner, his head almost touching the floor. "Okay, let it rip!" he called out. A mouse click activated the motor controller, sending a 100-pound wheeled mass of steel and wood whizzing past Ben's nose.

"Hey, watch your head!" called out Lea, a Gunn High School senior in charge of robot programming, from behind her laptop.

Unfazed, Ben remarked, "I see the problem," and reached for a wrench. "I'm going to tighten the chain—try turning up the PWM on the left motor."

The noise of the milling machine echoed from the adjacent shop, where three other students were finishing construction of the basket latch mechanism. Bill Dunbar, the engineering tech teacher, surveyed the activity and wondered if he would have to start kicking everyone out of the Industrial Arts area soon. It was past 11 PM, and there were only a few days left until the robot shipping date. Most of the 15 high-school students left were either machining or testing their robot components, working on the programming with Ken, an engineer from a local high-tech company, or sprawled out on a ripped-up car seat doing homework in their spare moments while waiting for a part to be finished. One of them was doing drawings and calculations of torque on the aluminum arm they had just designed. None of the students had any intention of leaving their engineering project until they absolutely had to.

Mr. Dunbar pondered the curious problem of trying to convince his students to stop working on their school project and go home. Quite a few of the robotics team members had worked past midnight every day for the past two weeks, including weekends. It was getting more difficult to get them to leave at night, but he decided that 2 AM was going to be the limit for today, no matter how much they protested.

Figure 8.1

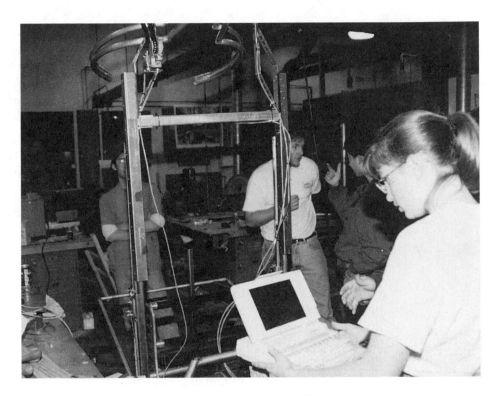

Programming the onboard microprocessor to detect elevator stop sensors.

Does this sound like any high-school science project that you remember? Where are the cardboard posters, the dioramas, the magic markers, the last-minute data fudging? These students are using math and physics to design complex electromechanical devices. They are using English and communication skills to write scripts and give presentations. They are using art and computer skills to create first-class animations. They are embracing challenging problems well beyond their experiences. They are thinking and learning!

What these students are working so hard on is their entry for the FIRST Robotics Competition (see Figure 8.1). For the past three years, researchers from the Xerox Palo Alto Research Center along with other engineers from Silicon Valley companies have partnered with students from Henry M. Gunn High School in Palo Alto, California, to build a large, complex, maneuverable yet strong robot to compete against teams from around the country.

This chapter describes what we discovered as school teacher and engineering mentors during the students' experience with the robotics competition. We observed young students working harder than they had ever worked in their lives and having the most fun they had ever had. We saw their dedication to the project spill over, often dramatically, to their work, school, social, and home lives. In the process they learned organizational skills, teamwork, how to work on big projects with lots of uncertainty, science and engineering, self-confidence, and balance (or the consequences of imbalance) of work. We analyze some of our observations here. While we believe that the events and philosophies expressed here are representative of many other people and programs involved with FIRST, the true range of experiences is as diverse as the thousands of student participants and the communities they represent. The opinions and experiences presented in this chapter are those of the authors and not necessarily those of FIRST, nor of Xerox, nor of Henry M. Gunn High School.

8.2   What is FIRST?

FIRST stands for "For Inspiration in Science and Technology." It is a nonprofit organization created by Dean Kamen, successful inventor/entrepreneur and president of DEKA Research Corporation, along with Woodie Flowers, professor of mechanical engineering at MIT and former TV host of the PBS series *Scientific American Frontiers*. FIRST's mission is to generate an interest in science and engineering among today's youth. Their current primary means of accomplishing this goal is through the annual robot competitions. The program is modeled after the MIT 2.70 mechanical engineering design course in which students are given a kit of parts with which to build a device that solves a particular problem (such as moving objects beyond barriers and up a hill). How well these college students have done their work is very publicly demonstrated in a wild competition on the last day of the class.

In order to adapt this very popular college course to the high-school level, FIRST introduced a key variation, that of engineering mentor participants. The resulting program is described in this excerpt from the FIRST Web page (*www.usfirst.org*):

> The FIRST Robotics Competition is a national engineering contest which immerses high school students in the exciting world of engineering. Teaming up with engineers from businesses and universities, students get a hands-on, inside look at the engineering profession. In six intense weeks, students and engineers work together to brainstorm, design, construct and test their "champion robot." With only six weeks, all jobs are critical path. The teams then compete in a spirited, no-holds-barred tournament complete with referees, cheerleaders and time clocks.

The partnerships developed between schools, businesses, and universities provide an exchange of resources and talent, highlighting mutual needs, building cooperation, and exposing students to new career choices. The result is a fun, exciting and stimulating environment in which all participants discover the important connection between classroom lessons and real world applications.

Each year, the competition is different, so returning teams always have a new challenge to look forward to. However, the details are kept secret until the unveiling at the Kick-Off workshop. This provides a high level of excitement as everyone sees the new challenge for the first time and ideas immediately begin forming in people's minds.

It's not a coincidence that the competition has a strong resemblance to the way a corporation or an agency like NASA conducts its engineering projects. In this way, volunteer engineer mentors feel confident in guiding students through processes familiar to them, while the students are acutely aware of the future career implications of what they are learning.

However, improving career options does not motivate students to spend weeks laboring and to forgo sleep nor does it inspire the intense devotion we have seen. There is something more here than constructing something from a kit of parts. There's the feeling of doing something new and big and very real.

For many folks, designing and building a real thing that moves is off-scale satisfying. If you make something that moves as you command it, the experience is even more intense. If you work with a team of friends to design and build something that, under your control, does complex high-tech stuff successfully, despite other robots' efforts to stop it, the whole process is getting near peak. If all this happens while a few thousand dedicated fans cheer, you've got a FIRST Competition!

Building a robot is a very creative act. I think being creative is one of life's few fundamental sources of satisfaction.

—Woodie Flowers, Pappalardo Professor of
Mechanical Engineering, MIT

8.3   The Competition

Just like a typical industry engineering project, the rules and specifications for each FIRST Robotics Competition fill hundreds of pages, and updates and changes arrive via the Internet up until the last day of building. At the

FIgure 8.2

The 1999 FIRST West Coast Regional Competition held at NASA-Ames Moffet Field, Mountain View, California.

annual kickoff meeting for each new contest, participants receive a kit of parts that includes motors, gearboxes, mechanisms such as hinges, bearings, and raw materials, as well as the control electronics used for the robot. The participants then have roughly six weeks to design and build the robot before competing in regional and national competitions (see Figure 8.2).

FIRST is not the only high-school robot competition. Strikingly different from other competitions, however, is the size of the FIRST robots. A typical high-school robot project is on the scale of a house cat, able to be carried by one person. The robots in the FIRST competition are on the scale of an adult human. For example, the 1998 contest allowed robots to weigh up to 130 pounds and measure up to $36 \times 30 \times 48$ inches tall in its initial state. In order to compete effectively, the robots often extended mechanisms that effectively tripled the robots' height (see Figure 8.3).

The robots are usually strong enough to knock over a large person and are often made of welded steel. The size, speed, and interaction of these robots require a robustness of design that may not be as necessary in competitions with smaller robots (see Figure 8.4, Color Plate only). This is not like building a toy or mock-up with hot melt glue and foam core. Students must learn about robust mechanisms and strength of materials. The rules allow

Figure 8.3

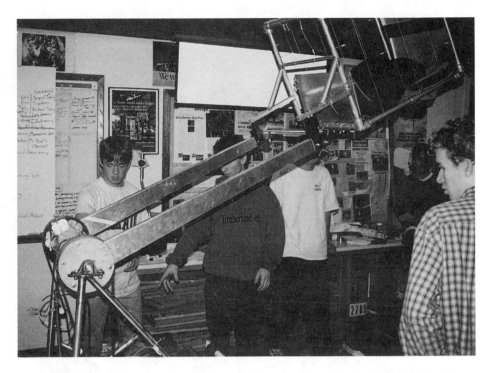

Initially designed to raise a basket, the aluminum arm turned out to add multiple functionality to this robot.

for additional structural elements to be constructed from materials such as sheet aluminum, steel tubing, wood, and wire.

In the arena, the robots are teleoperated by students via radio control. The element of programming is limited to creating software to link the user interface, typically joysticks, to control the robot. Although some robots are controlled entirely through the joysticks, the kits contain enough microprocessor power and input sensors—gyro, limit switches, and potentiometers—to present an opportunity for fairly sophisticated control software and some autonomy. In the 1999 national competition, Gunn High School won the Honeywell Leadership in Controls Award for their implementation of closed-loop feedback control with a gyro to stabilize the position of a four-foot-long arm on their robot.

A typical team entry combines a robot, two student drivers, and one student human player. The human player is attired in protective clothing and limited in movement to a small area just outside the robot playing field (see Figure 8.5). The objective is usually to retrieve large objects, such as automobile inner tubes, and to place these objects on structures within the enclosed playing field (see Figure 8.6). To score the maximum points, it is often necessary to extend the robot's reach beyond eight feet vertically, while

Figure 8.5

Human player prepares to fetch "floppy" for insertion into robot basket. A last minute adjustment added a remote-controlled motor-driven floppy hold-down bracket, shown in its retracted position here.

starting with no dimension larger than four feet. Typically there are three or four robots placed on a playing field at the same time. Both the human player and robot can score points within the two-minute rounds.

Since the competition is a skill contest and not a demolition derby like some robot events, deliberately damaging competitors is not allowed. However, the best teams engineer their point-scoring systems to the limits, and in the heat of battle when robots go for the same territory, there is often plenty of physical contact. Fractions of an inch or fractions of a second often decide matches. The combination of fast and powerful robot capabilities along with the drivers' skills and human-player physical skills and judgment makes for intensely exciting matches for the students and engineers, and a terrific show for the spectators (see Figure 8.7).

Figure 8.6

Robots prepare to place inner tubes onto spinning metal structure in the middle of the arena. Extra points are scored if inner tubes are raised directly above the central column.

Figure 8.7

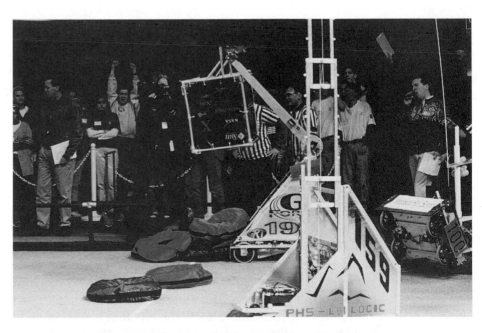

In real-life environments, engineering designs are put to the test. Motors overheat in the Florida sun, fuses blow because of heavy loads, and metal latches can fail as shown here.

8.4   Xerox PARC and GRT

In 1992, the first year of competition, 28 teams from the northeastern United States participated in the FIRST Robotics Competition. The program caught on quickly and in 1999 over 200 teams, comprising over 10,000 people, traveled to Epcot Center in Orlando, Florida, to match their robots against those from teams across the United States and Canada. Xerox PARC began its involvement with Henry M. Gunn High School's Gunn Robotics Team (GRT) in Palo Alto, California, in the first year of Gunn's participation (1997) and has been a supporter of their team since.

The philosophy from the PARC engineering mentors has been that the "students do everything, or at least they think they do." Just as a coach of a football team would never run on the field and make a play, we believe the roles of engineers are to advise, train, and coach. Thus, the students feel ownership of the robot. To maintain "invisibility" on the playing field is not always easy or possible, especially with this complex a problem and no "right" answers. Yet, we have tried to maintain a coachlike status most of the time, and we believe this is one of the key motivators in this project for this team.

8.5   Other Venues of Competition

In addition to the physical robot competition, there are many other components to the overall annual event. For example, Autodesk Corporation sponsors the Excellence in Engineering Creativity and Communications Award (often referred to as the animation award). In this competition, students use Autodesk 3D animation software to create a 30-second computer animation that best communicates the principles of the robot the students are building. Each year, students have been pushing the limits of what PCs are capable of producing in terms of first-rate animation. In recent years, judges have had to look not only at technical quality, which is often excellent and rivals productions of professional animation studios, but also at story and even character animation quality. Since winning this award in 1997, Gunn students have made animation a year-long activity, on their own initiative, gathering in garages to do animation training over the summer (see Figure 8.8; see also Figure 8.9, Color Plate only).

The most prestigious award, the one that is presented last at the awards ceremony by the chairman of the FIRST Corporation, is the Chairman's Award. By creating this award, FIRST has brilliantly presented solutions to two problems, one practical and one philosophical. As a practical matter, as

Figure 8.8

Members of the animation team screen a motion test of their work for other members of GRT.

teams get larger, it becomes clear that only a small number of people at any time can have their noses buried in robot innards. Because of its emphasis on documenting, communication, and community outreach, the Chairman's Award appeals to a group of students who might not otherwise be interested in a robotics competition. The Chairman's Award has motivated Gunn students to travel to other local schools (see Figure 8.10) and contribute to science education at an elementary-school level (see Figure 8.11).

On a philosophical level, the Chairman's Award makes explicit the question "What is the role of a scientist in the world?" As the students begin to realize the privilege of participation in FIRST, so do they start to discover the responsibility that belonging to "the community of science" entails. While the physical robot teaches the principles of engineering and science, the Chairman's Award motivates students to search for the highest principles of citizenship.

8.6   GRT Is Different from High School

Students participating on the Gunn Robotics Team find that their experience in the program is quite different from the rest of high school, and while both high-school classes and robotics teams are effective in their own way, it is

Figure 8.10

*The robot is brought to the gymnasium for a demonstration
to the entire school.*

worth looking at how the two programs differ. High school is structured to
keep students in class for about six hours a day, moving from class to class
every hour or so. The robotics team is more task-centered—students are
expected to work toward a common goal for long periods of time. While the
high-school day is set up like a series of one-hour meetings, meetings for the
robotics team merely punctuate the work sessions. Many high-school
classes adopt the university method of teaching: a "sage on the stage"
imparts knowledge to students. Here, the pedagogical model is closer to that
of a coach/team relationship: a "guide on the side" helps students to acquire
their own knowledge.

> I really like the [fact that it's] student led, student designed, just the engineers
> not actually designing it and the students building it, but the students design-
> ing and building it, getting help along the way if they get stuck. Just using the

Figure 8.11

GRT members traveled to area elementary schools to demonstrate their robot and to teach younger students what engineering design process is all about. Some of these elementary students may be future GRT members!

engineers as mentors more than people who actually do it, design and build it. I really enjoyed that structure.

—Thomas Fuller, GRT 1999

Most of [the engineers] knew when to let us just do our thing and when to jump in and say, "Oh that won't work" and "You're going to waste a lot of time." And they gave a lot of process advice. Instead of just "Do this," they said, "try things in this way and see how that works." It was very good.

—Rebecca Hinden, GRT 1998, 1999

And while the primary objective—teaching students—is the same, the scope of the student work is profoundly different. Typical high-school math and science homework consists of a series of similar problems to solve, each doable in 3 to 15 minutes. Extended projects may include lab write-ups, research reports, and the occasional long-term experiment. The problems encountered when building a FIRST robot are very different. Unlike typical homework, the problems the students solve are neither short nor repetitious.

They are interdisciplinary and are seldom one-dimensional. The robot must work as a whole, so it is impractical to approach design problems one at a time the way homework problems may be approached. And unlike typical high-school extended projects, the robot is big, strong, and extremely ambitious. The students know that if they do not solve all of the design and manufacturing problems effectively, there is a very real possibility that their project will fail.

> Just seeing how much of like a real, tactile, professional thing it is you're doing, how intricate the whole thing is, and how well it works and looks and the complexity of it. And the fact that we're able to get it done and make it work is just, is what is really sort of completely different from anything you can do in high school.
>
> —*Daniel Broderick, GRT 1999*

> Learning things in class is still useful, you know, like I learned how to program and how to do the math, but it can be sort of discouraging. Sometimes you spend your time learning things that you can't even envision on how to apply. So GRT really gave me an opportunity to take what I'd learned and apply it. Learning things in class, the theory, is important, but it doesn't stay with you and you don't really understand it until you've tried to do it. And the stuff I had to apply this year in robotics is stuff that I'll know forever, whereas stuff like in chemistry class or something will be out the door the day summer begins. I think that the opportunity to apply it really sort of ingrained it into me.
>
> —*Ben Hebert, GRT 1999*

Work Level and Obligations

Students must perform at a very high level in order to be successful with our robotics project, and the process is arduous and time-consuming (see Figures 8.12 through 8.17). To new team members and to those outside the team, this is the one dominating feature of robotics.

> Sleep. Eat. GRT!
>
> —*Haru Yamamoto, GRT 1999*

Students are torn between their responsibilities in school and their commitment to the robotics project, and even though we have brought in a stress-management expert to help the students strike a balance between their school life and robotics life, some students have trouble. The school

Figure 8.12

GRT gathers together a few hours after the competition rules are released, on a weekend, ready to get started on their designs.

Figure 8.13

Within a few days of the kickoff, competing groups present their models for design review by engineers and the team.

Figure 8.14

The base group members literally put their noses to the grindstone.

newspaper ran an editorial featuring a graphic of the GRT robot tipping the scales over all of their other schoolwork. The editorial described some members of the team who "use robotics as an excuse when putting off other obligations with the idea that they can cruise through life while taking on far more responsibilities than they can possibly handle." The editorial condemned students who "whine and complain after a late night of robotics work" and who use robotics as an excuse to slack off in school. Even though the program is overseen by a full-time physics teacher at the school, some other teachers are threatened by the program. It is not possible for teachers in a typical class to compete for the attention of students who have become hooked by the sexiness of robotics.

> [One thing] I didn't really realize until three-fourths through it, was that how much you get out of GRT totally had to do with how much you put in it. Because if you were doing another sport and didn't have time to show up, sporadically you'd get there and have no idea what was going on. It wasn't as cool if you were there like all the time. You got so much more out of it. I think just being there and being there all the time and just being able to know that your ideas will get on the robot, and seeing the thing progress; then when problems start you can help and figure it out. It's just so exciting you don't notice you've been there for eight hours and suddenly it's 11 o'clock and you have

Figure 8.15

Working in parallel means sometimes demonstrating the robot when subsystems are not yet finished. Here, a cardboard box stands in for the basket.

five hours of homework to do or something. You just don't notice because you're so enthralled with what you're doing, so into the work.

—Daniel Broderick, GRT 1999

GRT took a lot of my time actually, during the six weeks I didn't do anything else than GRT pretty much. Everything else sort of went into the background and wasn't very important. Although we had finals, I didn't really study for finals because I wanted to do GRT instead of studying. I didn't do that bad I guess. I didn't go home until late in the night and I didn't eat at home. I eat at classes. I just went home for sleep and came to school, went to my classes. Then after going to classes I would go to GRT and put most of the energy into it. Then I would go until late night and then go home. That kind of day repeated everyday.

—Haru Yamamoto, GRT 1999

Figure 8.16

Although prototyping is extremely important, it doesn't prevent every unpleasant surprise. In this full-scale wooden mock-up, the conveyer mechanism is working well enough to move to the next stage, but in the final version the conveyor added too much weight to the robot and had to be eliminated.

> This year I put in a huge amount of time, it was crazy. I had my 83-hour all-nighter, where on the way home I fell asleep while I was talking three times. So it really depends on how involved you are. It doesn't really demand that much commitment. If you love it, that's what you're going to put in.
>
> —*Daniel Lehrbaum, GRT 1997, 1998, 1999 (co-leader)*

However, the robotics program at this school is not meant to somehow supplant traditional education. It is intended to complement it. During the robotics "season," the coach distributes a list of robotics students to all of the teachers in the school and asks them for feedback should any grades drop. Students get the message that schoolwork must come first, and students who let their grades fall too far are suspended from the team until their grades come back up.

Robotics versus Classes

It is important to note that this is not some sort of panacea for the ills that plague education. Unfortunately, team members' grades sometimes go *down*

Figure 8.17

The assembled final version of the robot is complex and impressive, but before the final competition, GRT members will add banners and anodize the aluminum arm black for the right competition "look."

while students are involved in the project, and many teachers have complained how robotics students in their classes are overextended and have become less involved with the day-to-day activities that students are expected to participate in.

And yet the robotics team can be described as a superb educational motivator. While some teenagers sneak around doing drugs or hanging with gangs, we had students sneaking *into* school. On one late night, past midnight, a student came into school saying he had to sneak out of the house and left a note in case his parents woke up saying he went for a walk.

Not only is it difficult for a traditional high-school class to compete with the "coolness" of the Gunn Robotics Team, it would be very hard to find another class where the students learned as much.

I would say that I learned more in six weeks of robotics, more useful stuff, than I did in all four years of high school.

—*Thomas Fuller, GRT 1999*

In school we only get to learn about fundamental sciences and fundamental math, and you don't [learn] applications of either of them very much inside school. And GRT helped me learn a bit about mechanical engineering and how things get applied, like a lot of physics especially. And so it was really good to know that not only was I interested in theoretical sciences and math but also applications of them, so it helped me know what I wanted to go into in the future.

—*Cecile LeCoq, GRT 1998*

It's probably the most worthwhile thing I've done at Gunn. Some of the other cool classes I've done have gotten me interested in things. This was much above and beyond these other things.

—*Daniel Broderick, GRT 1999*

Rather than attempting to supplant all of the traditional math, English, and science courses offered, the robotics program complements traditional high-school education by tapping into emotions and behaviors that we sometimes try to suppress in the regular classroom.

Publicity

All this activity has garnered the team plenty of publicity. They have been featured on local TV news, network TV news, Spanish-language news, and a syndicated show on high-tech innovations. They have been covered by several major newspapers and by a robotics magazine. They are famous, in a way. When one of the team leaders, an accomplished cellist, gave a solo performance with a local symphony, the concert program described his robotics accomplishments in as much detail as it described his musical accomplishments.

It's nice to be recognized for what you're doing. And, you know, that people agree with us that it's something valuable and important.

—*Ben Hebert, GRT 1999*

This publicity motivates the team still more. The students know (or soon find out) that they will have to make trade-offs between the time they commit to the robotics team and the time they spend on other extracurricular activities, and they often chose robotics over ski trips and dance committees. While the robotics program is meant to complement the academic program at this school, not compete with it, it is worth looking at how robotics motivates students so much more than the typical high-school class.

Role Models

FIRST expects high-school students to work on this project with mentors from industry. Just as young basketball players learn about basketball by watching professionals in the NBA, so Dean Kamen expects young students to learn about engineering by working with professional engineers from successful companies. Since they are working with professionals, the students are almost obligated to work at a professional level, and they can see how things are *supposed* to get done. An additional benefit of working with professionals is that the students can develop role models and heroes from the real world—people with attainable jobs, as opposed to sports and media celebrities, whose jobs are one in a hundred million.

Do the students embrace this opportunity to work with professionals? Only to a certain extent at Gunn. They *like* working with the engineers, they learn from the engineers, and they respect the engineers, but they want to build their robot by themselves.

> Engineers, the shop workers, they were just absolutely amazing. They treated us as professionals and they gave us as much respect as we gave them. And it was just a really amazing experience, they really knew what they were doing, they taught us what we were doing, and they would always help us when we were going to screw up.
>
> *—Damien Hendricksen, GRT 1997, 1998*

> First of all, they're like textbooks. You can run ideas by them and they'll tell you if it's going to work or not. And the transition between the mind, paper, and wood to actuality, they helped each step along. If we didn't have them [engineers], we'd have to go through all the steps to find out some things wouldn't work.
>
> *—Ken Horne, GRT 1997 (co-leader), 1998 (team leader)*

> I'm in awe, like some of them have saved my ass from screwing up so many times, it's countless. It's amazing how quickly they can help you. They're always there, they're willing to lend a hand, they're just great people. They got me excited about the field, really. They're an inspiration to me.
>
> *—Zack Fisher, GRT 1999*

If we did something wrong, they would see if we could see it first, which I really liked, they'd ask, "Do you think this is really going to work, is the math working out? Is that going to be possible? Do we have the right materials for it? Can you even build it?"

—Eugene Kim, GRT 1997 (co-leader), 1998

Students often comment that they learn more and do more on our team than they ever did in class. While this creates something of a conflict for students who are expected to attend high-school classes for six hours a day before they can start work on their robotics project, the results in the end are well worth it.

The structure is rejuvenating for the adults as well. Hank Schwoob, a master machinist from NASA who works with the team, commented that he often spends his days writing code for the CNC machines at NASA instead of doing hands-on machining as he was trained to do. Now he says that he really enjoys getting out and working with high-school students, teaching them the operations of metal-working machines. It is clear that the students also enjoy their working relationship with this expert.

GRT Is Intensely Fun

One of the things that astonishes new student team members and mentors is how exciting and intense the whole project becomes because of the competition. You start by solving problems and building a few mechanisms and suddenly it is like you are on the stage at a rock concert, or on the field at the Super Bowl. Marching bands, cheerleaders, and the press all want to celebrate your science project, and Mickey Mouse personally shakes your hand (see Figure 8.18).

Certainly, having human drivers and including a human player contributes a sports feel to the event. The cheering of the spectators rivals that at many sporting events; the emotional involvement of the spectators is especially intense as they are the very students and engineers who put an incredible amount of time and effort into building the robot (see Figures 8.19 and 8.20).

In wrestling, it's a competition sport where you're going to matches. It's a lot the same because when I was out there driving the robot I would feel the same adrenaline rush as I would when I was out on the mat wrestling, and it's a lot like a sports competition where you're head to head, competing with someone, not just like competing for grades, but you're really in there competing with an opponent in an engineering competition.

—Chuck Anderson, GRT 1997, 1998

Figure 8.18

Teams gather at the main stage of the national competition to witness the final matches. To stand out, teams carry banners and noisemakers, wear matching T-shirts and buttons, and cheer like crazy for their robots.

Once the competition's started, I don't even remember what I do, I just, like, focus. I can't remember anything I did, afterward. We were watching a video-tape of our match, and we actually played with Woodside [High School], and I don't remember any of it. I don't even remember if they were our allies or what. It's like, whoa.

—*Alvin Cheng, GRT 1999*

When we got into the finals, a couple of us on the pit crew got to come in and wait backstage with all the tools in case something went wrong. So we're right behind where it's happening, very close-up view, closer than we got before, we got a great view of everything that's happening, and it's just, just so damn nerve wracking, and you get so anxious, I mean, it's stressful, you're worried if things are going to work, you really want everything to go right, it makes you nuts, and I want to do it again!

—*Zack Fisher, GRT 1999*

Figure 8.19

GRT's method of standing out in a crowd was unusual hair styles and a special yell.

Well, I don't think it would fascinate me as much as a sports-playing robot would. It's different from what I had expected engineering to be. It's a lot more exciting than creating a product and possibly making money off of it. Tossing balls. Competition adds a lot more to it. It's exciting and intense.

—*Kevin Gabayan, GRT 1998, 1999*

I guess the whole thing is fun because maybe to me I've never done this before. It's all new. The whole thing just has a huge impact. This is my first time and yet I felt I'm doing something that's very solid, rather than watching TV or doing passive stuff. I felt like part of this whole GRT organization. I'm doing something that's—there.

—*Haru Yamamoto, GRT 1999*

Figure 8.20

NASA is a major supporter of FIRST, and its Ames Research Center sponsored the first West Coast Regional in 1999. They were able to capture much of the excitement of the national competition.

Parental Involvement

The typical high-school parent knows little about the day-to-day things that happen to their children at school. It was interesting to watch over the years as the amount of parental involvement grew.

The first year, 1997, was marked primarily by disappointment at the small amount of time that parents were seeing their children. Many of the students would go for many days without ever seeing their parents, as they were at school at all times except when they slept, and in some cases, even then.

The next year, 1998, started to have more individual parent involvement as Mr. Dunbar realized that this was a resource that should not be ignored. Parents were responsible for managing the group finances (banks prefer to deal with people who are over 18). Parents helped to supervise the students' work hours. One parent noted that the time he spent in the school brought him much closer to his son.

In 1999, parents were even more devoted to the class. Many of the parents started their own booster club to help finance the travel. Parents also realized that their children were not coming home for dinner and were usually eating fast food or snacks to get by. Many of them started to bring breakfast and dinners for the 40 or 50 students working there. By feeding everyone they guaranteed that their children would eat well. They brought turkey dinners, home-cooked pasta, salads, full meals. All the students as well as the adult volunteers were very thankful to these generous parents.

My father is an engineering type. He came in the shop with my mom and when she asked when we would be home that night, I said, "Late" and she said, "By 11?" and I said, "Ummm," and my dad said, "Yup, see you at 11 AM!" and then they walked out. It was kind of funny. My mom saw how much me and my brother loved it and they've been supporting us. They bring us food. They brought full turkeys twice and they paid for our trip to Florida and they haven't given us too much grief over staying up late.

—*Brad Pflum, GRT 1998, 1999 (co-leader)*

I spent a lot of time, too much time for my parents. They disagreed in some respects, they disagreed with the fact that I was staying a little late and that I was using a little time. But they like that I got involved and I was learning. They were actually amazed that we did so well and it was good that I contributed.

—*Sherri Dairiki, GRT 1999*

8.7   Students Do Everything—Almost

When we say the GRT students do everything, in fact students are the main instigators for everything from raising funds, to organizing the team, to running meetings. They design every component of the robot; cut, machine, and weld the parts; and assemble them. The students use AutoCAD and early prototyping in wood to get started, then progress to sheet metal bending, machining on a lathe and mill, arc welding, and other tooling operations. This is not to say that the adult advisors don't contribute to the success of the project, but the students set the tone and direction for most of the tasks and vastly prefer it to be that way.

GRT Is Student Run

Something about owning the robotics team motivates students profoundly. Some of the students had never really pushed themselves, never launched themselves heart and soul into a project before they joined the group. During robotics, they become possessed. They come to the robotics lab first thing each morning. They eat lunch in the room, work there during class breaks and after school, eat dinner there, and stay there until someone kicks them out.

> My philosophy, I think students learn the best when they are put on the same level as engineers because it's so intimidating to sit next to someone with a Ph.D., someone who is just, like, brilliant—they know how to solve these problems. "Why should I be able to think of anything better than that, there's no way I could be better than these guys." To some extent, people have a huge amount of talent and some people may be really good at it, but other people can think of things that are just as good or better even if they don't have necessarily as much experience.
>
> And I think if students are put in a position where their opinions are valued and their designs are valued and people listen to them, suddenly they can rise to that new level. I think the one thing is that people fill the shoes that you put them in. If the engineers and advisors put them in really big shoes, they are going to fill them. They will do the things they need to do to get the job done. Especially if they are, you know, dedicated to the cause. People can do incredible things.
>
> They're not always going to come up with something brilliant, but they're always going to come up with something to be proud of in the end. And I think the biggest part of this project is this, to be able to do something you're proud of. To accomplish something.
>
> —*Daniel Lehrbaum, GRT 1997, 1998, 1999 (co-leader)*

Because GRT requires interdisciplinary approaches to problems, it encourages and empowers students to look more broadly for solutions. A GRT member relates that he was on a team of three students for a physics class in which they were to give a physics demonstration at an elementary school. He saw a large rod of brass, weighing hundreds of pounds, in the industrial arts room and realized it would be ideal for their demonstration. The other students wouldn't have presumed to ask to use it, he surmised; however, our GRT member knew he could since Mr. Dunbar was also the physics teacher.

> In GRT, you're allowed to use the materials at hand. There's no one there to say you can't use the material like "You'll probably waste the materials, you'll probably do something stupid with it." It's assumed that you'll probably do something right. If you do it wrong, you'll do it better the next time. The material and everything in the entire program is there for the student.

There's no rules limiting you. It's your judgment whether you think it's smart or not. That's something that doesn't usually happen with teachers in school. They usually think like the student doesn't have good enough judgment to decide this, so they'll give these guidelines of rules.

—*Daniel Broderick, GRT 1999*

Adult-Run Teams

This entirely student-run philosophy is not true for all teams participating in the FIRST Robotics Competition. It is one extreme of student participation. In the other extreme, a team of adult engineers design and build the robot with minimal student involvement except for the required student drivers and human players. It is logical that new teams would start out with heavy adult involvement and as a knowledge base was built over a few years of competing, the teams would move toward being more student-run. We find that as adult advisors, the fear of disappointment and failure is a strong force that pushes adults to intervene at sometimes inappropriate moments. It takes enormous wisdom to know when to back off and let students make their own way, and we have learned painful lessons when we did it wrong.

The formula for teaming industry with schools usually works very well, though this is not always the case. We witnessed one instance during the 1997 competition where several young students were visibly distraught. They were frustrated that they had no input in the design of their robot, little input on the building, and worst of all, their robot was not faring well in the competition. This extreme, however, is now rare. The bulk of the teams share the design and building between students and engineers to different extents. The fact that other teams typically have more engineer input on the design and building of the robots actually makes the competition more special to the GRT students.

It's really great that the students work on this. Like when we just played [another team], when we broke their basket, you see engineers out there fixing it and not students. I think that's one thing that's really great about being in a student-run thing, and even though it seems like it's hard to have a student leader, it shouldn't turn out bad.

—*Alvin Cheng, GRT 1999*

It's a point of pride that when you look at the GRT team before, during, and after a match, there are students who fix the robot and not swarms of adults. The students realize they are at a level where they not only can build a complex robot, but they can compete at a professional engineering level.

> When you watch your robot out there that you spend all that time doing and you know that it's 100% you and that no one else, other than the team, did it, then it's really amazing because it gives you a much greater sense of pride because you know that you made it and you were able to make it work perfectly without anyone coming in to hold your hand. You know that what you are seeing is a product of only you and your teammates, and that is what makes it all worthwhile.
>
> *—Daniel Broderick, GRT 1999*

Each team eventually has to find the best balance of adult-student interaction in its own way. What we believe is that, although it is tempting for adults to step in and produce a successful robot, there are possibly greater-lasting benefits to be had by trusting students to perform beyond expectations.

8.8   How GRT Affects Students

Through their participation in robotics, the students gain many skills including mechanical intuition, importance of communication in large groups, leadership, time management, presentation, and self-confidence (see Figure 8.21). Many are affected deeply by the social contacts they make, change their outlook on engineering, and gain the enthusiasm to start projects on their own.

Move a Molecule, Change the Future

Nearly every student involved in GRT will say that GRT has either solidified their desire to go into engineering as a college major or pushed them in that direction. Many feel that GRT will be a strong part of their memories of this period of life.

> Because I joined GRT I got a better look at engineering. I kind of wanted to go into medicine earlier on, but now I kind of want to go into medicine that has an engineering aspect to it. And so I'm thinking of going into biomedical engineering, and I think it's going to be a booming field and I think GRT has helped me come to that decision.
>
> *—Elaine Lu, GRT 1998*

Figure 8.21

The entire team turns out for a nighttime practice round.

Bess and I, since we're both seniors going to college next year, going into engineering, we talked a lot with [engineers] Mark and Geoff about what field we should go into, which college would be better for what we're studying.

—Kristen Jesse, GRT 1997

The biggest influence of GRT is that it has made my mind up to major in mechanical engineering. There's no question now after going through this competition for 2 years, it's what I want to do, and that's a pretty big influence that's happened to me.

—Chuck Anderson, GRT 1997, 1998

Oh, it definitely was a direction-changing kind of experience. This has changed everything about what I'm going to do in the future. I've learned, picked up, so much practical knowledge from trying to do this, about engineering, it's great.

—Zack Fisher, GRT 1999

This is a big thing in my life, and I probably will always reflect on it and what I learned—not only about the technical aspects, but also about myself as a person.

—Eugene Kim, GRT 1997 (co-leader), 1998

Figure 8.22

Making repairs to the robot in the pit at Moffet Field's Hangar One.

Mechanical Engineering

Students get an intuition about mechanical engineering that is missing in even many undergraduate curricula. They get a hands-on gut feeling for what will work and what won't work when designing and building mechanisms (see Figure 8.22).

> You could speak volumes about the stuff I've learned. This is all practical application stuff, I've never built something this complicated before. Like it's the whole process, you have to design it, you have to make it work, you have to prototype it, you learn how things are going to fit together, you learn about the real world by building stuff in the real world.
>
> I was kind of floating before, I was thinking computers, programming, stuff like that. But, I got so much time with some hands on, building stuff in the shop, it was just great.
>
> *—Zack Fisher, GRT 1999*

I came in freshman year without knowing what the word "torque" meant. I probably know more about forces than many people who haven't done robotics in my grade. I'll look at something and say, "Oh I could make that by doing this." I came in knowing nothing about that two years ago, but now I have a lot more mechanical knowledge than before.

—*Rebecca Hinden, GRT 1998, 1999*

It wasn't until this project that I actually discovered that I liked engineering, the process of planning and building a robot, or something that does a task. I surprised myself by looking forward to 15-hour days working on the robot. So definitely, in college I'm going to be doing some sort of engineering.

—*Ben Chui, GRT 1997, 1998*

It's probably going to decide my college major. I'm really thinking of mechanical engineering right now.

—*Justin Bertain, GRT 1997, 1998*

Before I was thinking of majoring in computer science, which is already toward that direction, but now I might look at a double major, in computer science and maybe some engineering field.

—*Kai Huang, GRT 1997, 1998*

Self-Confidence

By building a very complex robot, something that many adults and engineers have never done, the students learn a great deal of self-confidence. This also stems from the "students do everything" philosophy. The students are proud of this team.

I think the biggest influence that GRT has had was working with a lot of people on a unified goal. The robotics team showed what a group of people could do together that worked hard, and that definitely influenced me towards the future, showing me that I can go out and take on bigger, more ambitious challenges. And that's sort of what I did after the first year of GRT, I did this summer animation project that I wouldn't have thought of doing before.

—*Daniel Chuang, GRT 1997, 1998*

There was a lot of "We can do anything now. we can build anything." I really do think we can do a lot.

—*Gabe Rotberg, GRT 1999*

This experience beyond anything really boosted my confidence in math and science. Like when you really see these things applied . . . because when you're sitting there in physics class and you say, "Oh, that's torque, that's really nice. It's like an arrow." But when you actually see it applied onto this arm of your robot, and you see it being pushed . . . it's just incredible.

—Betty Seto, GRT 1997

Social Interactions

We have observed an interesting social dynamic on this team. Students have a really good time. The Gunn Robotics Team has provided a place on campus where it is cool to be enthusiastic about technology, where it is cool to spend extra time at school. These students have their own social life within the group, and students from different parts of campus get to know each other and become like family.

For me it was a lot of the people too, not just the building the robot. I got to meet people I didn't know before and I got to be really good friends with everyone on the team. And that was a great experience for me. It was one of the best things about the team, that's what made it great for me.

—Gabe Rotberg, GRT 1999

Here the students are accepted for who they are with much less emphasis on social cliques than elsewhere on campus. The team members have diverse backgrounds—there are cheerleaders, prom queens, special education students, jocks, geeks, artists, musicians, wealthy, not-so-well-to-do. The grade point averages of the students varies from almost failing to above 4.0. Despite this diversity, many of the students find a bond among themselves. They start to hang out together (see Figure 8.23).

Yeah, the interaction was really important. And with robotics, you get a really wide spread of cultures and people from different schools. There's a lot of cliques at school, and with robotics a lot of the barriers come down. They're just working on the project and not really worrying about who they're working with.

—Eric Henderson, GRT 1998, 1999

At the end, many would state that though they never knew each other before robotics, they now are the best of friends.

Figure 8.23

A team good-luck ritual.

Community

The students on the team are active in the school and the community, and they are quick to volunteer as a group to do community service or help out with school projects. The parents get involved, too, and this is one place on campus where whole families feel involved and welcome.

Because of the Chairman's Award, students have started to integrate social service into the fabric of GRT even between competitions. Each year they take the previous year's robot on a tour of area elementary schools, doing presentations for hundreds of students about their GRT experience and then running a mini–design competition for the elementary students to give them the feel for what the GRT does. This is especially heartening for the adult advisors in seeing that the students become advisors themselves. In the fall of 1999, a group of GRT students became mentors to a group of physically challenged elementary-school students in the FIRST Lego League Competition.

Leadership

Since GRT is a student-run organization, many of the students learn leadership skills. They learn that effective leaders do not merely boss other people around all of the time, nor do they do all of the work themselves. Team leaders delegate *responsibilities*, not tasks. Everyone on the team must be responsible for something—the students must *own* the robot.

> Something I learned about being a leader is that you have to be the bad guy a lot of the time and it's definitely not fun. And if you try to please everyone, it backfires and you make a mess of things.
>
> —*Brad Pflum, GRT 1998, 1999 (co-leader)*

> I think this whole project taught me a lot about leadership and about how it's completely a juggling act. Just keep everyone happy, and they'll get the work done. I learned a lot from this project. And I'm still thinking about engineering, maybe cinematography. Maybe both.
>
> —*Yisha Zhang, GRT 1997 (animation team leader), 1998*

Large Projects and Time Management

This project teaches the students about completing projects of large complexity and magnitude. They learn that teamwork is essential, and they learn what it feels like to be responsible to a group. They learn that they must set priorities and make trade-offs in their lives. They cannot just dabble superficially in a myriad of activities, the way many high-school students do in an effort to embellish their college applications.

> GRT helped me know more what I could do and what people my age could do, and I had never really done something that big before, that was so much of an undertaking. And I was really amazed how we could get corporations to listen to us, and to give us money. And how we could do this whole big thing.
>
> —*Brid Arthur, GRT 1998*

> I really know now that you can't procrastinate, I mean, sometimes you can during school, but like this, if you try to procrastinate, you're kind of really messed up.
>
> —*Natalia Loyola, GRT 1999*

Group Organization and Teamwork

Often with large complex projects comes the coordinated organization of groups of people. This experience is unique in an academic setting where individual evaluation is stressed and cooperation often considered cheating. In real engineering situations, group work is the norm and an essential skill.

> You learn so much, you learn how to work with a group of people that you may not necessarily agree with, and you sort of learn a bit of humility when things don't go the right way.
>
> *—Rebecca Hinden, GRT 1998, 1999*

> I got a ton of experience working in large groups, and that's something I've never done before, making decisions in large groups, and stuff like that, and just people relationships and working with people. I learned how to work and that you have to really work to show and convince people that what you think is what they should do.
>
> *—Thomas Fuller, GRT 1999*

> Through GRT you could see that, just with the 40 people, you needed someone to organize it, and even with 40 people and all the organizing and planning that went on in the weeks before the competition began, there were a lot of problems. There were times when people just wouldn't come to this or that. The gripper wouldn't fit because it was too large and there was a miscommunication. And that showed how important communication really was and how organization was even more important. And this was just with 40 people. And it gives you a better idea of how the real world works with huge organizations, such as Xerox, where there's hundreds or thousands of people, just working. It gives you a better idea of how much organization is needed to make something like this work, for little parts to actually work together to make a better whole, a better product in the end.
>
> *—Anand Karsan, GRT 1998*

Presentations and "Total Writing"

Team members give many presentations during the year—to companies during fund-raising and to large groups during community outreach. From preschool show-and-tell to high-school English classes, students are taught that presentation skills are important, but when GRT members realized that funds to make the robot came directly as a result of their presentations, they were suddenly very motivated to become effective communicators.

> I especially learned how to give presentations because we did a lot of campaigning to get money, and at the first presentation I was really nervous, like

what do I say? But by the last one it was like clockwork, so I'm glad I had that experience, that should prove useful.

—Rebecca Hinden, GRT 1998, 1999

The model for fund-raising for the students is not the typical bake sale and car wash that sports boosters use. Since Gunn sits in the heart of Silicon Valley, where start-ups and IPOs are commonplace, the students approach industry as if they were start-up companies looking for venture capital. In 1998 the students raised over $40,000. This is more money than Gunn's entire science, math, and English departments' budgets combined. Although this is a lot of money, many FIRST participant teams raise far more in contributions.

One of the research topics within PARC is looking at how reading and writing will change and grow with the maturing of new technologies. Many students today are learning Web design and multimedia production as part of future "total writing" and authoring skills. A group of GRT students used PARC's video resources to edit together documentaries, computer animation, and promotional video materials for them to use in presentations. Here they learned the value of being able to tell a good story with visual tools for a wide variety of audiences.

GRT has pointed me toward engineering as my major or as a career, but that's not definite. It's given me ideas of what I want to do, like maybe I want to go into media and do documentary, it's given me a lot of things to look at.

—Kei Park, GRT 1998

Outside of the Competition

The students' motivation and dedication to the program has empowered them to perform miracles outside the boundaries of GRT. Not only do they build a robot and produce a computer animation for FIRST, but they have purchased a pickup truck and converted it to electric power. They have built props for the theater department. They have hosted engineering challenges at local elementary schools. They have entered and dominated the "Sand Hill Challenge," the local high-tech soapbox derby. They have designed balloon drops for dances and spectacular homecoming floats. They have made presentations to the top executives at major companies.

One summer about 10 students formed a little company to make a feature-length computer-animated movie. They were inspired by their animation experience and by *Toy Story*, a movie that took many millions of dollars and many thousands of computer hours and hundreds of programmers to create. The students didn't quite succeed in producing a full feature, but they met almost every day during the bulk of the summer and created a respectable trailer.

Another year a group of students decided to spend their summer building a holonomic mobile base. This is currently the study of many Ph.D. graduate students in robotics. They spent time learning the principles and then took an existing design and successfully implemented the base. Again this was all on their own initiative, contacting and visiting research centers, acquiring parts, and designing and building it on their own time.

Sportsmanship

We expect students to learn about sportsmanship, too. All of the teams in this competition work hard, and all of the teams experience the pain of losing a match at some point or another. We have had some negative experiences, and the students who have learned so well how to deal with setbacks in mechanical systems must also learn how to deal with setbacks in competitions.

> The success of the robot means a lot. In the regionals when we first started and we had a lot of trouble, we felt bad about it, but I think the success doesn't mean as much as the fact that we really did it. If we didn't do so well, I think we would have been heartbroken, but we knew what the robot could do and we knew that we had done a really, really great thing, and I think that would have been enough for at least some of us.
>
> —*Gabe Rotberg, GRT 1999*

8.9 Corporate Involvement with Schools

As with sports programs, a robotics program of this magnitude does not achieve success without a tremendous amount of support from the school, parents, and the community. A program like GRT would not be possible if it were to use the standard support model of a school class or a club. FIRST, by setting an extraordinarily high expectation for learning and then backing up those expectations by delivering a truly exciting experience for students and engineers alike, has opened possibilities for funding and support that are as creative and diverse as the design projects themselves.

The FIRST competition arena alone is itself an enormous engineering project, tantamount to building a sports or concert arena from scratch, complete with television support, sound systems, lighting, concession stands, parking, and a giant pit area for all the robot machine and repair work that needs to be done. As a nonprofit organization, FIRST depends on the largesse of some pretty big names from multi-billion-dollar companies to raise the money it needs to put on this level of production—people like Paul Allaire, the CEO of Xerox Corporation and chairman of FIRST; David Brown, a VP of Fidelity who was lured to be executive director of FIRST; Ralph Larsen, CEO of Johnson and Johnson and member of the FIRST board—and on organizations such as Disney and NASA. FIRST does this by appealing to contributors not at the guilt level, but at their highest level of altruism. The prospect of contributing to such a positive learning event has a great gut appeal to anyone concerned with education and the sciences. At the national competitions, you can see board members, casually dressed CEOs of multi-billion-dollar companies, beaming with pride at the level of excellence achieved by the high-school teams and at the enthusiasm of the crowds.

> In an age where technology turns fantasy and fiction into reality, and the need for a qualified workforce becomes even stronger, FIRST has developed a program to capture even the most disinterested students, and create in them an interest in science and technology. FIRST provides young people the opportunity to work with professionals from industry and education to build a working task-oriented robot. It develops a student's ability to work as a member of a team, stay focused on a task, think creatively, test ideas, and learn hands-on technology skills.
>
> As chairman of the FIRST board, I have watched FIRST have a profound effect on the lives of its participants. Other members of the FIRST board such as Gary Tooker, chairman of Motorola; Vernon Loukes, chairman of Baxter International; and John Alele, chairman of Boston Scientific, have witnessed the same. Engineers have experienced a renewed commitment to their profession, students are demanding a stronger curriculum in science and technology, and communities have rallied around the teams from their district. FIRST has renewed hope in creating technology heroes and celebrated science.
>
> *—Paul Allaire, CEO of Xerox Corporation, chairman of FIRST*

At the local level, teams face a large financial challenge. Robotics turns out to be a project that involves tens of thousands of dollars, which goes toward travel, parts, shipping, entry fees, machining, documentation, videotape, editing, posters, computers, software packages, and matching T-shirts. As the teams become more popular and get larger every year, the total costs increase proportionally.

Teams also need help with engineering. Many schools that would like to participate have more than enough enthusiasm and energy but lack the engineering expertise within the group to design and build a successful robot. This is not a project whose requirements are contained in the standard high-school curriculum. Rather, it needs expertise in machining of metal, materials science, structures, electric motors and pneumatics, control systems, embedded programming, as well as video production, editing, graphics, 3D software. The people with these skills are found in corporations. For both the financial contributions and engineering expertise, it becomes an obvious thing to form partnerships between high schools and corporations. And this is how FIRST designed it to be.

It is often difficult to envision how corporations and schools can interact. Schools have been described as the "tightest of oligarchies," over which local school boards exert complete control. If you were, say, a financial specialist and wanted to teach a rudimentary course in money management at your local high school, there would be no mechanism that would allow you to do this. Corporations are often very tightly guarded entities as well. If a school were to approach a corporation for a donation, there is often no mechanism in place that would even allow such a contribution to be made.

GRT's involvement with Xerox PARC began slowly, at the grass-roots level, when a few engineers became involved with the team as volunteers and mentors. As the scope of the project grew, it became clear that the project had taken on a life of its own, and the engineers started asking other coworkers to help out in their own areas of expertise, such as video editing. At the conclusion of the first year's competition, the volunteer engineers sponsored a presentation, featuring the entire GRT team and the robot, to all of PARC. This brought the project to the attention of the senior staff.

It was this activity that inadvertently set the stage for the next level of fund-raising. Flushed with success, the then-junior members of the team planned a strategy of fund-raising that would surpass anything ever seen before. Determined and fearless, they presented a proposal to the mentors. Being meek engineer types, the mentors were aghast at the amount of money they were asking for and suggested they tone the whole thing down. Then, thinking better of the idea, the mentors asked if they would be willing to do a practice presentation to some people with more experience in fund-raising. The mentors brought two of the team members together with a senior staff member and another senior member, Dr. John Knights, a physicist who had been involved with both educational research and had managed a start-up company.

The GRT presentation went something like this: "This is a deserving project. We work hard and would like your support. Please think about us and if you can spare some money, we really can use it."

The critique came back loud and clear: "Be bold. Be clear you want to be the best. Put down the biggest number you can think of. Strive for the top. Go for the gold and ask for the world."

The new strategy paid off, and soon after the presentation to PARC's senior staff, GRT was informed that a significant fraction of their proposal was approved. The GRT fund-raising team went on to present to many other companies. Sometimes they were successful and sometimes they were not, but they learned an invaluable lesson in the world of business that nobody could have taught them in a class.

The robotics project turned out to be a starting point for some other corporate-school intermingling as well. One of the engineers, Ken Kreiger, so enjoyed his involvement with GRT that he offered a short course on designing digital circuits to the robotics team members after the competition in Florida. The PARC mentors were able to hire GRT veterans as summer interns on various projects within PARC, knowing that they were fully capable of working on a complex project with deadlines. The students continue to use PARC facilities and personnel to produce documentary video for the project, and GRT is currently on the road demonstrating their robot to PARC and other companies. Both the school and the corporate organizations have been able to benefit from these relationships (see Figure 8.24).

As an industrial research institution, most of PARC's energies are focused on striving to provide impactful science and technology innovation in support of Xerox's strategic intent. At the same time we recognize the benefits of engaging the expertise, know-how, and talent of our community in support of outside individual and local endeavors, particularly ones related to science, technology and education. We increasingly understand that as small as these activities might be, they contribute not only directly to our local surroundings, but also indirectly to the nurturing of those diverse resources from which our enterprise will hopefully draw upon in the future. The FIRST robotics program is an example of such an opportunity that was proposed through the initiative and interest of our staff. It represents a synergy between technical and creative content and promotes shared values of teamwork and competition. It is an example of what we strive to be about.

—*Dana Bloomberg, Xerox PARC vice president of operations*

It is important to remember that corporate resources and mentors' time are not infinite. Time limitations become clear when the students want to work around the clock and need adult supervision, and there aren't enough adults that want to stay up past midnight. Contributions of cash or in-kind donations are subject to internal corporate manipulations and are not always a constant, dependable source of funding. As we learn more about

Figure 8.24

Corporate sponsors are acknowledged with a tasteful display of logos on the robots themselves.

how these programs are received, we can suggest some ingredients for successful corporate-school relations:

- *A corporate champion:* There should be a senior person with budgetary authority that can say, "Yes, we support this project. We want involvement in this to be part of our work culture." Many corporate champions are heavily involved with education or the sciences and see the value to a program like this immediately.

- *Grass-roots champions:* These are the engineers and other mentors that spend hours with the students working together and solving problems. These mentors need great discipline not to take over and do the task, but let the students solve the problems, often in a nonoptimal way. It is not uncommon for this involvement to be an official part of an engineer's work responsibilities, but often it is done completely during after-work hours and weekends.

- *Student outreach:* Students are their own best emissaries for publicizing this project. It is extremely effective to have students in corporate situations to present their work. This builds a bridge of familiarity that works its way into the corporate fabric.

- *Planning ahead:* As with all projects, it is important to make clear the budget requirements during the budget planning cycle for the next year. Cash support is not always the only way to help. In-kind donations are very important for supporting the team activities.

 ## 8.10   Ingredients for Success

If we measure the success of an educational program by the amount that students learn and the extent to which the program influences their lives, clearly we have stumbled upon a formula for a successful educational program. The students, parents, and members of industry rave about how delighted they are with the GRT experience. The structure of the FIRST competition, coupled with the parental and corporate support described above, provides the foundation for the project. The freedom of the students to run their own group is a key component in our own recipe for success. The rest of the formula may be characterized by the breaking of barriers that crop up in traditional education.

What Is Cool and What Is School?

This project blurs the distinction and breaks the barrier between what is cool and what is school. When our team displays their projects, hundreds of students turn up to watch. We generate bigger crowds than do the spirit rallies. It is cool to be on the robotics team, and GRT must turn away many applicants each year.

> I was in Mr. Dunbar's physics class, and he showed us the promotional video from last year, and it just looked so cool, you know, all these people, these kids, all involved in doing this really cool thing. I mean something that I had never seen kids do before and I didn't know that people my age could do that sort of thing, and it just sounded so neat.
>
> *—Brid Arthur, GRT 1998*

> It's the experience working in teams and stuff like that and building a robot and seeing the stuff you made go out and whup other robots. It's fun. It's cool. Before I was on GRT, I saw the robot on the quad, and wow, that's really phat! I'm going to build one of those next year.
>
> *—Daniel Broderick, GRT 1999*

Teacher/Student Barrier

GRT breaks the teacher/student barrier, too. The teacher and the adult mentors are on the students' side. It is us—all of us—against the robot. Students report again and again how much they enjoy working *with* the adult engineers with the team, rather than *for* them.

> I worked with Ken Krieger and Mark a lot and I really enjoyed that, that was a lot of fun. It was really great to come up with ideas and have them critique them, and not just say, "This is what you can do," but say, "You might want to think about this." And as you come up with more ideas, have them critique it again, and have them working alongside of you, really respecting you, respecting your decisions. It was really great.
>
> —*Thomas Fuller, GRT 1999*

The next challenge is to get school administrators on board. While the level of corporate giving is often astounding to school administrators, this project does not fit into any of the tech-prep categories that they are used to.

Social and Gender Barrier

By interacting and bonding with other students whom they might otherwise never get to know, the students break social and gender barriers. GRT and FIRST strive to get a diverse group of students involved in science and engineering. By reaching out to female and minority students while they are in high school, and giving them this opportunity to gain confidence in design and manufacturing, the young adults on GRT arrive in college with quite a head start on many of their classmates.

Curriculum Barrier

GRT also breaks curriculum barriers. There are rigid artificial distinctions among science, math, and English courses in school: They are taught in different buildings by different teachers who may or may not coordinate their programs. Since these and many other studies are essential to the building of the robot, it would seem silly to try to separate a math problem from a science problem. Physics, calculus, material science, statics, and dynamics problems come up daily, and the students do not have time to reflect upon the fact that most of them have never even taken these classes yet. They break the curriculum barriers by diving in and solving problems by hook or by crook.

8.11   Academic Motivation

In regular classes many teachers try to use grades to motivate students, and sometimes they miss the mark. It is best for students to push themselves to excel, so teachers give exams to test student achievement and attach a grade to motivate students to do their best. But one of the real problems of high-school education is that grading standards vary widely and continually slip downward. At the same time, students would seem to be foolishly wasting their time if they did anything more than the *minimum* required to get an A in a class. There are plenty of expressions that students use to describe those who do more than they need to in a class—all of them derogatory.

So while grades may provide incentives for students not to do horribly in a class, they may not give students any incentives to truly excel. We all know of students who skate through high school without ever having to work particularly hard to get As. We hear people say that they never really had to work hard—in fact, did not know what hard work was—until they got into college.

So what really does motivate students to learn as much as they can, to work as hard as they can, to truly push themselves to be great? By unleashing the pent-up demons in students, GRT empowers them to *attack* this project. Among the demons released are the following.

Cutthroat Competition

Educators are well aware of the potentially harmful side effects of competition within a class, and books have been written on classrooms without competition. But extracurricular competition is as much a part of high-school culture as cafeteria food, and teachers would be foolish to ignore the power of healthy rivalry. If football players will spend all summer running up and down the field with 15 pounds of pads on so that they may play a game, why should we be surprised that students will put 500 hours into a robot that competes in a similar way?

Assertive Self-Reliance

The students of the GRT manage their own affairs. They raise their own money, buy their own supplies, structure their own organization, and write their own rules. They arrange the furniture. They line up their own supervision and set their own work schedule. The adult members of the team treat the students like adults and they expect them to act like adults. By the time the actual project starts, the students simply expect to design, build, and operate their own robot.

Fear

So often teachers try to shield their students from the disgrace of failure. Even on this team the adult mentors do everything they can to steer the students away from potential traps, but this project is different from typical high-school projects in that the possibility of abject failure looms large as the project progresses. The students know that if their project fails, all of their effort will have been in vain.

Pride and Vanity

Looking good is perhaps the most powerful motivator high-school students ever encounter, and GRT does as much as it can to make this group of students visible on campus and in the community. The students design their own shirts and wear them often. Each year many of the students carve the letters "GRT" into their hair or otherwise distinguish their looks as a team. We want these students to be as proud to be on the Gunn Robotics Team as gang members are to be in a gang.

> A lot of them think it's more cultish, sort of a cult we're all staying there odd hours doing weird stuff at [the industrial arts room] IA5. A lot of them see it as something positive. Some people think that it's something cool that smart people are doing. It's really sort of mixed. I think that one of the reasons that people think it's cool is that the application to news stories we're hearing everyday is more obvious than say a math or science class. It's pretty clear that people could go from building a robot in GRT to building robots for NASA or something. So people see it's cool that high-school students are doing stuff that, you know, the same stuff that highly paid professionals are doing.
>
> —*Ben Hebert, GRT 1999*

8.12 No Losers

The FIRST robotics project is easily the most positive, most educational, most motivational high-tech program that Gunn High School has ever had. The enthusiasm of the students, parents, and mentors is palpable. On cam-

Figure 8.25

At our school's graduation, where individualism is rather discouraged, the members of the Gunn Robotics Team decorate their hats and proudly sit together. In a sea of black mortarboards, the letters "GRT" stand out prominently. Robotics is their identity now, and we are tremendously proud of them.

pus the Gunn Robotics Team's progress can be monitored on the school's marquee and on the daily announcements. Less obvious but even more profound is the progress of the students as they mature through the program.

It's easy to forget what it's like to be a teenager. Teenagers possess all of the intellect, creativity, and physical stamina of adults, but they are largely voiceless and powerless in our communities. The excess energy they possess is phenomenal, and our robotics program gives students a way to channel this energy in a spectacularly positive way. As mentors of the team, we have seen students undergo a distinct transformation as they progress from followers to leaders of the team. Their demeanor and attitude change, and they take a giant step toward adulthood (see Figure 8.25).

For us, the experience has validated our optimism for young people. The three of us share a desire to teach and mentor high-school students, and this program provides a vehicle for us to connect with these students that normal school cannot provide. The students in the Gunn Robotics Team have demonstrated through their work that they can achieve far more than we would normally expect of them in school. This inspires us and reaffirms our faith in the quality of our youth. They are not the slackers, hackers, and gang members so often seen on TV.

Everyone who pays attention to what is happening has figured out that informed creative thinking is the ticket that gets you "in." No matter where you come from, whether you are female or male, no matter what your skin color, if you are sincere and offer new ideas that are factually correct and sensitive to others, folks will thank you and reward you. Informed creative thinking opens doors.

—Woodie Flowers

Whatever you do, it's all worth it for Gunn Robotics. No matter how late the nights, no matter what you're doing, it's all worth it.

—Damien Hendriksen, GRT 1997, 1998

Kid's View

   Trapped with Robots

By Kate Murphy, age 12

What do you think when I say, "Robots"? Do you think about the *Terminator* or *Terminator 2*? Well that's cool, but that is not what I think. Well then, what do I think? Two words, "trapped" and "mom." Why? Let me tell you.

Imagine that you are trapped under a bed in a very messy room. The reason that it is a pig-sty is because an earthquake has hit your city and ruined your home. You're trapped under the bed, and nobody can get to you. Can't imagine that? Well, think about the movie *Twister* when the tornado hit Joe's aunt's house and trapped her so she couldn't get out. That's where my mom comes in with her robots.

Yes, robots! My mom bought a Power Wheels toy jeep from Toys 'R Us, and then made it into a search-and-rescue robot called Silver Bullet. Silver Bullet has about $20,000 of circuits, computers, cameras, and sensors. She (all of my mom's robots are female) can operate by herself, so when something happens to a building and humans can't get in, she can. She carries a "baby" robot and then when she gets to a place were she can't get in, she lets out her baby.

Yes, her baby! As I said, the mother robot lets out a baby robot, just like a kangaroo mommy carries her joey and lets the joey out. The joey robot is named Bujold. Bujold has cameras for eyes to see somebody or something. She doesn't have a computer, so she has a tether to Silver Bullet. Grad students like Jenn Casper and Aaron Gage can radio Silver Bullet, who sends the directions to Bujold through the tether.

My job is to pretend I'm injured and trapped in an earthquake and then get rescued by Bujold. You could say that I have an acting career, but it's not like I'm Drew Barrymore or Lisa Kudrow. Also being in robot demos is nowhere near being in movies, but it is nice to think of that. It is fun to work for my mom because I go to places that I would never dream of, I get to be on TV and in magazines, and when I meet people I get to tell the most amazing life story.

What I do is really just an easy trick that some dogs can do: play dead. Mom asks me to be the victim because I'm small and can fit in hard-to-get-to places. Also, she needs a live person because they give off heat, so Silver

Bullet can see the person with her heat sensor and drop off Bujold. If we're in Tampa, mom has me hide under a bed that used to be mine in a "search and rescue" room at her laboratory. If I'm with mom at a robot conference, I might lie down under a table or be covered up with stuff that looks like sheet rock. The trick to doing this is to just lay down and not make a sound. This can be hard if you have so much you want to say. I recommend thinking of all the fun things you have done and want to do again, and to try not to fall asleep.

Oh, the Places You'll Go is a good book, and I can really relate to it. I have gone to some really awesome places like Montreal, Canada, and Portland, Oregon, for the AAAI robot competitions. I have made some cool friends at these competitions, but most of them are not kids. There's rarely any kids, but there's lots of really neat and smart adults who I want to be like. I love going with my mom on these trips because of how I am helping out.

I have gotten my fair share of publicity (what is a fair share I don't know, but who's counting?). I have been on an Austrian TV show and the local news. I was in some AI magazines a few times. I found out I was more famous than I thought. In the summer of '99, I was lucky enough to go to Space Camp. That was about a week after one of the robot competitions in Orlando. One of the counselors had seen it on the day that I was there with my mom doing my "survivor" act. One day he started talking to my group, "When I was in Orlando, I saw a little girl and her mother with robots. The mother was talking and the girl was playing dead while the robots were trying to find her." As I was leaving his talk, he said, "Oh Kate, the girl looked like you." And I said, "It *was* me!"

One of the many things I've learned is that nobody is perfect doing anything all time, even robots. So yes, I have gotten "robo boo-boos." I remember one time when one of the students was working with Bujold and drove her right at me. Bujold kept on going and hit me in the arm. The robots will do that from time to time when they are being teleoperated and the driver can't see me very well. Mom and her students want to make Bujold autonomous so it won't bump into people, but seeing distances is hard. When you get hurt, the best thing to do is to make a joke out of it, because the person probably didn't mean to. If you don't get up and yell, he or she won't feel really bad over some little scrape.

The robots have become my wire and metal friends. I would be crazy not to be friends with them, because of all the things I have done with them and for them. I have given them so much of my love, my time, and even some of my toys. Once I bought a wolf mask while shopping after a robot conference. Just for fun, we put it on one of my mom's bigger robots that has two cameras like eyes. It fit around the eyes and made the robot look really funky. The students really liked the mask, so I loaned it to them. The mask was used in a robot soccer competition that I didn't go to because it was in Japan. They just now gave the mask back.

Weird is what I am sometimes called by my schoolmates. Sometimes you can tell when it is a joke. But when it is not, I just think that at least I know what is happening in the world and what we can do to help people. And they'll be ones working at McDonald's.

I also get to help with other robot demonstrations. Are you ever stuck having to serve food at a party? Well, at one robot competition, the robots were giving out food, and I was the one who was bringing the food to them. Boy, I ran a lot that day! I learned to have a lot of food on hand, because people like to eat and they like to eat from robots.

As I have said earlier, once you get used to robots, you learn to love them. Other people, especially teachers, love them too. Some teachers will give you extra points if you are able to tie robots into a learning activity. Once I brought in my mouse robot for extra credit in geography. And I have another small robot that you too can get. It's called the LEGO Mindstorms.

Technically, I'm not trapped with robots, they just trap me into working with them because they're fun to be with. You may see robots as bad evil creatures in the movies, but in real life they are good and can save your life. With robots you get a better view of what's to come in the future. And robots have made me more interested in becoming a scientist.

Chapter Nine

Robocamp

One Hands-on Week of Exploring Science through Robotics

Robin R. Murphy
University of South Florida

Michael Rosenblatt
Carnegie Mellon University

Abstract

This chapter describes our experiences conducting a one-week-long science summer camp for sixth to eighth graders since 1997. The camp uses artificial intelligence and robotics as a unifying framework in which to explore the biological and physical sciences. The target audience was preteens who did not necessarily have a significant exposure to science or computers. The camp is designed to handle up to 14 participants at a materials cost of $125 per person or less. The day camp covers a diversity of topics, including the differences between industrial manipulators and AI robots, locomotion, perception, behaviors, gears, Global Positioning System (GPS), and simple circuits. Participants build and keep a working robot, visit a zoo to research locomotion and camouflage behaviors in animals, construct individual Web pages with links to the most interesting robot sites on the Internet, program simple robots, build circuits to represent behavioral programming, and navigate with GPS. Concepts are reinforced through a scaffolding of guided exercises, indoor and outdoor games, bike riding, documentaries, science-fiction movies, and a personal robot project. Participants present their project and Web page to parents and friends during a wrap-up party. The chapter covers our syllabus, exercises, equipment, and lessons learned. It is expected that middle-school teachers, home schoolers, or parents can either duplicate our camp in its entirety or select particular themes of interest. The chapter suggests ways to adapt the camp exercises for use with other kits, videos, and newer technologies such as the LEGO Mindstorms robotic construction system.

9.1   Overview

Since 1997, the Colorado School of Mines (CSM) Office of Special Programs and Continuing Education (SPACE) has sponsored a one-week-long summer day camp on robotics. The pedagogical objectives of the camp are for students entering grades 6–8 to have a general science experience with a robotics theme while learning about career paths and expectations in science. The best overall introduction to the camp is the handout provided to parents in Appendix A (at the end of this chapter).

The Robocamp approach is to create a breadth of interrelated activities enjoyable by everyone, including students signed up by parents who were more excited by robots than their children. The activities are intended to help campers (1) develop basic skills and confidence such as reading directions, assembling kits, and conducting incremental experimentation and (2)

Figure 9.1

CSM Robocamp 98

Call of the Techno-wild!

Robocamp T-shirt showing robots in the CSM Mobile Robots Laboratory out on a camping trip.

provide opportunities for campers to express their creativity. Specific learning objectives for each day build on topics introduced on prior days, and the camp emphasizes connections of the robotic material to the biological, social, and computer sciences. As part of the camp fees, the students get to build and keep a mobile robot and receive a "Robocamp: Call of the Techno-Wild!" T-shirt, shown in Figure 9.1.

Activities fall into one of four categories. Many of the robot activities offer an opportunity to increase student skills in *traditional* educational assignments, such as laboratory work and a science-fair-like project. Several activities encourage campers to integrate robotics with more *liberal arts* types of skills and opportunities for creativity and expression. Another set of activities is tied into the *media and social perceptions of robots*. Even *physical exercise* is melded with the robotics theme; for example, campers compete in sack races mimicking a series of four-legged gaits developed for robots. The camp makes a conscious effort to balance learning styles and social preferences, with some activities being done individually and others in teams.

From an instructor's viewpoint, the use of robot technologies to motivate a broad science education has been successful and exciting. In Robocamp, robots provide the motivation for learning about biology, mechanics, and circuits, as well as developing Web pages, presentations, and considering societal issues. Robocamp has been a success from both a participatory and an administrative perspective. Its enrollment has increased from 10 in 1997 to 14 (full capacity) in 1998, and 14 in 1999. It was the first camp offered by CSM in the 1999 season to reach capacity and have a waiting list. It is expected that the camp will be offered both by CSM and by Young Middle Magnet Math, Science, and Technology School in Tampa, Florida. There is a demand for more sessions at CSM in 2000, but the instructors' schedules cannot accommodate them.

This chapter attempts to provide enough information to permit others to duplicate all or part of Robocamp. First, it describes the target (and actual) audience and the instructors. The organization and daily syllabus is presented in detail, followed by descriptions of each of the major activities. The lessons learned are discussed and recommendations are offered for readers who wish to duplicate some or all of Robocamp. The appendices at the end of the chapter cover sources of materials, including robots, video documentaries, television shows with teachable content, and websites of interest.

9.2   Target Audience and Instructors

CSM has a long tradition of sponsoring science day camps in geology and physics. The idea for Robocamp stemmed from an informal survey of CSM faculty regarding what other kinds of science camp they would like to see CSM sponsor for their own kids. Robotics emerged as one of the top ideas, in part because of the high visibility of the mobile robot laboratory at CSM directed by the first author (including a segment on CNN) and its K–12 activities.

The original audience was students from the metro Denver area entering grades 6–8. This age group was chosen because there are almost no science camps for that group in Denver, ensuring good enrollment. It was also hoped that such a camp could influence participants to take more science and math courses in high school, leading to a career in the sciences. Another consideration was that this age group was easier to work with than high-school groups, where social dynamics have more impact.

The camp was advertised in the *Denver Post* as part of a "directory to camps" special issue and in the CSM faculty/staff and alumni newsletters, and flyers were distributed to suburban middle schools. The fee for the camp was $275, making it nearly twice as expensive as a Denver YMCA or scout day camp. Campers were enrolled on a first-come, first-serve basis, with a maximum of 14 students. This number was chosen because it was the maximum number of students that could be transported in a school van for field trips, and it appeared manageable for two instructors.

The demographics of the camp reflected the higher fee, the advertising decisions, and societal trends in science. In 1997, the camp consisted of 10 white students; 8 males and 2 females. The majority of the students were from families associated with CSM, either as faculty or alumni. In 1998, there were 12 white students and 2 minority students; 11 males and 3 females. The larger enrollment in 1998 reflected an advertising campaign that started earlier in the school year. The 1998 enrollment requests were high enough to justify a second session, but the instructors' schedules could not accommodate it. The small number of female students in both years was a disappointment. It was expected that since the director was a woman the negative perception that "robots are for boys" would be offset. The 1999 camp followed these trends with an enrollment of 14 white students; 12 males and 2 females. There were no prerequisites for the camp (e.g., no minimum grades, no specific science courses, etc.), and the students appeared to represent a normal distribution of abilities

At the beginning of the first day of the camp, each camper completed a survey including questions as to why they were attending the camp. Although the exact number was not recorded, a significant number each year indicated that their parents had been very excited about robots but the camper was not as excited. This suggests that just because campers are attending a robot-oriented camp, it isn't wise to assume they all are highly motivated by robots. At the other end of the spectrum, at least one camper each year came with a detailed sketchbook of robots they had designed and imagined, implying their interest in robotics existed well before they learned of the camp.

An important characteristic of the campers was that in both years, the majority did not show much familiarity with tools or have much spatial comprehension. They were uncomfortable with screwdrivers and often had great difficulty translating assembly diagrams. Each year, only two or three campers (always male) had any experience building kits or models. One impact of this in 1997 was that during the robot kit building activity, the campers often could not figure out how to screw things in, were easily frustrated, and assembled the kit incorrectly. In following years, this problem was alleviated in two ways. First, as a pre-exercise, the campers practiced using tools by screwing in a wide range of screws (both Phillips and slotted) into predrilled wood. The screw heads started large and worked down to smaller sizes, requiring increasing dexterity. Second, because of the 1997 experiences, the instructors were able to anticipate the problems with connecting diagrams to physical reality and therefore work with individual campers more effectively.

Robocamp is ideally taught by two instructors: one with experience in robotics and science, who can answer conceptual questions and take advantage of "teachable moments," and an assistant who helps provide individual attention. The assistant does not need to have a robotics background. It is hoped that this chapter's descriptions of camp organization and activities, as well as the suggested supplemental reading material, will permit instructors of similar camps in the future to have only a general science background.

The lead instructor in 1997 and 1998 was the first author, Robin Murphy, who was an assistant professor in computer science at CSM. In 1998, the second author, Michael Rosenblatt, joined the program. Rosenblatt was an undergraduate majoring in mechanical engineering at CSM. (Both authors have since left CSM; Murphy is now an associate professor at the University of South Florida, and Rosenblatt transferred to Carnegie Mellon University.) In 1999, Rosenblatt led Robocamp with a CSM undergraduate, Karlan Schneider, as an assistant.

It may be interesting to comment on the impact of teaching a Robocamp on an academic career. The primary motivation for the first author for taking on the additional responsibility was a commitment to K–12 education, especially with a daughter in the Robocamp age group. While the CSM Academic Affairs (provost) office encourages K–12 educational outreach, the attitudes of individual departments vary. In this case, it was clear that taking a week off from summer research was viewed by the head of Mathematical and Computer Sciences as at best a career-neutral event, one that would not be treated as a plus for tenure but might be counted as a negative. While educational outreach is attractive to many institutions, assistant professors should be aware that such efforts are not always supported in fact by their home departments.

9.3 Organization and Syllabus

Robocamp went from 8:30 to 4:00, Monday to Friday. One or both of the instructors were usually present from 8:15 to 4:15. The pedagogical strategies for each day were organized around one or more learning objectives. The learning objectives were met with short lectures, a hands-on activity, and a follow-up discussion or video. As part of the hands-on activities, the campers were expected to completely assemble a robot "mouse" from a kit, program a Movit Navius robot in binary, construct a Web page with links to robots, go on two field trips, use a handheld GPS receiver to navigate like a robot, and complete a project with the theme of "my ideal robot."

Each day was generally structured as follows:

- *While campers were arriving:* Campers watched videotapes of robot documentaries or science-fiction TV shows with robots, or worked on projects.

- *Morning session (9 AM–noon):* Campers worked on cognitively challenging activities and topics suited for individual work.

- *Lunch (noon–1 PM):* Campers ate their bag lunches outdoors and then played one or more robot-themed games as a physical outlet.

- *Afternoon session (1 PM–4 PM):* Campers worked on projects, less structured activities, and more group work. They had free time if they finished early.

- *While campers were winding down, getting ready to depart:* Campers again watched videotapes of robot documentaries or TV shows.

The daily structure attempted to follow the campers' natural attention span and predilections, while also keeping them busy. Since the majority of campers were early adolescent males, the robot-themed games during lunch seemed to satisfy the need for physical activity and "roughhousing." Video documentaries were frequently shown as part of the motivation for the concepts addressed in a particular exercise. The campers often found these videos fascinating and liked being able to see them again. In addition, some TV shows and movies provided a natural basis for discussing societal implications of robotics. For example, questions posed included: How do you know something is intelligent? Is it OK to treat an intelligent robot like a slave? What is realistic about robots in the movies and what isn't? A list of videos and TV shows used in previous Robocamps is given in Appendix B.

The five-day syllabus for the camp was largely the same in both 1997 and 1998. The 1999 camp shared a similar syllabus for the first three days, but dedicated Thursday and Friday almost entirely to independent projects using a variation of the LEGO Mindstorms (see the section entitled New Technological Advances). Presented below is the five-day syllabus from 1997 and 1998, but you are encouraged to modify it (or abandon it) as called for by changes in technology or other factors.

Monday

The focus for Monday is on the parts of a robot. The morning exercises concentrate on discussions, and in the afternoon, the campers assemble a mouse robot from a kit. The campers get to decorate and keep their mouse. (Making and keeping a robot that others outside the camp are unlikely to have seems to have been particularly important to the campers. Based on observations of the first author's daughter, the robot reappeared for use in science projects during the academic year and in general one-upmanship.) The campers are also given research notebooks on the first day in order to encourage them to role-play thinking and taking notes like a scientist or engineer.

8:30–9:30	Introductions
9:30–10:30	What Can Robots Do?
	Strange Universe video, instructor-led discussion
10:30–11:30	What Are the Parts of a Robot?
	Minilecture
	"Through the eyes of a robot" activity (using an Armatron or a remote-controlled toy)
11:30–12	How Do Robots Move?
	Clips from *Robots Alive* and *Destination Mars* showing rolling, walking, flying robots
12–1:00	Lunch; gait control game
1:00–3:30	Build a Robot
	Pre-exercise with tools
	Build mouse robot
	Decorate
	Race in mazes
3:30–4:00	Introduce Project

As part of the science experience, the campers complete a small-science-fair-like project that encourages them to think about what they have learned, how to apply it to a real-world problem, and how to communicate it effectively to a general audience. The campers have to design a robot for a task of their choosing, for example, explore Mars, help people who are paralyzed, or even clean their room. By the end of the week, they are required to create a poster describing the robot and an electronic "brain." The campers must work on their project individually. On Monday, the students are expected to start working on answering two questions about their ideal robot: What is the purpose of your robot? What does your robot use for each of the parts of a robot (power source, sensors, effectors, controller)?

Tuesday

The focus for Tuesday is to explore the biological foundations of intelligent robots. Material for the minilectures was based on the "reactive" or behavioral movement in robotics popularized by MIT robot scientist Rodney Brooks. Most mobile robots are programmed using behaviors, which are similar to stimulus-response type behaviors in animals. The major activity of the day is a field trip to the Denver Zoo, led by docents who point out interesting behaviors in various animals and discuss how different animals move. After the campers return, they are expected to write up at least three behaviors that their ideal robot will have in order to accomplish its task. In particular, they have to decide what the robot would sense and what it would do in response to sensing an event or thing.

8:30–9	Biological Inspirations for Robots Minilecture on intelligence emerging from behaviors
9:00–9:30	Examination of robots in Mobile Robot lab, discussion of how they are like animals
9:30–2:30	Zoo Field Trip
2:30–4	Write-up for part 1 of project: what behaviors will your robot have?

Wednesday

The focus for Wednesday is on controlling a robot, either through a program or a circuit. The campers program a Movit Navius robot to execute complex motions, including making a square and figure eights. The programming is simple; the campers darken squares to indicate when the robot should turn and in what direction. After lunch, the campers ride their bicycles while learning about gears (the campers were asked to bring their bicycles to camp for the day). Immediately following the bike-riding session, the concepts about gears are reinforced by working with LEGO gears and doing the mathematical gear analysis of a toy's drivetrain. The afternoon session then returns to the idea of controlling a robot and behaviors. Campers are shown how to construct a printed circuit board out of aluminum foil, batteries, resistors, and LEDs. They then make a simple circuit where a switch corresponds to the stimulus and the LED to a behavior. By creating more complex circuits, the campers work on representing the behaviors for their ideal robot in circuit form.

8:30–9:30	Discuss behaviors for ideal robots, answer questions about behaviors

9:30–11:30	How Do Robots Think?
	Robots Alive and *Robots Rising* video clips
	Behaviors as stimulus-response
	Program Navius Robot
11:30–12	Lunch
12–2	How Do Gears Work to Move Robots?
	Bike riding
	Gear demonstration and analysis
2–3:15	How Do Robots Use Circuits?
	Foil circuits; flowcharts to behaviors to circuits
3:15+	Build circuit brains for your project

Thursday

Thursday's activities make use of two of the newest technologies in consumer electronics: the World Wide Web and the Global Positioning System (GPS). In the morning the campers learn to surf the Web (many already know how, but invariably several do not) and then construct their own Web page using Netscape Communicator. In the afternoon, the campers work in teams of two or three to participate in a "treasure hunt" using handheld GPS receivers (loaned by the CSM Engineering Division).

8:30–9:00	Sojourner Truth: The Little Robot That Could
	Clips from *Destination Mars*
9–11	Surf the Web
	Search for Sojourner, unmanned aerial vehicles, unmanned ground vehicles
11–12:30	Build their own Web page with links to robot sites
12:30–1	Lunch
1:00–3:00	GPS Treasure Hunt
3:00-4:00	Work on projects

Friday

The push on Friday is to wrap up the projects. In both 1997 and 1998, the campers wanted to spend all the time on the Web constructing Web pages.

The morning session attempts to satisfy that urge, while trying to focus the campers on how teams of multiple robots might solve problems that single robots cannot. Robot soccer has emerged as a popular venue for multiple robots, and campers begin their Web session by looking at related sites. The afternoons in 1997 and 1998 were spent in the CSM Mobile Robot Lab, where the campers participate in interactive demonstrations of search and rescue robots. The campers are allowed to teleoperate most of the research robots in the lab, including a kangaroo-like robot that carries a smaller robot inside. The poster presentations and a cake and punch reception were set up in the lab so that the campers' parents could also see the mobile robots. During the reception, the instructors spoke briefly to the campers and parents about careers in robotics (and sciences) and types of courses that the participants will need to take in high school to get on that career path. Each camper receives a certificate of completion.

8:30–9	Work on projects
9–12:00	Teams of Multiple Robots Search for robot soccer competitions on Web Free time Print out home pages
12–1	Lunch; robot soccer game
1–2	Finish projects
2–3	Field trip to CSM Mobile Robot Lab
3–4	Presentations and reception for parents in Mobile Robot Lab

 ## 9.4   Activities and Equipment

The following is a detailed discussion of the activities and equipment. It is intended that one would be able to recreate these activities and make educated decisions about equipment from the information provided. A material list is provided in Appendix D, including price information and distributors.

"Through the Eyes of a Robot"

Materials: a video camera, a television, and one of the following: a Radio Shack Armatron Robot, or a remote-controlled toy vehicle (the remote controlled construction vehicles available at larger toy stores are particularly well suited)

Duration: 1 hour

The goal of this activity is to provide a fun gamelike activity that will stimulate thinking about what is intelligence versus teleoperation. A good way to accomplish this is to let campers "be the robot" in a task-oriented situation and discover for themselves the value of intelligence. This is done in two steps. The first is a teleoperation game, where campers pair off and sit facing each other. One camper pretends to be an industrial robot with no sensors and no intelligence, while the other camper is the human controller. The "robots" have to close their eyes and can only move their arm in direct response to commands. Once the "robots" have closed their eyes, the "supervisors" put a pencil or other object within reach of the arm (but in an unknown position to the robot). The supervisors then give commands to direct their partner to pick up the object. The robots have to pretend they can't feel the object. The pairs then swap roles and repeated the exercise. A discussion follows where the campers discuss the problems with teleoperation. These observed problems are then related to the correct scientific terminology. The most common problems the campers encountered are ambiguous commands (this leads to a short discussion on why computers and robots are so literal), different frames of reference (left and right often get confused as the pair are sitting facing each other), the lack of perception, and the need for macros for repetitious tasks. All campers agree that teleoperation was tedious.

The lessons from the teleoperation game are then reinforced by having campers operate Radio Shack Armatrons (a toy robot arm) to move objects around the arm's workspace. Their only view of the space is through a video camera attached to a TV screen. Because the video camera's angle gives a "worm's eye view" of the arm, the task of moving the objects becomes even more challenging due to the unfamiliar perspective. The following discussion concentrates on how the video camera is analogous to a robot's sensors, used for input, and the arm they are controlling is an actuator, used for output to the world. In interpreting the input and controlling the output, they themselves are taking the place of the robot's brain, usually a computer.

The Radio Shack Armatron is close to ideal because it looks like and is presented as a toy robot. However, it appears that it is no longer produced, making it nearly impossible to find. A good alternative is a remote-controlled construction vehicle available at larger toy stores. These vehicles tend to be relatively slow (allowing operation in a constrained space), and wire controlled as opposed to radio. An interesting addition might be to mount a small CCD "quick cam" or PC camera (which can be bought for less than $100) directly on the remote-controlled toy.

Build and Decorate a Robot "Mouse"

Materials: Tamiya Robot Mouse Kits (require one C cell battery), screwdrivers, scissors, decorations (fake feathers, pipe cleaners, plastic eyes, paint, glue, glitter, etc.), one soldering iron and solder (used by instructor). Optional: 2 × 4 lengths of wood in 3-foot lengths to create mouse mazes.

Duration: 3 hours

A robot kit reinforces the concepts of the parts of a robot, builds skills, and gives the campers physical proof of their accomplishments. The Tamiya mouse kit is the kit of choice for the first robot-building activity for several reasons. First, since it is a model of a mouse, it helps build the connection between robots and biology. Second, it provides a demonstration of how simple stimulus-response mechanisms can produce seemingly complex behaviors. The mouse kit produces a robot-shaped plastic mouse about the size of a hand. The mouse has one whisker; the whisker controls the robot. If the whisker is depressed, it turns left. If there is no pressure on the whisker, it turns right. This produces a wall-following behavior, and the campers had great fun making mazes, discovering under what circumstances it couldn't follow a wall, and seeing that the robot went in circles if it was not placed near a wall.

The Tamiya kit is also inexpensive (<$35), appropriate for the age and skill level of the campers, and comes unpainted with the intention that the builders will personalize it with their own decorations. Although there is no computation, a reactive behavior is achieved with a simple switch circuit allowing the mouse to follow walls. This was perfect for the camp curriculum because reactive behavior is one of the fundamental topics in robotics, and the switch circuit is simple enough for the campers to understand. One disadvantage, however, is that the kit instructions call for "twist" connections of the wires to the motor and battery terminals, which easily come undone and are electrically unreliable. This is easily fixed by soldering the connections, but that takes an instructor's time (about 3–4 minutes per robot) and soldering equipment. Campers are not permitted to solder because of the added instruction time, need for supervision, and extra equipment.

The activity begins with a practice exercise driving screws into wood. When a camper has successfully fastened all screws, he or she receives a kit and a few tips for following the directions. It is repeatedly stressed that the wiring diagrams in the instructions require careful attention. The instructors had both built mice of their own prior to running the activity that proved instrumental in anticipating potential problems and troubleshooting errors. (The second author, wrongly assuming that he would not need the directions, encountered almost every problem that arose from the 14 campers combined, and was well prepared to assist.) Campers' abilities to assemble the kits appear normally distributed, with most campers requiring occasional help, a few working totally independently, and a few needing help on almost every step. With the 2:14 instructor to camper ratio, instructors are busy, but no one has to wait long for help. However, since the demand for help is initially higher than the supply, some of the faster working (more experienced) campers are usually very willing to help their peers, leading to a natural collaborative learning experience.

Despite the help and the instructors' cautions at the beginning, many of the robots did not work right away. This also proved to be a very positive thing. Most of the problems arose from incorrect wiring, and resulted in run-time errors (i.e., robots moved, but the behavior was incorrect). When such problems occurred, instructors discussed potential causes with the campers including reversed motor wires and circuit "logic." It was helpful here that the instructors had at least a fundamental understanding of circuitry. Provided with an explanation of the circuit on the blackboard (drawn roughly to scale) and suggestions of potential problems, most campers are able to solve their problems themselves.

The deeper understanding that resulted from working through these problems inspired some campers to question what other behaviors could be created by rewiring the circuit (i.e., wall avoidance—bounce off the wall). Creating new behaviors became a competitive goal for some of the male campers, and designs for new behaviors were traded like valuable commodities. After completing construction of the robots, campers had time to paint and decorate the robots, and completed robots were brought home that afternoon (a few came back the next day with newly engineered behaviors or more extravagant decorations).

It was interesting to note that the groups seem to be evenly split between campers using the free time to play with the wiring versus decorating the robots. The division does not appear to be gender based; boys are as likely as girls to paint and decorate their robots. Part of the enthusiasm for decoration appears to be a desire to personalize the robots. Also, it may stem from campers having more familiarity with the glue, paint, and other art supplies and feeling more comfortable experimenting with that rather than with wiring.

The mouse robots can be used effectively with younger groups for robot demonstrations. Younger students may not be able to construct the robot, but they can operate it. To help illustrate the principle of stimulus-response, prior to the demonstration, each student can be blindfolded and given a strand of uncooked spaghetti. They are told to imagine that they are a cockroach with a whisker and the spaghetti is their whisker. Then they have to follow a hallway, including a turn, using only the feel of the whisker on the wall.

Project

Materials: poster presentation board, handouts of the six topics, tape

Duration: 3–6 hours, mostly done during free time

The motivation for the project arises from many sources. A project with a poster board presentation is used to reinforce communication skills and help the campers gain familiarity with science-fair-like activities. It also is used to help focus the campers' attention on the material by having them relate what they are learning to a robot of their own design, regardless of whether the robot can be built or not. Finally, the project lets campers concentrate on the parts of a robot that fascinate them: the mechanics or the intelligence.

The students are given the following handout on the first day:

As part of the Robocamp experience, you will design your own robot and present it to your guests at the party on Friday. There is time and materials allotted at various parts of each day to work on it. You should be sketching and writing down ideas in your journal throughout the week during free time. *We want you to daydream about your ideal robot as you learn more about what robots are, what they can do, and how they can do it!*

Some of the camp activities during the week will help you with your project. For example, you will make a circuit out of aluminum foil on Wednesday that will represent how your robot's brain would work; you will use that as part of your display. On Friday, you will be given poster board and markers to do your poster. On Friday, you will also need to draw your robot on a sheet of paper. If you want, you can construct a model (or sculpture) of your robot out of cardboard, pipe cleaners, or whatever you want to bring from home. Art material will be available starting on Tuesday.

The main thing is you get to decide whatever you want your ideal robot to do: explore Mars, help people who are paralyzed, or even clean your room. It's your choice. It doesn't matter if someone picks the same purpose for his/her robot.

Regardless of what you decide your robot should do, you will have to explain (on your poster) the following:

1. What is the purpose of your robot?

2. What does your robot use for each of the parts of a robot (power source, sensors, effectors, controller)?

3. What are the behaviors of your robot, and for each behavior, what does the robot sense and do in response to it? You have to have at least 3 behaviors but less than 6.

4. How does your robot move and why?

5. What animal is your robot like and why?

6. A drawing of your robot.

7. As an option you can write a story about what you and your robot would do or build a model of your robot.

On Friday the campers are given sheets of paper with the headings to help the campers organize their thoughts. Figure 9.2 shows the poster components. The campers write on the sheets and then tape them to the poster board. One or two campers typically opt to build a model, and no camper has ever written a story; the majority preferred to make baroque foil circuit designs.

Trip to the Zoo

Arrangements: docent tour guides

Duration: 6 hours

Since the late 1980s, designers of artificially intelligent robots have relied on studies of animal intelligence. One does not need to share this opinion to see that animals provide excellent examples and inspiration for building robots. In the case of robot camp, the animal-robot analogy proves to be commutative, where robotics provides an excellent perspective towards studying the biology of animals. Once at the zoo, campers are challenged to ask themselves: "What if animals were like robots? Could we build them? How do they move? Are there cause-effect type relationships that define their behaviors?" Before taking the camp to the zoo, these ideas are shared with zoo staff in order to enable docent guides to focus on animal behavior and locomotion. The docent tour lasts about an hour, after which campers pair up and leave for free time around the zoo. After regrouping, but before leaving the zoo, a discussion on everyone's observations is conducted.

Figure 9.2

<table>
<tr>
<td>

All robots have a purpose.

ROBOT NAME:

ROBOT'S PURPOSE:

</td>
<td>

All robots have four parts.

POWER SOURCE:

SENSORS:

EFFECTORS:

CONTROLLER:

</td>
</tr>
<tr>
<td>

A robot's intelligence is based on behaviors. A behavior is a pattern of action that is triggered by a stimulus observed by a sensor.

Behavior   Name   Stimulus   Action
1
2
3
4
5
6

</td>
<td>

Artifical Intelligence is often inspired by biological intelligence.

MY ROBOT IS LIKE THE FOLLOWING ANIMALS BECAUSE:

</td>
</tr>
</table>

Samples of four of the poster handouts. Note the use of "reminders" in the upper-left corner of each.

Program a Binary Robot

Equipment: assembled Movit Navius robots (~$50), or assembled Movit Wao-II robots (~$75).

Duration: 1 hour

Movit robot kits range from about $25 up to $100 and are made by OWI Inc. Most of the kits are single-function reactionary robots, but the two top models, the Navius and the Wao-II, are programmable. While assembling these more advanced kits would not have been practical to do during the camp given their complexity, they can be operated and programmed with very little instruction. This allows campers to get results with only about five minutes of getting-started tips. The only guidance needed beyond the initial instruction is to suggest activities: "Can you get the robot to do a zig-zag through soda cans?"

The Navius robots, the ones used in Robocamp, are particularly well suited for beginners because the programming method is very concrete and easy to understand. Programming is done with a paper disk with two concentric rings printed on it. A person blackens spots on the rings to make the robot drive. One ring controls the right motor, the other, the left motor. The disk goes into the robot and is constantly spun by a separate motor (not the wheel motors). As it turns, each ring is monitored by a sensor for white or black, and relays commands through some control circuitry to the motors. The disk is a form of "memory," just like punch cards, and is physically visible, allowing campers to "see" what is going on.

An alternative that is used at a robotic camp at the Carnegie Science Center in a fourth- through sixth-grade camp is the Wao-II. The Wao-II has a microprocessor and is programmed with a keypad on the back of the robot. The keys represent BASIC-like commands, which are stored in RAM and can be executed by pressing the *Run* button. While this makes its inner workings more abstract, the Wao-II is a much fancier and more capable robot. This added capability comes at little penalty in terms of operating complexity. However, the Wao-II costs 50 percent more than the Navius.

Gear Exercises

Materials: preassembled LEGO vehicle with motor and drivetrain (or other gear example), gear assembly diagram handouts (see Figure 9.3), camper provides bicycle and helmet

Duration: 1/2 hour for bike riding, 1 hour for discussion and gear analysis of example vehicle

A look into gear mechanics provides an opportunity to integrate math skills into the camp's curriculum. However, the math behind gear mechanics can be confusing even to undergraduate engineering students, so gears are introduced to campers through a familiar medium: their bicycle. After lunch, everyone takes their bicycles to an outdoor basketball court. Campers are asked to ride around and shift gears, thinking about what happens with each change (i.e., faster, slower, easier, harder to pedal). After having some time to do this individual testing, all campers line up along one baseline of

Figure 9.3

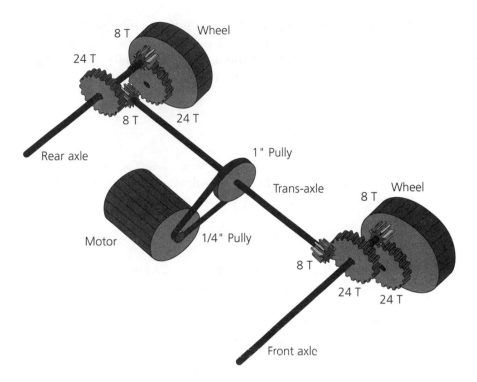

Drawing of LEGO gear assembly (used for handouts).

the court, shift the bikes into the easiest gear, and count the number of pedal revolutions (no coasting) it takes to get to the other end. The count varies between campers due to errors and difference in bicycles (wheel size and gearing), but everyone counts at least 20 pedal revolutions. We repeat the exercise with the bikes in their hardest gears. This time the count is usually less than 5. While doing these tests, we encourage the campers to notice the gear size at the pedals (the input) relative to the gear size at the rear wheel (the output).

After returning to the classroom, campers look at another gear system: a LEGO vehicle equipped with very low gearing, enabling it to climb steep inclines. The analogy is made to climbing a steep hill using the low gears on a bicycle. The campers are given a drawing showing the gear connections and the number of teeth on the gears, and are challenged to calculate the speed of the motor. The exercise begins by calculating the gear ratio between the motor and the wheels as a group. Campers take turns working on the blackboard as we dissect the problem. Campers appear to have more diffi-culty conceptualizing the problem than actually doing the math. Once they can calculate the final ratio of the drivetrain, they figure out how fast the wheels were spinning in revolutions per minute. This is done by having one camper measure the time with a stopwatch and another count revolutions. The campers multiply the measured wheel RPMs by the gear ratio, to calculate the motor speed in RPMs.

Foil Circuit "Brains"

Equipment: 12×12-inch (or bigger) cardboard squares, 9-volt batteries, 9-volt battery clips, LEDs, 380-ohm resistors (1/4 watt), aluminum foil, and Scotch tape

Duration: 2.5 hours

The motivation for this activity is to both reinforce the concepts of behavioral control and provide a low-cost, low-manual-dexterity introduction to electrical circuits. In this activity, the campers create simple circuit boards out of aluminum foil and cardboard. The activity begins by passing around circuit boards and talking about how thin the traces are, and how they serve the same purpose as a round wire. Next, a simple diagram is drawn on the board of how a stimulus-response behavior might be implemented, with the stimulus as a switch and the response as a LED. The power supply and resistor are inserted into the diagram, then the diagram is turned into a circuit diagram using electrical symbols. The campers are then shown a circuit made of foil cut like a trace and glued to cardboard. The leads of the 9-volt battery clips, resistor, and LED are taped or glued to the foil. Switches are pieces of aluminum foil glued to one foil lead and bent up for the off position. The campers then build the identical circuit. Afterwards, how to construct parallel (each behavior is triggered by a different stimulus) and serial (multiple stimuli must be on for the behavior to be on) behaviors are described. After showing competence with building the foil circuits, the campers are asked to work on the circuit for their project.

One advantage of the foil circuit boards is that they are cheap to make (practically free compared to the $15–$40 needed to purchase breadboard, wires, etc.), and the campers can make them at home. Another is that the campers do not have to conceptualize the layout of a breadboard, nor experience as many problems inserting wires and keeping the circuit in working order. Many campers seem to enjoy making interesting patterns out of their foil, exploring curves and spiral traces. This suggests that the foil circuit boards are a worthy exercise even for a camp without financial considerations and might make an excellent pre-exercise before a more rigorous breadboarding exercise.

A disadvantage of this exercise is that the campers tend to hook up things incorrectly (remember to explain about the different lengths of the legs on LEDs) and go through many LEDs. A grab bag of LEDs seems to work best, as the campers like to pick colors and sizes to personalize their circuit.

Web Page Building

Equipment: Web access, Netscape Communicator, a computer for each camper, user accounts on the local computer network (if applicable)

Duration: 4 hours (in 2-hour sessions)

This activity begins with a formal introduction on how to surf the Web. This includes an introduction to the Netscape browser (entering URLs, clicking on links, bookmarking sites), and a tutorial on how to find and use search engines effectively. While this was a review for most campers, it was new to some. Campers are given some free time to practice surfing, and some good robot-related websites are suggested (see Appendix C for a list) as well as keywords for search engines.

When campers are comfortable with using the Web, the exercise moves on to building personal Web pages. (Note: To do this, prior arrangements had to be made for campers to have user accounts on the Colorado School of Mines computer system, and for these accounts to have Web-authoring privileges.) Rather than trying to teach campers the intricacies of HTML, the campers use the Composer feature built into Netscape Communicator. Composer allows a user to visually lay out a Web page, automatically generating the HTML code "behind the scenes." Additionally, Composer is easy to learn and easy to teach; campers are able to get started with it given only a few minutes of instruction. The lessons progress from simple lessons of creating a new file, changing the background, adding text and sectioning bars, and move on to demonstrating how to add pictures. Adding pictures is particularly important, since campers collect pictures from other sites on the Web and digital pictures of activities from throughout the week.

The campers clearly enjoy surfing the Web and especially building their own pages. About half had surfed the Web before, but in 1997 and 1998 none had built their own home page. The only complaint about the exercise was that the home page did not persist after the camp since they were on temporary accounts at CSM.

It should be noted that this exercise requires a great deal of supervision to help campers follow the directions. In 1997, a camper who had some familiarity with the Web ignored directions and repeatedly attempted to use commands and search engines he used at home. This crashed the computer at the camp due to incompatibilities three times in a row, causing lengthy reboots. As a result he did not finish his page. In 1998, this type of behavior was brought up as an example of why it was important to follow directions, and there were no problems. The majority of time-consuming questions or problems came from campers who had some experience with the Web and were experimenting.

Robot Gait Control Races

Materials: soft rope cut into 1-meter lengths, two pieces of rope per camper

Duration: 30 minutes

The gait control game is a popular after-lunch physical activity (see Figure 9.4, Color Plate only). Prior to lunch on the day of the gait control game, students have already been introduced to some walking robots and how many of them exploit natural gaits in animals to simplify control. In order to make the gaits less abstract, the campers compete in four-legged gait races for *pacing, trotting,* and *galloping.* Each of these gaits essentially decomposes control of many legs into controlling pairs of legs. For the races, each camper locomotes on hands and feet, but the appropriate pairs are tied together to insure that a particular gait is being used. Figure 9.5 shows the gaits and where to tie the ropes. After the races, the campers discuss which gait seemed fastest, most tiring, better suited for what situations, and so on.

GPS Treasure Hunt

Materials: hand-held GPS receivers, compasses, preplaced "treasures"

Duration: 2 hours

The purpose of this activity is to consider how robots navigate, as well as to introduce the campers to an emerging technology (GPS). This activity is preceded with a brief discussion of how robots (and aircraft and boats) use the global positioning system to navigate, and an explanation of some of the science behind how GPS works (i.e., use of satellites, ranging, triangulation geometry). The campers are taken outside and form groups of three campers. Each group is given a handheld receiver and a short explanation of how the units are operated. Each unit has six locations stored in its memory

Figure 9.5

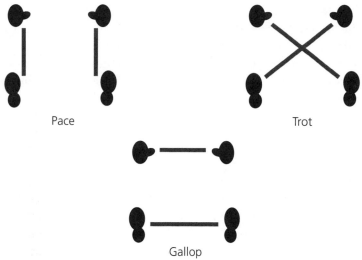

Rope configurations for gait races.

(preset by the assistant earlier in the week), and campers set their units to track these stored waypoints with a built-in *goto* function. The units tell the campers the range and heading to the target points. Points are spread out around the Colorado School of Mines campus, and at each point there is a poster that gives an interesting fact about CSM's history or the area's geology. Each team member has a turn at navigating to a specific leg.

Campers have about a 50 percent success rate in finding the waypoints due to noise and consumer-grade GPS units, but all have a good time trying. The merits of this activity are that it exposes campers to a modern piece of technology and allows for some time outside. The campers also begin to realize that all technology has limitations.

This activity may be beyond the scope of other camps because of the costs of receivers; even consumer-grade GPS units are in the $150–$300 price range. The CSM Civil Engineering Department lent the camp expensive GPS receivers at no charge. Also, setting up the receivers and laying out the course takes some time.

9.5   Discussion

Our experiences with Robocamp suggest that robots can serve as motivation for a broad educational experience integrating both the sciences and liberal arts. Simple, inexpensive robotic kits and household materials can stimulate thinking about biology, ethology, and zoology as well as computer science. The activities show that robotics can be incorporated into almost every traditional school subject. Robocamp raises important pedagogical issues, which we will discuss below. Also, since educational robotic technology is rapidly changing, we discuss the LEGO Mindstorms robots and how they might be integrated into Robocamp.

Pedagogical Issues

From a pedagogical standpoint, Robocamp raises two issues for an instructor to consider. The first issue is, *How much focus should be placed on robotics, versus using robotics as a tool to motivate general education?* The answer to this issue is influenced, of course, by the goals of the educational enterprise. In the case of Robocamp, the goal is to have an interesting science camp and to encourage students to go on to pursue a science-oriented career. Therefore, Robocamp is designed to have a broad curriculum where robotics serves as a theme. Regardless of goals, the demographics of a day camp suggest a broad curriculum may be more beneficial than one with a more rigidly robotic-centric focus. In all years, a significant number of campers were registered because of their parents' desires, rather than their own deep interest in robotics. Furthermore, the majority had no experience with robots or electricity even at the simplest kit level, and their impressions of robots came only from the media. It seems clear that parents look at Robocamp as an opportunity for their children to gain exposure to the types of skills they would need to enjoy a later camp with more of a focus on working with circuits, gears, and programming.

The issue of how much focus a more general educational experience should receive in a robotics curriculum can be turned around to ask how much robotics can enhance an educational experience. We have found that robots can add spice to just about any aspect of learning. Despite the less-than-overwhelming enthusiasm for robotics expressed in the initial camper surveys, the intrinsic "wow!" factor associated with robots kept almost all the campers' attention for every activity in the camp. Only one camper in three years proved to be unwilling to participate wholeheartedly in the exercises; this camper had a history of behavioral problems and was eventually dismissed from the camp for discipline problems. The norm is for the campers to work on their foil circuits, robot decorations, or robot project in the evenings and return to class with new things to show. Integrating robots into the educational experience also provides an important opportunity for the campers to gain hands-on skills needed for future laboratory work, reading directions, interpretation of two-dimensional (paper) representations of three-dimensional objects, and general confidence.

The second pedagogical issue Robocamp raises is, *How much structure and how much free play are appropriate in a robotics experience?* One of the many attractive features of robotics is that it seems to stimulate creativity, which would argue for scheduling large amounts of free play. The experience with the 1997 camp suggested that the campers do not yet have sufficient confidence and skills to use a large amount of free play. Activities generally included an extra 30–45 minutes for campers to tinker and experiment. Even with a set of questions (What happens if . . . ?), this was often too long for the average student, who many times resorted to just play (e.g., crashing robots into each other). In the 1998 camp, there was less free play and more goal-directed suggestions (Who can make it do *x*?). However, campers were encouraged to work in the evenings and try out new things to show in the morning. This seemed to work more smoothly, since campers who were highly motivated still had an opportunity and an outlet. This also suggests that creativity and learning may be better served if the camper owns less expensive equipment and has complete access to it, rather than has limited access to more expensive tools that must remain at school or camp.

Although it is impossible to generalize from such limited numbers, the behavior of the three females in the 1998 camp reinforces the issues in structure versus free play. It appears that girls in particular may need encouragement and a formal structure in order to experiment and be creative. Two of the three girls sat together, worked quietly and quickly, rarely asked for help, and usually completed their assignments early (except for assembling the robot kit, at which they were noticeably at a disadvantage). Upon completion of the assignment, they would put aside the robots or materials and pick out a book from their backpack and begin to read. They would do more advanced exercises only when specifically asked. However, the advanced assignments had to be formal; when encouraged to explore or make up things to do with the circuits or robots (Can yours do something different than anybody else's?), both of them typically appeared confused. One actually asked, very politely, if she *had* to experiment or if she could just go back to reading. This was in sharp contrast to the other male campers who often failed to complete a task within an activity because they had found something "cooler" about robots, programming, or foil circuits to show off. Indeed, in those cases, competition seemed to spur creativity. In terms of overall performance and ability to repeat the academic concepts covered in the Robocamp, the two girls were clearly outstanding. In terms of operationalizing the concepts and being able to build on them, it was not clear that they had gotten as much out of the camp. They may have gotten more if the camp had included a more structured free play component.

It may be that the answer to these two issues depends largely on the expected abilities of the campers. A group of sixth through eighth graders

Figure 9.6

a

b

c

Robots used in the 1999 Robocamp: (a) a LEGO "photoseeker" using Cricket controller, loaned from the MIT Media Lab, (b) Movit Hyperpeppy kit robots, and (c) a LEGO robot for moving a tower of soda cans.

drawn from the middle-income class at large may have different attributes than a group with some type of selective filtering (grades, robotics experiences, etc.). However, these population attributes influence only the degree of emphasis on robotics and the amount of free play, not the intrinsic advantages of integrating robotics into educational experiences.

New Technological Advances

The 1999 camp used a variety of robots, as seen in Figure 9.6 (see also Figures 9.7 and 9.8, Color Plates only), including the LEGO Mindstorms Robotic Building System. This takes the LEGO Technic System, which already includes bricks, gears, and motors, and extends its capability by adding computation in the form of a small computer built into a brick (called the

RCX Brick). With the RCX, you not only build their LEGO model, but you also program it to sense, "think," and react to its environment. Before Mindstorms there were no tools, appropriate for middle-school children, that allowed for fast start-up time, ease of use, and reasonable cost (a Mindstorms kit costs about $200 in toy stores).

The 1999 camp used a variation of the Mindstorms technology, called Crickets, which is currently being developed at the MIT Media Lab (see Chapter 1). The impact this had on the syllabus was to dedicate Thursday and Friday entirely to projects done with the Crickets and the LEGOs. In this two-day, largely independent activity, students worked in pairs to build, program, test, and demonstrate robots. They were required to define a task for the robot prior to building. This culminated in a final presentation Friday afternoon that parents and siblings were invited to. Upon presenting their robot, they demonstrated their robot working and explained its systems, including sensor choice, unique output attributes (lights, sounds, motors), and the "intelligence" they implemented in their programs.

Resources for more information on Mindstorms is found in Appendix E. It might even be reasonable to expect campers to (1) have or purchase their own Mindstorms to bring to camp and (2) have completed the tutorial prior to the first day of camp. This would allow the instructor to focus on more hands-on activities using the same robot throughout the week.

Ratings of the Camp

Course evaluations of the camp are available only for the 1998 session. The evaluation procedure consisted of forms given to the campers and parents at the end of the camp. The forms are filled in by the campers, and the parents can attach notes. The results from the 8 families (out of 14) responding in 1998 are shown in Table 9.1 and were the highest of any camp offered by CSM that summer.

Campers were also asked to list what they liked best and least about the course. The most popular activities in order of frequency mentioned were: building the mouse robots, the GPS treasure hunt, going to the zoo, and building Web pages. The most frequently cited disliked activities were: going to the zoo and the GPS treasure hunt. The dislike of the GPS activity seemed to stem from the camper not liking GPS in general due to the inaccuracy of GPS and losing the signal in urban canyons.

Only three parents added comments to the evaluation: two expressed appreciation for the course and the other thought that allowing the campers to construct a model of an ideal robot for their project out of art supplies and trash was a waste.

Table 9.1   *Course evaluations of the camp.*

	Yes	*Undecided*	*No*
I learned new things as a result of this class.	8	0	0
The classroom activities were interesting.	8	0	0
Field trips were worthwhile.	6	2	0
The instructor was helpful.	7	1	0
I would recommend this course to friends.	8	0	0

9.6   Summary

For three years, the popular CSM Robocamp has exposed sixth through eighth graders to robotics, artificial intelligence, biology, and engineering, while enhancing their hands-on laboratory abilities and encouraging the development of presentation skills. A secondary goal has been to encourage students to pursue a science-based career. Although it is too early to determine if Robocamp has made a difference in the participants' education, anecdotal evidence indicates that a one-week science day camp in robotics can be effective and inexpensive. The CSM Robocamp is a for-profit venture, with campers charged $275 for the week. Of that, less than $125 was spent for equipment, field trips, a party, and so on.

The Robocamp approach is to treat robotics as a theme unifying contributions from the general sciences. As the topics progress from the parts of a robot through how a robot is controlled, the camp emphasizes how each of the sciences has contributed to each topic. Another important component is making and keeping an autonomous mobile robot, which gives campers a sense of ownership in their learning. Finally, Robocamp also serves as an introduction to the scientific profession, where campers are expected to take notes in a research notebook and relate what they have learned to an individual project on the "ideal robot." The use of video documentaries and TV science-fiction shows fosters discussion and critical thinking, which is another novel aspect of Robocamp.

Robocamp should be reproducible by most organizations. Although the CSM Robocamp made use of an on-campus robotics laboratory and a nearby zoo, the lack of these facilities might be compensated for through videos, use of the Web, and newly available technologies such as LEGO Mindstorms. While both instructors had background and interests specific to robotics, we believe that science-inclined middle-school teachers, home schoolers, or parents are qualified to either duplicate our camp in its entirety or select particular themes of interest. Experience suggests that participants may have little or no experience with tools and assembling kits, but pre-exercises help overcome that gap and increase confidence.

9.7   Acknowledgments

We would like to thank Gail Rust and Linda Baldwin of the CSM SPACE office for their assistance in creating, administering, and maintaining Robocamp; Mary Bertsch of the Carnegie Science Center for her comments and suggestions; and Cari Kaufman for help with editing. The first author would like to thank Dale Hawkins, Kummi Ka, and the U.S. Space Foundation for their help in earlier iterations of many of the exercises.

Appendix A: Robocamp Parent's Information

The objectives of the camp are for the campers to be exposed to general science through robotics, and to have fun. As part of the science experience, the campers will have a small science-fair-like project that will encourage them to think about what they've learned, how to apply it to a real-world problem, and how to communicate it effectively to a general audience. The campers will have plenty of time to do it during camp, but we're encouraging them to discuss what they've learned and what they're thinking about with you. So be prepared to listen and to ask questions!

The campers won't be desk potatoes, though. In addition to building a robot, programming robots, and building Web pages, there will be physical activities planned for each day that tie into our robot learning objectives. So you may want to have your camper bring sunscreen every day, not just the days when we know we'll be outside with field trips.

Although the majority of the campers won't have any experience with robots, some may have built a kit robot or have models of robots. They are welcomed to bring them to camp for informal sharing anytime they'd like, although they should be prepared for the wear and tear of 13 other campers (and two instructors) handling it!

Here are some of the highlights of the camp by day.

Monday

Objective: Campers will be able to define robots, list their parts, and identify what makes the difference between an artificially intelligent robot and a regular robot.

Fun stuff: Campers will build their own "mouse" robot, as well as work with a robot arm to learn more about the parts of a robot.

Tuesday

Please have your campers wear their robocamp t-shirt and bring a backpack suitable for carrying their notebook and lunch.

Objective: Campers will be able to compare intelligent robots to living things.

Fun stuff: A trip to the Denver Zoo, where docents will discuss how animals move, perceive, and think. (The kids don't need to bring any money unless they want to get a soft drink; we won't be going to the gift store despite extensive pleading.)

Wednesday

Please have your campers bring their bike, helmet, and a lock. (Please leave the bike outside the Brown building, locked in one of the bike racks near the Brown building parking lot.)

Objective: Campers will be able to describe how a robot thinks and explain the mechanics of their moving parts.

Fun stuff: Campers will build foil circuits representing a robot brain; program a miniature robot with simple binary commands; and learn about gears, first by examining and experimenting with their bikes, then seeing how gears are used to allow robots to traverse slopes.

Thursday

Campers will be outside for most of the afternoon. Please have them bring sunscreen!

Objective: To learn what robots can be used for (including robots in space), and how robots can use GPS to localize themselves.

Fun stuff: Campers will build their own Web page of links to sites on the World Wide Web about different robots and their uses; participate in a GPS-based treasure hunt using handheld GPS receivers.

Note: Our Web browser may be set up to use different search engines, etc., than what a home or school computer uses, so if your campers are familiar with the Web, the CSM access may be confusing if they don't pay attention to our directions. And if the camper tries to use the wrong commands for the CSM computer, the camper may spend all of his or her time rebooting instead of getting to do interesting things. If your child is computer-savvy, please feel free to remind him or her that the CSM set up may be different.

Friday

Campers may bring a soccer ball if they want for robot soccer.
Objectives: Teams of robots working together for applications as diverse as robot soccer to urban search and rescue.
Fun stuff: Campers will program simulations of robot swarms; see demonstrations of BEAM robots built by undergraduates; play with Bujold and Willis, two search and rescue robots; and present their projects at *a party for parents and friends in the Mobile Robotics Lab at CSM, Brown 154, 3–4 PM.* Due to high Web traffic on Friday afternoons, we may or may not be able to browse the campers' Web pages, but we will have printouts of the Web pages and URLs of all links.

Appendix B: Robot Videos Appropriate for Sixth through Eighth Graders

Documentaries

Scientific American Frontiers: Robots Alive

PBS special "Show 705." This 1997 special narrated by Alan Alda is particularly well done, covering in detail robots that walk, roll, and fly. The VHS tape can be purchased by calling 1-800-315-5010. Transcripts and extensive teaching guides are now available at *www.pbs.org/saf/*.

Discovery Channel: Robots Rising

This 1998 two-hour special covers more types of robots than *Robots Alive.* The science takes a back seat to a more MTV-like editing and Linda "Terminator" Hamilton narrating, but there are enough robots and details to keep even the most jaded roboticist's attention. The VHS tape can be purchased from the Discovery Channel's website at *www.shopping.discovery.com/product/712570.html.*

Discovery Channel: Destination Mars

Another 1998 two-hour special. While the video focuses on human exploration of Mars, it has excellent segments on why robots are needed to explore a planet prior to human landing and on the challenges of autonomy and mobility on Mars. The VHS tape can be purchased from the Discovery Channel's website at *shopping.discovery.com/product/701318.html.*

TV Episodes

Star Trek: The Next Generation, *"The Quality of Living"*

In this episode, the android Data discovers that a set of miniature robots are actually intelligent. Then he's asked to sacrifice the robots in order to save Picard's and Geordi's lives, a contradiction of what Picard has been trying to teach him. It presents an interesting ethical dilemma, the tests for intelligence are quite reasonable, and the robots' creator is a woman. Maturity: No violence, no bad language, just a thought-provoking episode.

The Outer Limits, *"I, Robot"*

An android robot goes berserk and kills his creator who was performing a mysterious operation on him. Leonard Nimoy is the lawyer who is engaged in the robot's defense, and who eventually moves from believing the robot is just a clever piece of hardware to believing it is intelligent and should be accorded the same rights as a human. There's a nice, classic *Outer Limits*–style twist at the end. Maturity: There is the initial violence, which isn't bloody and consists of a lot of pushing through glass and so on. Occasionally the robot loses its temper, just when a person would, but the point is that it is acting just like a person. (Trivia: This is actually a remake of an episode of the old *Outer Limits*, where Leonard Nimoy played the robot. Adam Nimoy, Leonard's son, directed the new version.) Can be ordered from *directvideo.com/science.htm.*

X Files, *"War of the Corophages"*

Cockroaches infecting a town may actually be miniature robots sent by aliens to survey a planet. The idea of insectlike robot explorers isn't far-fetched. MIT AI Laboratory director Rodney Brooks pitched the idea to JPL years ago, and it was the motivation for Sojourner (although Sojourner doesn't look like an insect, it is programmed at about that level of intelligence). The main roboticist whom Scully and Mulder turn to at the

"Massachusetts Institute of Robotics" is a cross between Stephen Hawking (he's in a wheelchair with a voice synthesizer), Joe Engelberger, who founded industrial robotics companies in the United States (he wears Engelberger's signature bowtie), and Rodney Brooks (his explanation of why the cockroaches might be alien explorers is almost a literal rendition of interviews with *Omni* and *Discover* magazines on insect robots). The episode is actually technically accurate. Maturity: Scary in a fun way with cockroaches crawling everywhere. There is one possibly objectionable scene where teenagers are experimenting with getting high off of manure-induced methane fumes; the teenagers come to a bad end and drug use is definitely put in the most negative light. (Suggestion, just fast-forward.) A couple of uses of the word "shit," mostly as a play on the alternative fuel source for these dung-eating robot insects. Can be ordered from *directvideo.com/science.htm.*

Appendix C: Robot Websites Appropriate for Sixth through Eighth Graders

Websites with Resources for Educators

Robohoo (a portal managed by Yahoo)
www.robohoo.com

American Association for Artificial Intelligence
www.aaai.org

Websites with Interesting Robots and Movies

NASA Jet Propulsion Labs (Sojourner)
www.jpl.nasa.gov

Carnegie Mellon Robotics Institute
www.ri.cmu.edu

Carnegie Mellon Field Robotics Center
www.frc.ri.cmu.edu/

Carnegie Mellon Robot Learning Lab (Xavier and Minerva can be teleoperated over the Web!)
www.cs.cmu.edu/~rll/

MIT AI Laboratory (insect robots plus a humanoid robot)
www.ai.mit.edu

MIT Leg Laboratory (walking robots)
www.ai.mit.edu/projects/leglab/

Appendix D: Special Equipment

The following table gives a list of special equipment for camp activities (items such as screwdrivers, a video camera, and batteries are not listed, but are noted in the activities and equipment section of the chapter).

Item	*Activity Used In*	*Approximate Cost*	*Vendor*
Tamiya Robot Mouse Kit	Build a Robot	$35	MondoElectronics
Armatron Robot	"Through the eyes of a robot"	$30	Radio Shack
A remote-controlled construction vehicle (e.g., a bulldozer or crane)	Alternative for "Through the eyes of a robot"	$40	Toys R Us and other large toy stores
Movit Navius Robot	Program a Binary Robot	$50 (unassembled)	The Robot Store *www.robotstore.com*
Movit Wao-II	Alternative for Program a Binary Robot	$75 (unassembled)	The Robot Store *www.robotstore.com*
Netscape Communicator	Web Page Building	Free for educational purposes	Netscape *www.netscape.com*
Garmin handheld GPS receiver	GPS Treasure Hunt	Starting at $150	Recreational Equipment Inc. *www.rei.com*
LEGO Mindstorms Robotic Invention System	New technology for future use	$200	Lego *www.legoworld-shop.com* or local toy store

Appendix E: LEGO Mindstorms Resources

LEGO Mindstorms Home Page

www.legomindstorms.com
This is LEGO's official Mindstorms page including links to lots of information, ideas, and a community of users, young and old.

Fred Martin's Mindstorms Info Site

fredm.www.media.mit.edu/people/fredm/mindstorms/
Here you will find some useful notes about what Mindstorms is and is not, and some ideas for expanding its capabilities. Fred Martin is a member of the Epistemology and Learning Group at the MIT Media Lab, which played a role in the development of Mindstorms.

Part III

Future Visions

Kid's View

   Hobatu: Punisher Droid,
a Day in the "Life"

A short fictional story by Bob Milstein, age 12

"PRAISE TO YOUR EXCELLENCE. WHAT IS THE CURRENT POSITION OF YOUR WELL BEING?" Leg after sturdy metal leg lifted itself from the hold of the castle's artificial gravity, then sank quickly back down to crash on the floor several feet closer to the table. The process sent the boulders of the castle foundation vibrating with force; each of the robot's three legs weighed two thirds of a ton.

The head cook of Castle Jenek looked up to meet the hidden gaze of her conversationalist. "I'm fine, Hobatu. How are you?" She focused her attention back onto the dish in front of her, a plump shrew head smothered in breaded cabbage, which she had prepared herself in Bine Jenek's honor.

"NINETY-SEVEN PERCENT. HOBATU PUNISHED EIGHT TODAY. VIEW." With this, Hobatu aimed the palm of its hand at the table and projected from it the data taken from the various security cameras in the castle.

"Let's see it."

The vision of a holding cell appeared on the satin tablecloth. Hobatu activated his outgoing sound system, and the audio data loaded and then began to play through Hobatu's "mouth."

"Armande DiCollo." The voice of the security camera calmly stated. "Crime: cannibalism, first-degree murder, arson. Punishment: torture, level seven. Application by Hobatu 3. Begin Procedure."

A large, eyeless man huddled in a corner as the droid lumbered into his cell. Armande had removed his own eyes the day before upon hearing the level of torture he would receive, as he did not want to see it coming. Also, a droid would make it much more painful if he gave *it* a chance to rob him of his sight. Thank God for healing herbs.

"PRISONER NUMBER 1066, ARMANDE DICOLLO: YOU HAVE BEEN GIVEN YOUR LAST OPPORTUNITY TO BEG FORGIVENESS OF BINE JENEK AND HIS KINGDOM WHICH YOU HAVE DISGRACED WITH YOUR AFORE-

MENTIONED ACTS. HOBATU WILL MAKE YOU SUFFER." As the droid advanced, a small compartment slid open in its chest.

As Armande stood blindly in the corner, his mind was rapidly flipping over the horrible possibilities of what that sound of sliding metal could mean. *Great*, he thought. *I'm even more frightened than I would be if I could see. What the hell's going on? I should have cut my whole Goddamn brain out. The scary thing is, doing that would have probably saved the Punisher this trip. . . .*

"That was probably the most grotesque thing I have ever seen. And while I'm eating lunch, too!" Nauseous, the cook turned back to her feast and jabbed a chopstick into one of the eyes of the half-eaten shrew, then proceeded to remove the eye and plop it into her mouth.

"HOBATU WAS NOT CREATED TO CONSIDER HOBATU'S ASSIGNED TASKING GROTESQUE. IT IS NECESSARY."

"You used a nail gun on the guy for five minutes. He looks like Goddamn *Hellraiser* for crying out loud! It's amazing you didn't kill him." She paused, and looked thoughtfully back at the projection on the table, the projection of a man on the floor, bleeding from thousands of wounds, not appearing to breathe. . . .

"You did kill him! Oh, for Pete sake, what the hell did you do that for? You aren't supposed to actually kill anyone! What happened?"

"PRISONER NUMBER 1066, ARMANDE DICOLLO, RECEIVED THE DEATH SENTENCE FOR CANNIBALISM AND FIRST-DEGREE MURDER. PRISONER NUMBER 1066, ARMANDE DICOLLO, RECEIVED THE TORTURE LEVEL SEVEN SENTENCE FOR ARSON. PRISONER NUMBER 1066, ARMANDE DICOLLO, WAS ON DEATH ROW. HOBATU KILLED PRISONER NUMBER 1066, ARMANDE DICOLLO."

"Oh." She didn't feel like arguing with something as deadly as a Punisher Droid, at least not one that didn't have an emotion chip. This particular Hobatu did not possess any feelings, and thus could turn around and kill her without giving the act a second thought. And by now she had finished with her meal, so she pushed away her plate and left the table. On the way, she tapped a hidden alert button by the exit. The cook knew that droids were not supposed to kill humans, no matter what the circumstances. It broke the first law of robotics—she couldn't allow such behavior to continue. Sure, the law could be bent for the injury of humans, and had been, but this was *killing*. *And in a moment*, she thought to herself, *the castle security would be by to dismantle Hobatu.*

Everything was taken care of perfectly, it would never happen again, she said to herself as she turned the corner and found herself facing Hobatu's blaster barrel.

Chapter **Ten**

Robots for Kids

The Landscape

Ray Hammond

Author, Computers and Your Child *and*
Forward 100: A New Way of Learning

Abstract

It is hard to think about the future because we lack the necessary tools—the spoken, written and visual languages. The robots our kids will be using in the coming decades will emerge from a technological landscape that will be startlingly different from the present. Robots will become "companions" that will eventually share most of their owners' childhood experiences and, in time, are likely to "grow up" alongside their human "friends." They may even become our childrens' lifelong companions.

We have no language for the future, and where there is no language, there can be no thought. So it is with *Robots for Kids*.

Although the editors of this book have no choice but to apply language that is in common usage today, our current concepts fail to prepare us for what will, in fact, be the arrival of a new form of intelligent companion on earth. Inside a decade they will be ubiquitous, and a few years later, it will be difficult to remember what it was like for humans to be the only communicative and intelligent species on this planet.

Some machine creatures of the future will, indeed, be "robots," with all of the ambulatory and mechanistic characteristics implied by our present understanding of the word. But many more will be "companions"—friendly, funny, cute creatures, who will captivate the young and befriend the old. If we must, we can continue to refer to them as "robots," but it is better to think of them as pets, playmates, and helpers. The learned researchers whose work appears in the other chapters of this book are struggling to find ways to make competing technologies compatible, to ensure that these new devices are as open as possible, to find ways of engaging children with machine-based "life" and exploring how such creatures can extend the armory of education professionals. Just *how large* a place creatures with machine intelligence will occupy in our lives, and in the lives of our children, is hard to imagine from the perspective of the present.

It is clear that humans have a deep and continuing need to anthropomorphize nonhuman creatures and inanimate objects. The much-loved car, bicycle, or boat is often given a name and spoken to kindly (and, sometimes, angrily), but it is pet owners who most clearly project human qualities onto their long-suffering, loyal, but largely dumb pets. It will be the exploitation of our anthropomorphic desires which will propel "robots"—or, as I will call them from now on, intelligent companions—into the mainstream of life a few years from now.

When I first started studying how children interact with computers, I was drawn to the work of Seymour Papert and others at MIT who had created the Logo Turtle to help children visualize mathematical concepts (Papert 1980);

see Chapter 1. Although in 1982 I was still laboring under the delusion that it would be helpful to teach children about computers (rather than the other way around), I nevertheless watched class after class of preteen children draw eyes and make tails for what were (at the time) very unappealing clear plastic domes meant to represent "turtles." But the message was clear: children have no fear and no discrimination about what pleases and engages them. From then on I understood that we would be sharing our future with intelligent machines.

Within a decade children will have interactive companions that are soft, furry, and funny (some of the early generations are described earlier in this book). They will also have companions who will play games with them, research on networks for them, engage in realistic conversation, and, in some situations, companions who will demand quite sophisticated nurturing and attention from their young owners. Although it is outside the scope of this work, it is also worth pointing out that the elderly will enjoy the company of cuddly and communicative machine pets, who will provide "someone to talk to" while monitoring their owners' physical safety and physiological status. Network connections will provide links to human caregivers. It is in our "second childhood" that many readers of this book will come to understand the value of intelligent companions first-hand.

But it is children and their enthusiastic and generous anthropomorphization of toy companions—as evidenced by so much field research that appears in this book—who will attract society's attention.

As I write this chapter I am breaking off from a new work of fiction, which I have set in the year 2015. In my story I imagine that children of that time will be able to choose from a wide range of "Furry" companions, which learn from their "owners" but which also teach and protect. As children grow, so a Furry's software is updated as programmers achieve ever more capable "simulations" of companion behavior. Even though upgrades are regularly retrofitted, all of a Furry's experiences and memories of life with its childhood owner are protected and form part of the basis on which child and machine companion communicate. The Furries of my imagination are immortal and will survive all rigors their owners inflict. Even total physical destruction does not bring an end to their existence as all of their memories and capabilities are constantly backed up, ready to be transferred to an identical replacement companion.

It is likely that children may want a new external appearance for their companion—a red caterpillar is less appealing to an 11-year-old than a 7-year-old—but the knowledge and "personality" of the companion will be transferable to all representations. Companions will also provide recording and retrieving facilities, and as the cost of storage tumbles, it is likely that companions will keep a continuous audiovisual record of their lives with their young masters and mistresses. It is possible that intelligent machine companions may grow and mature with tomorrow's children to become life-long servants, companions, and friends, growing "older" with their owners.

I have deliberately chosen *not* to make such imaginary creatures ambulatory as, contrary to other contributors to this book, I believe motion is not central to the role that intelligent companions have to play in the lives of children (or the old). Some fun companions will undoubtedly display locomotive and other physical abilities, but it will be some time before our ability to emulate biological movement and environmental coherence in machines becomes sufficient to make such creatures wholly convincing.

In my novel my central "companion" character is a red caterpillar called Jed who lives with seven-year-old Tommy. Jed is about a foot long and has excellent speech recognition and speech simulation capabilities. Jed can see and hear and, as well as providing an otherwise lonely Tommy with a friend, Jed is permanently connected to the networks (by wireless, of course) and can answer many of Tommy's questions.

I can imagine that some parents, teachers, and even a few researchers may be horrified at the concept of a future for children in which they are "sat" by machines and in which "normal" play interaction with other children and adults is replaced by "robots." I believe that, although such reactions are understandable, they are rooted in a misunderstanding of what it is to be human and they are formed from within a bias of present thinking from which, I am the first to admit, it is extraordinarily difficult to escape.

I am certain that our future, our near future, will include a burgeoning relationship between humans and intelligent machines. I do not see this as a "cyborg" future, nor do I see it in the overly dramatic science-fiction terms of a potential future competition between humankind and machine. Such common scenarios are usually created by imaginative but technically under-educated writers. It is clear to me that the arrival of new nonhuman virtual intelligences is a wholly natural step for humankind. Machine intelligence is, by definition, virtual, but before you dismiss that as unreal, I want to suggest that the very essence of our humanness is virtual. We are merely about to meet the projections of our own virtuality. I predict it will be highly satisfying. I will risk a detour in this chapter to make an attempt at presenting my argument for why I am sure that humanness is virtual and that virtual intelligences, generated by machines, will prove to be comfortable, engaging, and, ultimately, challenging companions on this planet.

Because we have no language for the future, I have had to invent a phrase to help me imagine the digital "e-vironment," "e-cosmos" or "infocosm" (take your pick from these unsatisfactory neologisms) which we are building in the networks and satellite systems around our planet. The Internet is only the start: the near future will provide us with a low-cost, high-capacity, ubiquitous digital space, which we will access by dozens of different devices. We will interact with it by ordinary human speech as well as by keyboard, drawing pads, touch screens, soft toys, physical monitors and many other access technologies. I call our future domain "global virtuality" because it will be both truly global and wholly virtual.

I see nothing sinister, unusual, inhuman, or worrying about the development of global virtuality. I do not worry about the alienation of our children, nor the threats to long-standing social and cultural institutions such as nation states, cultural identity, income taxes, and personal privacy. All are issues that need to be addressed, but I regard human occupation of the digital networks and the creation of nonhuman intelligence as something entirely natural. Man is a virtual creature and to understand why we should all feel comfortable about our forthcoming migration to global virtuality, we have to go back to the very beginning of human life.

This planet is between four and five billion years old. Around four million years ago our first closely recognizable ancestors in Africa's Rift Valley started to lean back on their hind legs and, step by step, began to walk in what anthropologists now call "plantigrade fashion." Thus began the process, which led to modern humans.

In our fully upright posture we tilted our heads back in order to see further, gravity elongated our skull, our brain started to expand, and our larynx fell to the bottom of our throat. Here it found more room to enlarge, to grow a nervous system, and become mobile. The range of sounds that could be produced expanded dramatically and thus, through language, we stumbled upon our most important ability, *the interconnection of a single mind with many other minds*. Language provided the feedback loop, which sent the human brain on its runaway evolutionary progression, and it was language—spoken, unspoken, written, symbolic, and conceptual—that was the trigger. This is why natural language interfaces will lie at the heart of our relationships with intelligent machine companions.

Language is the essence of humanness and it was the first external symbol, simulation, representation, or *virtual* element to appear in what had been until then a wholly physical world. This uniquely human form of shared consciousness that, with all other forms of representational expression and storage I chose to collectivize as "virtuality," began the moment Man named himself, another, or an object in the outer world with an abstract, but mutually understood and agreed upon, unique sound comprehensible to others in the group network. Naming something, for example, the condition of "global virtuality," is always humanity's first step to understanding the new. Successful and sustainable neologisms are signposts to progress.

Language created our ancestors' past and their present and gave them a few tools with which to try to imagine their future. This proceeded from earlier personal forms of virtuality such as thought, memory, and dreams, which are now known to be constructed as "virtual reality" models in the brain rather than stored as complete ideas and experiences.

For example: there is no intrinsic color in the external world. Humans create color internally as reactions to specific wavelengths of visible radiation. Light falls onto receptors in the eye that contain red, green, yellow, and blue pigments. Color is generated internally for us within the eye and the optic nerve. This occurs for reasons closely connected to our evolutionary survival: color coding is the fastest way to identify danger, or water, food, or fire at long distance. The glories of golden sunsets and green fields do not exist in the nonhuman, noncognizant world. They are part of human-created virtuality.

But, by definition, our language has limitations, and it does not automatically equip us for imagining the future. Such tools as we do have must be incomplete, a shadowy group of symbols and projections, and it is the lack of commonly shared notions, more than the uncertainty of prediction, that makes the understanding of probable future developments and implications so difficult. In essence, we find it hard to imagine possible futures because of the bias of our current symbolism—we think from the perspective of the present.

We must also come to understand that our world, our concepts of what is "real" and what is not, and, most importantly, our sense of self and identity, are all *products of human language* as it has developed so far. The first virtual representations of the world were probably prehistoric cave paintings. The earliest found so far were created about 35,000 years ago in caves near the village of Vallon-Pont-d'Arc in the Ardèche region of France. The colored paintings had been created over a period of 1,300 years and depict the diverse menagerie that made up the real world of these "modern" humans. These paintings are among the earliest known steps into externally recorded (extrasomatic) virtuality. The artists had created a representation of their world of rhinoceroses, bears, owls, and mammoths, and they have certainly passed all tests required to be considered "permanent." These representations can be described as symbols, simulations, or virtual expressions.

Then there was a very long gap. It took the wealth and stability generated by the agricultural revolution to foster the human intellectual interaction necessary to invent a common storage method for human language and ideas. Writing, originally in the form of pictograms, was invented by the Sumerians (in today's Iraq) around 5,000 years ago, and modern phonemic alphabets appear to be descended from a system invented by the Canaanites around 1,300 years later.

Once these difficult technologies were mastered, people could express compressed ideas and knowledge in virtual form, on papyrus, slabs of stone, and so on and send them to the future for use and reuse. (Humans "decompress" written information as they reconvert the symbols to concepts.) Papyrus rolls and stone tablets may not seem particularly "virtual" in our contemporary use of the term, but this is to confuse the container, the carrier, or the medium with the message, which is, of course, wholly virtual. Despite Marshall McLuhan's famous claim, the medium is *not* the message, although until now our crude containers have colored it.

Writing technology started the process, which has brought us so far, so fast, and that now is taking us into a completely new form of existence. Civilization and the social force of culture stemmed directly from the discovery of virtual storage, which allowed all forms of wisdom, morality, information, and design to be captured for future generations to build on.

In particular, the concept of money, the ultimate form of virtual representation, was also invented in the Temples of Sumer about the same time as early forms of writing. Far from being the root of all evil (only Man, with his free will, can be that), I consider the invention of money to be one of humankind's greatest achievements. Everything civilization has achieved, and will achieve, is based on an agreement between people to bestow value on colored paper, coins, lumps of metal, or digital bits that have no intrinsic value and a collective cultural suspension of disbelief in the worthlessness of the imbued object. Even gold and other rare or precious commodities only have value if a society agrees to accord them exchangeable value. *Credit* is, after all, the Latin word for "he believes!"

The only absolute values that have always existed are water, food, shelter (land), survival goods (e.g., clothes and materials for tools and weapons), and labor (which is limited to two or three days' worth). To this list we must now add energy and knowledge, the latter a relatively recent product of cultural development and something that is becoming more valuable than most other commodities.

All else is wholly virtual and a product of human culture. Today, all of the money you own or owe is nothing but ones or zeros on computer disks scattered around the world. Money is the principal virtual commodity—invented, not discovered—and the "reality" and confidence bestowed on it by almost every community in the world is the clearest possible indicator of human willingness to accept forms of virtual representation as being "real."

The agricultural revolution, with its virtual tools of writing and money, produced wealth, which then supported the great civilizations of Egypt, Greece, Rome, and the later European empires, and, ultimately, led to the Old World's discovery of the New World. It took the industrial revolution of the 19th century to push growth forward once again.

These previous revolutions in social history have run deep rather than fast: the benefits and drawbacks of the agrarian revolution took thousands of years to be felt; the benefits and costs of the industrial revolution took two centuries. But I think that this latest development, our transition to global virtuality, will be both deep *and* fast.

In the digital space of networks and interpretation devices, growth opportunities—through the development of information products, vastly improved complexity-handling capabilities, and the reduction of friction in almost all transactional processes—will be almost infinite. These do not require further consumption of natural resources. We still have not yet realized the full and monumental inefficiencies of the processes of our giant organizations: in a few years they will appear to function like quicksilver, almost autonomously adapting and redrawing themselves to meet every new requirement. The friction created by physical transaction processes will have evaporated and economic growth will rocket. *This is why the migration to global virtuality is now taking place.*

The concept of a virtual transaction space in which humans can extend their society is not new. In 1867, as the electric telegraph was spreading to all corners of the world, Samuel Butler, the British essayist and friend and critic of Charles Darwin, wrote:

> We will say then that a considerable advance has been made in mechanical development, when all men, in all places, without any loss of time, are cognisant through their senses, of all that they desire to be cognisant of in all other places, at a low rate of charge, so that the back country squatter may hear his wool sold in London and deal with the buyer himself—may sit in his own chair in a back country hut and hear the performance of Israel in Aegypt at Exeter Hall—may taste an ice on the Rakaia, which he is paying for and receiving in the Italian opera house Covent garden. Multiply instance *ad libitum*—this is the grand annihilation of time and place which we are all striving for, and which in one small part we have been permitted to see actually realised.
>
> ("From Our Mad Correspondent," *Canterbury Press,*
> New Zealand, 15 September 1863)

Now that such a vision is actually being realized, the question is, How will people behave in a dimension that is virtual, instant, and global? What clues can be gleaned from evolutionary psychology (we're not going to shake off selected behavior for a while) and what can be learned from observations of the behavior and responses of humans who have pioneered living part of their lives over electronic networks? I am one of this latter group (as are many of my computer science colleagues and their students), and I think some early behavioral patterns of what might be termed "postphysicalism" can be discerned.

But although a few of us who belong to the older generation have spent 20 years or more working and living part of our lives connected to the electronic prosthetic, the most important group to study is the middle class American/European young—those between 16 and 26—who first encountered computers as young children and who have enjoyed Internet access throughout their college years and early working life. Their reactions, habits, and behavior provide our best clues to how individuals will shape a post-physical global culture out of apparent chaos. This appearance of chaos has caused sociologists to wring their hands about prospects for "Generations X and Y," but I contend that social scientists haven't grasped the fact that today's media culture is merely a transitional phase, one made oppressive because of the limitations of embryonic technology.

Accordingly, postmodernists argue that today's youth has little hope or faith in the future. They argue that human nature has given up (as against risen up) against a society driven mad by television and video games (especially in the United States) and suggest that a natural defense mechanism has made motivationless cynics of the young.

The influential British sociologist Dominic Strinati puts it this way (Strinati 1992):

> Television, which makes us what we are, which brings the world rushing into our living rooms, has similar effects (destroying identities) because it is, at one and the same time, individualistic and universal: it speaks to everyone and to no one in particular. And, like the increasing confusions over space and time, it prevents new collective bases for personal identity from being formed. People relate to TV as individuals watching everything, and TV relates back to people as individuals and/or as abstract parts of a universal order, in both instances ignoring, eroding and fragmenting any wider collectives to which people might belong and any legitimate ideas in which they might believe.

That 1992 view may have been partially valid at the time he wrote it, but TV as we understand it today is all but finished. As I said above, the medium has so far been shaped by its "container" (or "constrainer"), by the fact that it has to be beamed or conducted to us in linear, uncontrollable form. Our only choice has been the remote control, and a study of how humans use this when they are supplied with more than a few channels (and the temporary tenure of the video rental store) reveals that our future interaction with virtual information and entertainment will be very much more selective than despairing postmodernists might think. Encouragingly, Harvard biologist Edward O. Wilson describes postmodernism as "blissfully free of existing information on how the mind works." Equally, the case studies of young people interacting with technology that appeared earlier in this book make such depressing forecasts seem laughable. The problem is, such views are all too common.

It is only the limitations of geographic distribution and this strange squirted, artificially boxed delivery of electronic moving pictures that produces ratings-dependent economic vehicles. Entertainment, information, education, and stimulation in video or film form are now becoming available as nonlinear or linear, in real-time or non-real-time, on a global basis. Ratings for an arbitrarily beamed product (other than an important live event or breaking news) will cease to matter, and a much wider choice of high-quality programs will be available for audiences who choose to either pay or to watch targeted advertising. Talk shows featuring the emotional outpourings of disadvantaged people may still get made (and watched) in the United States and elsewhere, but as television ceases to be a mass medium and becomes a personally designed service, the way to the advertising dollar will become much more sophisticated. Instead of working on a "lowest common denominator" principle, programming will be closely tailored to its recipient groups.

In essence, fully interactive, easy-to-use, high-capacity, low-cost, global digital networks will restore the individual's say over the influences, actions, and transactions of an electronic society. Marshall McLuhan's famous meme, "the medium is the message," will finally cease to have any truth, as the message within the medium becomes our goal and the medium disappears into the fabric of our surroundings.

Writing in the 1960s, McLuhan despaired that Western society was entering a two-dimensional, machine-mediated cultural period as the early forms of electronic media beamed themselves at us. In "The Medium is the Massage" (he substituted "massage" for "message" in much of his writing) he said (McLuhan 1969):

> All media work us over completely. They are so persuasive in their personal, political, economic, aesthetic, psychological, moral, ethical and social consequences that they leave no part of us untouched, unaffected, unaltered. The medium is the massage. Any understanding of social and cultural change is impossible without a knowledge of the way media work as environments.

McLuhan understood that electronic networks are an extension of humanity long before any other 20th century commentator, but the limitations of the technology of his time made it seem fascistic, dominating, and destroying. He rightly identified "electronic media" as an extension of our biological nervous system, one that was "ablated" (outed), but he saw only human anxiety, stress, exhaustion, and bewilderment resulting.

It is understandable that from his viewpoint of 30 years ago, McLuhan saw it as humans receiving input, something that must drive people mad, whereas we now know it is as much about output, about creating ideas, things, and services (even if it's only a family video emailed to Gran), which we can send forth to grow and multiply in global virtuality, as it is about receiving.

I admit, however, we have been waiting a long time to see how electronic "media" would develop. Almost 20 years ago, I observed (Hammond 1982):

> Some cable TV stations are pioneering the development of interactive TV in which viewers participate in shows, but even when this two-way facility is fully developed it is unlikely to be used for more than vote gathering or armchair shopping. At its best, television is stimulating, challenging, and informative; but quality is rare, and most TV programming is mediocre and opiate both in content and stance. Most parents instinctively feel it right to steer their children away from such passive pursuits. Computing is the most mentally active pursuit it is possible to find, *providing the computer is used in the right way* [original emphasis].

The debate about "using computers the right way" has continued. Nearly 20 years later many observers feel that computers, in the form of video games, are damaging the young. Let's look at some evidence: Nearly 200 million video game and multimedia computers are in use around the world, often for several hours a day, to play computer-generated games. Over 90 percent of these are used by boys and men, and many of them are set in "the future." In these games the future is a grim and dangerous place, and the rule of almost all computer games is "kill or be killed." The themes are very restricted and usually feature aliens (which, of course, must be killed), enemy machines (which, of course, must be killed), or cyborgs, prison guards, or demented scientists all of whom must be . . .

The first video game was "Space Wars," which was created in Boston in 1961 on one of the first Digital PDP-1 minicomputers. The object was to show off the capabilities of what was then newly miniaturized transistor technology, and the programmers chose to show outlines of rocket ships moving against a stellar background. It seemed natural to these men that, to give the game a point, these ships should be firing torpedoes at each other.

In today's virtuality, the look and feel of such games has become more sophisticated, and all of them boast reasonable quality sound. Many offer hydraulic-powered seating for "the captain" for added physical realism, and we can be sure that every other sense will become involved in due course. I have suggested elsewhere that the hit Christmas present for 2005 may be a small, hydraulically powered seat that will download game movement instructions from the Web and allow the little darlings to play Captain Kirk, boldly going from "planet to planet" (website to website) in the space of global virtuality (Hammond 1996). Of course, he will be killing Klingons, not falling in love with an alien princess.

Interestingly, all types of "shoot 'em up" video games (and physical games) are played by all types of young men in *all* societies. This includes the groups who are considered to be socially excluded from access to virtual information. A visit to an electronics amusement arcade or a bar with video game entertainment will show you that large numbers of the group we might consider economically disadvantaged (and therefore probably socially excluded) are fully competent at playing these games. (As an aside, this points to a useful avenue for social inclusion policy and for interface design in the future.)

One universal point observable with video game players is that they would technically be considered to be in a temporary "state of flow," that is, totally absorbed by the activity, unaware of external events and, not to put too fine a point on it, happy. "Flow" is the term coined by Mihaly Csikszentmihalyi, professor of psychology at the University of Chicago. In my 1982 book *Computers and Your Child*, I quoted him as follows:

> Flow is described as a condition in which one concentrates on the task at hand to the exclusion of other internal or external stimuli. Action and awareness merge, so that one simply does what is to be done without a critical, dualistic perspective on one's actions. Goals tend to be clear, means are coordinated to the goals, and feedback to one's performance is immediate and unambiguous. In such a situation, a person has a strong feeling of control—or personal causation—yet, paradoxically, ego involvement is low or nonexistent, so that one experiences a state of transcendence of self, sometimes a feeling of union with the environment. The passage of time appears to be distorted: Some events seem to take a disproportionately long time but, in general, hours seem to pass by in minutes.

That passage comes from *Intrinsic Rewards in School Crime,* in which Csikszentmihalyi and his colleagues sought to understand what they then thought was a computer-produced aberration in teenagers (Csikszentmihalyi 1980). Over the last 20 years, Csikszentmihalyi has devoted a major part of his career to developing the theory of "flow" (two international best-selling books prove the subject's appeal), and he now considers that the condition is central to human happiness. He defines it as a condition enjoyed by people with a vocation, a form of artistic expression, or an otherwise engaging occupation that provides them with what he calls "optimal experience." (The condition of "flow" is clearly identified and described in Chapter 8.) He now attempts to teach people how to bring "flow" into their work, their hobbies, and their friendships. (To be fair to Csikszentmihalyi, he does distinguish between unconstructive and constructive forms of engagement, but he contends that all forms replace the misery of undirected consciousness.)

Despite this, many parents, some academics, and most legislators are alarmed by this aspect of virtuality. A 1991 book, *Video Kids,* by Eugene Provenzo, professor of education at Miami University, claimed video games were corrupting the world's youth by failing to foster a sense of community. He said, "Each person is out for himself. One must shoot or be shot, consume or be consumed, fight or lose."

By 1993 the U.S. Congress was debating whether such games should be restricted, and some American towns banned public video game arcades. The video game industry defused the situation by agreeing to a voluntary ratings system, but many parents, teachers, and socially concerned legislators remain very worried.

Are they right to be concerned that themes of brutal violence, which are at the center of 90 percent of the world's most frequently used computer simulations, obsess young (and not so young) Western males? They are not, and they reveal their bias of the present and their lack of basic psychological understanding: these young males have merely found the ideal dimension in which to satisfy and fulfill the urges for which evolution painstakingly selected. Provenzo's complaint about the activities involved in the games sounds familiar, doesn't it? For 99 percent of human existence a man's survival depended on his ability to kill or be killed. Now this evolutionary imperative can be expressed harmlessly.

To the consternation of my generation, our little boys and little girls born in the 1970s and 1980s stoutly resisted our attempts to correct what we assumed had been the unthinking sexual stereotyping we had suffered at the hands of our parents. When we bought our daughters science sets, they promptly swapped them for "My Little Pony" (always the pink one first), and our boys, denied of anything resembling toy guns, daggers, or swords, whittled and bent weapons of much greater ferocity from materials they found around them than any commercial toy would have possessed. In the last two decades the development of evolutionary psychology combined with personal experience has explained a great deal.

The video games available today are still crude in design. The use of graphics and sound is still limited by the speed of current microprocessors and the laborious effort required to render (to generate backgrounds and surfaces by computer) the environments. We are in a period equivalent to the early days of emulsion film when the limitations of the technology had to be overcome by dry ice, superimposition, and cutaways.

With the exception of young people with pre-existing mental problems, I do not accept that any of the games' players confuse today's crude computer representations with reality. It is a place for play and a place where otherwise dangerous impulses can be discharged. It is also a place where reaction times can be honed and machine-mediated communication can be understood. It is a place to prepare for our computer-aided future existence.

For those who are still worried that the violent, apparently pointless, and very two-dimensional world of the combative video game will corrupt our youth, I have a warning: Prepare to be really upset.

The exponential curve of microprocessor design has reached a point where I can safely predict that within the shelf life of this book video games will seem to mature "overnight." Those who wish to will be able to immerse themselves in environments as real, in some cases seemingly more real, than the physical world. They will be able to do this in their own homes (through virtual headsets fed by WebTV, PC-Net connections, etc.), in 360-degree entertainment rooms in arcades, at resorts, and in shopping malls.

The result will be millions of more young men killing things in virtuality, sometimes hunting in packs in global virtuality (recreating the cooperative mechanisms that made our species dominant). The virtual representations will also be rich enough to create the texture and feel of more rounded environments, but there is nothing in the selection process of women that leads me to think they will become significant users of fantasy projection games (other than sex, but this is a topic outside of the scope of this book).

Women are already showing us that they will use global virtuality to connect, or to use today's appropriate vernacular, to "network." Here we arrive at the most important contribution global virtuality has to offer the individual: personal growth and development through new cultures that will emerge independent of nation state, ethnic group, gender, age, and, of course, physical location. I predict that, in time, women will form the largest social group in global virtuality. Humans have never had this opportunity before, but our supreme achievements have come from our central desire to create culture, and now we are going to see that amplified on a massive scale. The results promise to be spectacular and may even lead to a form of global collective consciousness.

The possibilities for new forms of human behavior and cultures in the arena I call global virtuality have been apparent to researchers for some years. In her book, Allucquère Rosanne Stone, assistant professor and director of the Interactive Multimedia Laboratory (ACTLab) at the University of Texas, offers a very personal female view (Stone 1996):

> I am interested in cyberspace because it is a social environment. The networks are elsewheres where we can observe new collective structures risking themselves in novel conditions. These structures take the form of organized and moderated conferences, multiuser groups, anarchic chats, clandestine assignations. Some are trivial, some are definitely not trivial and have real

effect outside the nets. Some of the interactions are racially differentiated and gendered, stereotypical and Cartesian, reifying old power differentials whose workings are familiar and whose effects are well understood. But some of the interactions are novel, strange, perhaps transformative, and certainly disruptive of many traditional attempts at categorization.

Second I am interested in cyberspace because the kinds of interactions we can observe within the spaces of prosthetic communication are for me emblematic of the current state of complex interaction between humans and machines. Third, the identities that emerge from these interactions—fragmented, complex, diffracted through the lenses of technology, culture, and new technocultural formations—seem to me to be, for better or worse, more visible as the critters we ourselves are in process of becoming, here at the close of the mechanical age. I see these identities engaged in a wonderful and awesome struggle, straining to make meaning and to make sense out of the very idea of culture as they know it, swimming for their lives in the powerful currents of high technology, power structures, and market forces beyond their imagination. In this struggle I find certain older structures stubbornly trying to reassert themselves in a technological milieu that to them seems to have gone berserk. These are the structures of individual caring, love and perhaps most poignant, desire.

This is part of the landscape against which it has been my pleasure to reconsider the type of machine companions for children now under development in many laboratories and R&D facilities all around the world. There are dozens of reasons for needing such creatures: from the perspective of the editors of this book, education and childhood fulfillment are the most driving imperatives. But others want to provide toys, health monitors, and protection systems (for the young and the old), and, no less importantly, psychic companions for the legions of the lonely. All of these are worthwhile and worthy aims.

Semi-intelligent machine companions have been with us for nearly 20 years, but they have made little impact on our society because of the severe limitations of their capabilities. In recent years the arrival of Tamagotchi pets, Barney, Furbys, and so on, have begun to reveal what lies around the next corner. The capabilities of these "toys" will increase rapidly, but it will not be until high-quality speech recognition and speech simulation are practical in low-cost battery-operated toys that we will become fully aware of the potential for intelligent companions. This is likely to occur between 2002 and 2006, by which time both recognition and simulation will be fairly sophisticated.

Speech recognition must eventually become speech understanding, a very much greater goal, before intelligent companions can truly become our friends. But I believe that the barrier—described so well in the Turing test—is already a false goal. I believe it is now irrelevant. When Alan Turing devised his test in 1950, he wanted to create an experiment, which would allow humans to agree on the point at which machines reach or surpass the intelligence level of human beings. As most readers of this book will know, the test calls for a human to start a dialog with another unidentified "being" without knowing whether the interlocutor is human or a machine. If the human is unable to decide during the dialog with a machine whether the correspondent is a person or a machine, then the machine will be said to have passed the test.

In the last few years it has become clear that machines will slide around, rather than confront, the Turing test. It also seems laughable that we should be so anthropocentric as to consider that a "human" model of intelligence is the only one worth testing for, or even a worthy goal. I think it highly likely that the intelligences that will confront us will be definitely inhuman, but this does not mean they will be unacceptable—we control the parameters for that. It merely means that the idea of judging intelligence by our own standards is now irrelevant.

In the next few years intelligent companions will understand and respond to a limited range of spoken commands, but their own speech capabilities will be much greater. On request they will sing songs, tell stories, tell jokes, and, perhaps most importantly from the context of this work, will carry out research. Intelligent toys will be talking to the networks even as they are talking to their child companions. Seymour Papert once wrote about the exhaustion of knowledge that can occur within human teachers (Papert 1980). He asked what would happen to childhood curiosity if all of those wonderfully imaginative questions could be answered instead of swept aside. There *are* answers to questions such as "Why is the sky blue?" and "How do giraffes sleep?" and, I suspect, robots in the form of childhood companions will prove to be an important interface between children and the world's networks of information. They may even become our friends for life.

References

Csikszentmihalyi, M. 1980. *Intrinsic Rewards in School Crime.*

Hammond, R. 1982. *Computers and Your Child.* New York: Ticknor and Fields.

Hammond, R. 1996. *Digital Business: Surviving and Thriving in an On-Line World.* London: Hudder and Stoughton.

McLuhan, M. 1969. *Counter Blast.* Toronto: McClelland and Stewart.

Papert, S. 1980. *Mindstorms.* New York: Basic Books.

Stone, A. 1996. *The War of Desire and Technology at the Close of the Mechanical Age.* Cambridge, MA: MIT Press.

Strinati, D. 1992. Television. *Sociology Review* (April):2.

Index

H–J

About the Authors

Robbie Berg is associate professor and chair of the Physics Department at Wellesley College. His current research interests are centered on developing new computational tools for use in science education. In 1996 he was a visiting professor in the Epistemology and Learning Group at the MIT Media Lab, and he continues to collaborate closely with the group, working on the creation of a new generation of "Programmable Bricks" called Crickets. With Mitchel Resnick (MIT) and Mike Eisenberg (Colorado), Robbie leads an NSF-funded project called Beyond Black Boxes, in which children are using Crickets to design their own instruments for scientific investigations.

Mark Chow currently works in the Research on Experimental Documents Group at the Xerox Palo Alto Research Center. Recent activities include building a digital reading-eye dog for a museum exhibition, doing location sound recording for a feature film, and coordinating a school superintendent intern program at PARC. He has worked as a college instructor and as an assistant director at public television station WGBH-TV. He holds S.B. degrees in electrical engineering and in architecture and visual studies from MIT and an M.A. in education from Stanford University.

Robin Church, assistant vice president for educational programs at the Kennedy Krieger Institute, holds a joint appointment as an associate professor in the Department of Special Education of The Johns Hopkins University. As a member of the Maryland's Career Connections State Management Team, she remains actively involved in efforts to ensure school-to-work initiatives meet the needs of all students, particularly those with disabilities. Her research interests include reading disabilities as well as the use of technology with students who have disabilities.

Dr. Toshi T. Doi is a corporate senior vice president of Sony Corporation, a president of Digital Creatures Laboratory, and chairman and CEO of Sony Computer Science Laboratories, Inc. He led the Sony project team that developed digital audio, invented the DASH (Digital Audio Stationary Head) format for professional multichannel recorders for studios, and coinvented

371

the digital audio compact disc with Phillips. These accomplishments have earned him numerous international awards, such as the Eduard Rhein Award, the Michel de Conda Award, and the Audio Engineering Society Silver Medal Award for the compact disc and DASH format. After completing his work in digital audio, he developed the NEWS workstation, Japan's workstation market leader. At present he has overall responsibility for research within Sony Corporation, and he was serving as a director of DAVIC (Digital Audio-Visual Council), an ad hoc organization of more than 200 companies worldwide to settle an open standard for the Information Superhighway. He graduated from the Tokyo Institute of Technlogy in 1964 and earned his doctorate from Tohoku University in 1972.

Allison Druin is an assistant professor in the University of Maryland Institute for Advanced Computer Studies (UMIACS) and the Department of Human Development in the College of Education. She is a member of the Human-Computer Interaction Lab (HCIL), where her research focuses on the impact technology can have on children and the impact children can have on the design of new technology. Her recent work has been in developing new robotic storytelling technologies for children, with children as her design partners. In addition, she is editor of the book *The Design of Children's Technology* (Morgan Kaufmann, 1999) and coauthor of the book *Designing Multimedia Environments for Children: Computers, Creativity, and Kids* (Wiley, 1996). She received her Ph.D. from the University of New Mexico's College of Education in 1997 and an M.S. from the MIT Media Lab in 1987.

William Dunbar has a B.S.M.E. from Stanford and engineering experience at Lockheed and Intel corporations. He has been teaching physics, chemistry, and engineering in California for 12 years, and he is the executive director of the Stanford Teacher Institute. He wishes that robotics programs like this (see Chapter 8) had been around when he was in high school.

Masahiro Fujita is a system architect and a senior reseach scientist at Digital Creatures Laboratory, Sony Corporation. He received a B.A. in electronics and communications from the Waseda University, Tokyo, in 1981 and an M.S. degree in electrical engineering from the University of California, Irvine, in 1989. His research interests include modular robotics, agent architecture, visual and audio perception, neural networks, and evolutionary systems.

Ray Hammond is a London-based author and lecturer who studies the impact of computer and communications technology on society. He is the author of nine nonfiction books on the subject, including *The Musician and* *the Micro* (Blindfold Press, 1981), *Computers and Your Child* (Ticknor and Fields, 1982), *The On-Line Handbook* (Fontana, 1983), *Forward 100: A New Way of Learning* (Viking, 1984), and *Digital Business: Surviving and Thriving in an On-Line World* (Hodder and Stoughton, 1996).

He is a former senior fellow of the Advanced Computing Environments Laboratory at the University of Nottingham, a visiting lecturer at the City University Business School, London, and fellow of the Royal Society of Arts and Manufactures (FRSA).

James Hendler is currently working at the Defense Advanced Research Projects Agency (DARPA) as a program manager. At the University of Maryland, he is a professor and head of both the Autonomous Mobile Robotics Laboratory and the Advanced Information Technology Laboratory. He has joint appointments in the Department of Computer Science, the Institute for Advanced Computer Studies, and the Institute for Systems Research, and he is also an affiliate of the Electrical Engineering Department. He is the author of the book *Integrating Marker-Passing and Problem Solving: An Activation Spreading Approach to Improved Choice in Planning* (Lawrence Erlbaum Associates, 1988) and is the editor of *Expert Systems: The User Interface, Readings in Planning* (with J. Allen and A. Tate; Morgan Kaufmann, 1990), and *Massively Parallel AI* (with H. Kitano; MIT Press, 1994). He has authored over 100 technical papers in artificial intelligence, robotics, intelligent agents, and high-performance computing. He was the recipient of a 1995 Fulbright Foundation Fellowship, is a member of the U.S. Air Force Science Advisory Board, and is a fellow of the American Association for Artificial Intelligence.

Hiroaki Kitano is a senior researcher at Sony Computer Science Laboratories, Inc. and a project director of the Kitano Symbiotic Systems Project, Japan Science and Technology Corporation. He received a B.A. in physics from the International Christian University, Tokyo, and a Ph.D. in computer science from Kyoto University. Since 1988, he has been a visiting researcher at the Center for Machine Translation at Carnegie Mellon University. He received the Computers and Thought Award from the International Joint Conferences on Artificial Intelligence in 1993. His research interests include RoboCup, computational molecular biology, engineering use of the morphogenesis process, and evolutionary systems.

Richard J. Maddocks was born in Lancashire, England, and grew up in East Anglia. He has a mechanical engineering background and received an H.N.C. in mechanical engineering at Luton College of Technology. He has since been in the toy business as a designer for 29 years, 14 years with

Matchbox Toys and the past 15 years freelance. He has been involved over the past two years in developing the mechanism for Furby and other interactive toys for Tiger Electronics and Hasbro. He is now living in Maryland with his wife Nancy and 10-year-old son Andrew.

Fred Martin, a research scientist at the MIT Media Laboratory, develops educational robotics technologies and classroom practices. He cofounded the annual MIT "6.270" Autonomous Robot Design Competition, now in its 14th year. Working with Brian Silverman and Randy Sargent, he developed a series of robotics technologies that laid the foundation for the LEGO Mindstorms Robotics Invention System. His hardware and software designs (the Handy Board and Interactive C) are used in over 100 colleges and universities worldwide for engineering education courses. He is presently completing work on a university text, *Robotic Explorations: A Hands-On Introduction to Robotics and Engineering*, to be published by Prentice Hall in 2000.

Bakhtiar Mikhak, a theoretical elementary particle physicist, taught in the UCLA Physics Department before joining the Lifelong Kindergarten group at the MIT Media Lab. His current research focuses on the design, implementation, and study of new computational tools with the goal of rethinking science, engineering, and mathematics education.

David P. Miller received his Ph.D. in computer science from Yale University in 1985. He now holds the Wilkonson Professorship for Intelligent Systems in the Mechanical Engineering Department of the University of Oklahoma. Along the way he taught computer science at Virginia Tech, helped to develop Mars Rover technology at the Jet Propulsion Laboratory, and helped found IS Robotics as well as KISS Institute for Practical Robotics (where he still serves as technical director). He has worked with dozens of robots and thousands of students, teaching courses for kindergarteners through Ph.D.s (students, not robots).

Gabrielle Miller is the director of business partnerships and work-based learning at the Kennedy Krieger Institute and an adjunct faculty member of the Department of Special Education of The Johns Hopkins University. She has most recently been involved in the development of a technologically based school-to-work model designed for students with disabilities. Her research interests include teacher training and transition services. She is currently completing her doctoral dissertation at The Johns Hopkins University on the use of the Internet to support the career development needs of adolescents with emotional disturbance.

Jaime Montemayor is a Ph.D. student in computer science at the University of Maryland. He is a research assistant to Allison Druin, at the Human Computer Interaction Lab, and to James Hendler, in the Parallel Understanding Systems Lab and the Autonomous Mobile Robotics Lab. In addition to receiving an engineering degree from the University of California and a diploma from the French Culinary Institute, he also studied computer science at the City University of New York. His current research interests are in reasoning about uncertainty, in programming systems for robotic controls, and in methodologies for creating technology for children.

Robin Roberson Murphy is an associate professor in the Computer Science and Engineering Department at the University of South Florida, with a joint appointment in the Psychology Department (Cognitive and Neural Sciences). She received a B.M.E. in mechanical engineering and an M.S. and a Ph.D. in computer science (minor: computer integrated manufacturing systems) in 1980, 1989, and 1992, respectively, from Georgia Tech, where she was a Rockwell International Doctoral Fellow. From 1992 to 1998, she was an assistant professor in the Department of Mathematical and Computer Sciences at the Colorado School of Mines.

In addition to her active research program in sensor fusion and mobile robotics, she is involved in robotics education. She is a co-chair of the Educational Committee of the IEEE Robotics and Automation Society and has won numerous teaching awards, including a Colorado Institute Gender Equity Excellence Award for her efforts at the college and K–12 levels in encouraging women and minorities to pursue careers in the sciences. She is the author of a forthcoming undergraduate textbook, *Introduction to AI Robotics* (MIT Press).

Mitchel Resnick, associate professor at the MIT Media Laboratory, develops new technological tools and toys in an effort to bring about deep changes in the ways children think and learn. He led the development of the ideas and technologies underlying the LEGO Mindstorms robotics construction kit. He has also led the development of several projects (including StarLogo software and the Virtual Fishtank museum exhibit) designed to help people learn about complex systems and emergent phenomena. He cofounded the Computer Clubhouse, a network of after-school learning centers for youth from underserved communities. He earned a B.A. in physics at Princeton University (1978) and M.S. and Ph.D. degrees in computer science at MIT (1988, 1992). He worked for five years as a science/technology journalist for *Business Week* magazine, and he has consulted widely on the uses of computers in education. He was awarded a National Science Foundation Young

Investigator Award in 1993. He is author of the book *Turtles, Termites, and Traffic Jams* (MIT Press, 1994).

Michael Rosenblatt is currently an undergraduate student at Carnegie Mellon University in Pittsburgh, Pennsylvania, with an expected graduation date of 2001. Harboring a lifelong interest in building robots, he has participated in numerous robotics projects including Carnegie Mellon's efforts in autonomous demining. His research interests include using robotics as an educational vehicle and robotically enhanced toys. He was an intern at the Massachusetts Institute of Technology Media Laboratory during the summer of 1999 and also taught the Robocamp for a second year. When not surrounded by robots, he likes to be outside riding his bike or just generally exploring. His favorite muppet is Gonzo.

Brian Silverman is a visiting scientist at the MIT Media Lab. He was one of the founders of Logo Computer Systems Inc., the world's leading developer of Logo software. He has directed the development of more than a dozen commercial educational software products (including LogoWriter, MicroWorlds, and the Phantom Fishtank), many of which have won major awards from industry groups and publications. At MIT, he has been centrally involved in the development of StarLogo, Programmable Bricks, and Crickets.

Cathryne Stein cofounded KISS Institute for Practical Robotics back in 1994 when she discovered how effective robots could be in engaging young students in scientific inquiry. It seemed like a fun thing to do at the time. (It still is!) She has served as president of the KISS Institute since its founding. KISS Institute started out as an organization that occasionally built robots for exhibitions and sometimes gave robot demos to elementary-school classes. Under her direction, KISS Institute has developed several educational programs, including KISS Institute's Botball and Robotics in Residence programs, through which several thousand students have participated in some form of robotics activity.

Mark Trexler is a special educator at the Kennedy Krieger Institute who has worked with students with disabilities for the last five years. Using his previous professional experience as a corporate instructional designer, he has incorporated school-to-work principles into instructional activities throughout his teaching career. His research interests include the use of constructivist principles and technology with students who have disabilities.

Marina Umaschi Bers is a Ph.D. student in Seymour Papert's Epistemology and Learning Group at the MIT Media Laboratory. Her research involves the design of technological learning environments to support children's exploration of identity and values with a constructionist approach that integrates storytelling and programming. She has applied her research on educational technology projects in the United States, Costa Rica, Thailand, and Argentina. She is from Buenos Aires, Argentina, where she did her undergraduate studies in social communication. In 1994 she came to the United States, where she received a master's degree in Educational Technology from Boston University and a master of science from the MIT Media Laboratory.

Claudia Urrea is a Ph.D. candidate at the Epistemology and Learning Group at the MIT Media Laboratory. She holds a bachelor's degree in computer science and is completing a master's degree in educational media and technology. She is interested in understanding how children concurrently develop knowledge on different subjects (e.g., science, mechanics, math, and human values) through project-based work. Her main focus is formulating and implementing strategies to facilitate the creation of new educational programs for rural areas, especially in developing countries. Since 1990 she has focused on educational and technology projects in the United States, Latin America, and Thailand.

Mark Yim has been a researcher at the Xerox Palo Alto Research Center (PARC) since 1996. Currently, he leads a government-funded project building a modular, reconfigurable robot system at PARC. His work on MEMS and robotics has been featured in the *New York Times,* MSNBC, *USA Today,* the Discovery Channel, BBC News, and various other local and international news media. He has published in journals and conferences in the areas of mobile robot planning, distributed robotics, optimal control, MEMS, and haptic devices. He has authored over 20 patents. He has been chosen as one of the TR100, the top 100 young innovators, by *Technology Review* magazine. He received his Ph.D. in mechanical engineering from Stanford University in 1994.